IRVING BERLIN

A DAUGHTER'S MEMOIR

MARY ELLIN BARRETT

LIMELIGHT EDITIONS
New York

First Limelight Edition April 1996

Library of Congress Cataloging-in-Publication Data

Barrett, Mary Ellin.
   Irving Berlin : a daughter's memoir / Mary Ellin
Barrett.
            p.   cm.
   Originally published : New York : Simon &
   Schuster, c1994.
   Includes index.
   ISBN 0-87910-078-8 (pa)
   1. Berlin, Irving, 1888-   , 2. Composers —
   United States — Biography, I. Title.
[ML410.B499B37 1996]
782.42164' 092 — dc20
[B]   96-11445
                                              CIP
                                              MN

The author is grateful for permission to reprint the
following copyrighted material:
Excerpted lines from The White Cliffs by Alice Duer
Miller are reprinted by permission of the Putnam
Publishing Group. Copyright © 1940 by Alice Duer
Miller, Renewed © 1967 by Denning Miller.
Grateful acknowledgement is made to the Morgan
Guaranty Trust Company of New York as executors
of the Irving Berlin Estate for permission to reprint
correspondence, lyrics and other writings of Ellin
Mackay Berlin and Irving Berlin.
Additional permissions appear on page 305.

Photo on page 93 courtesy of the Billy Rose Theatre
Collection; The New York Public Library for the
Performing Arts; Astor, Lenox and Tilden
Foundations.

For my children and their children,
and my sisters and their children.

CONTENTS

PART ONE

THE GREAT AMERICAN ROMANCE

Mr. and Mrs. Irving Berlin, off on their honeymoon, January 1926.

I AM STANDING in what appears to be an attic, dusty and dimly lit, crowded with trunks, suitcases, and packing boxes; a curious sort of attic, with levels, steps up in one direction, down in the other. The steps are part of a broad corridor leading at either end to shadowy spaces piled high with unidentified objects. A bit of gray late-afternoon city light seeps into the corridor through grimy windows, not enough at first to see past the inundating clutter.

"Watch your step, careful, you'll break your neck," says the lady with the flashlight, my companion in exploration, who has run an ancient ironwork elevator up seven stories to this eerie storeroom that once, long ago, was the upper floor of a duplex apartment—the bachelor apartment of my father, Irving Berlin.

She fumbles and finds a switch. Now I begin to make out features in the lower room that are scarcely atticlike, the skeletal lines of living quarters: rusty sconces; a wrought-iron chandelier with a single bulb, suddenly lit, that hangs from the beamed cathedral ceiling. Graceful wooden balustrades, thick with dust, edge the steps leading down. Flanking the entrance are dark-wood alcoves with shelves. To the right is a fireplace with a crumbling stucco mantel. Along the front, on the far side of a pile of boxes and trunks, is a wall of leaded-glass windows and a wooden window seat that originally must have been cushioned—an inviting place for a small, dark-eyed man to stretch out with a book from the once-filled shelves.

Out there, beyond the dingy windows, lies present-day midtown Manhattan, Forty-sixth Street between Fifth and Sixth, a busy commercial street on the edge of the diamond district. But once, long ago, it was a quiet, residential neighborhood—well-tended brownstones and limestones, commerce restricted to stores at the street level—a part of town favored by theater people because it was so close to Broadway. And this desolate space where I stood was a Jazz Age landmark; the private sanctuary of a famous New Yorker—the man who in 1911, aged twenty-one, had written "Alexander's Ragtime Band," the theme song of a generation, and had been writing the nation's favorite songs ever since. But it was a gathering place, too, where friends dropped in at odd hours of the night to find the proprietor more likely than not at his piano, just finishing yet another song he was eager to share.

For as long as I could remember, I had known about this house, 29 West Forty-sixth Street, that my father bought in 1921, the year he and Sam Harris built the Music Box Theatre a few blocks to the west; another few blocks up Broadway were the offices of his publishing firm, Irving Berlin Inc. ("Sterling on Silver, Irving Berlin on Songs"). Fixing up for himself the apartment on the top two floors, renting out the rest, he had lived there for only a half dozen years. But the building was never sold—for sentimental reasons, so the story went. This was where he and my mother had courted. This was where they had spent the first days of their headline marriage, barricaded against a mob of reporters and celebrity seekers in the street below; and where they had packed for their escape to Europe, with no return in mind. It was also where, eleven months later, they returned from the hospital with me, their firstborn. Somewhere on this floor or the one below they had found a spot to accommodate a black-haired baby girl and her white-clad nurse.

But though I had walked by the building many times as a young woman working in the neighborhood, I had never gone to see my first home, not till this autumn afternoon in 1989, a month after my father's death, fifteen months after my mother's the previous summer. Who knows why not—lack of interest, shyness, a desire not to intrude on someone else's past.

Even now I felt like an intruder as I picked my way through the clutter, the framed, discolored posters of hit shows of long ago, the rusted filing cabinets, the trunks and cartons and iron boxes filled with papers and manuscripts; opening this door and that, looking into a small guest bathroom, into the remains of a bar with cracked red-leather walls, imagining ghostly voices, laughter, the sound of a cocktail shaker—a silence—then the piano, the sweet, wispy voice.

Back up the wide corridor, with its successive flights of steps, I passed a grilled recess, stuffed with packages, that might have held one of the intricately carved ivory objects that as a young man my father collected. There was a coat closet, more boxes, the remains of a pantry or small kitchen. Now I was in a back room with dark woodwork and yellowing walls where metal shelves held packets of sheet music. Facing the thick, arched doorway, Spanish in style, was an alcove designed to frame a bed. Grilled windows on either side and a crown of small skylights let in a bit of light. Other doors opened onto a large bathroom and a closet with polished wood armoires; a closet designed to accommodate the English suits and made-to-order shirts and many pairs of shoes of a well-dressed gentleman-about-town.

It was all a storeroom now, said my guide, the indispensable Hilda Schneider, my father's secretary for forty-three years, keeper of the flame and the gate, a small, pretty lady with red hair, trim figure, and a feisty spirit. Some of the formidable clutter came from the recent move. Just eighteen months earlier, the year my father turned 100, the offices of his publishing company, the Irving Berlin Music Company, moved out of high-rise quarters on Sixth Avenue into the lower three floors of 29 West Forty-sixth, which were remodeled to accommodate a still-thriving business. But the rest of those boxes and objects? How many years had they been there, waiting for this visit? "If walls could talk," said Hilda, "as they say," acknowledging the cliché. I put my arm around her shoulders, and we stood there, silently staring into the memory-filled gloom.

I couldn't stay long that first time. The rooms felt too haunted with their dusty walls and littered floors. Already for me they had evoked my young father; portraits and photographs came to life. At any moment I might see him, slight, dapper, and dark, in a gray or blue suit, meticulously tailored; olive in complexion, with glistening, slicked-down black hair, large brown eyes, heavy-lidded, heavily circled, arched eyebrows so thick and black they looked painted on, chiseled jaw, high cheekbones, thin but shapely lips. In coloring not that different from the charcoal sketch his friend

Neysa McMein had done around the time he met my mother that hung always in our living room or library. Almost film star material, the gentleman who lived in this apartment, except for the nose, beloved of cartoonists, which Cecil Beaton once said made Irving Berlin *impossible* to photograph (though photograph him Beaton did, more than once). Years later, in a novel, I described a hero, a young Frenchman, as almost too handsome, too romantic, except for his oversized nose, and my mother said I was describing, perhaps unknowingly, my father as he was when she first knew him. By the time I begin to remember him, he has lost that sheen. His good looks have taken on a quizzical cast, and he is always in motion, with a comical air about him, a bit like Chaplin in a speeded-up silent film. Certainly the man my mother fell in love with was quick and quizzical, too, but less so: something smoldering under the surface.

It was on my next visit that I entered the room where I felt my mother dwelt—the unoccupied streetside room on the floor below, which had been left to decay, untouched and empty.

Once again I was in a spectral space, a time warp. This downstairs front room, more formal than the one above, had chestnut-brown paneling, bookcases, a coffered ceiling with a faded design in gilt, old rose, and dusty blue. Opposite the fireplace, on the one unpaneled wall, a tapestry once had hung; part of its scene—trees, a reclining figure—by some mysterious alchemy still clung to the surface. Off this room was a mirrored foyer with flattened pillars edging the silvery panels, French in feeling and rather feminine, different from the solid masculinity of the rest. Could this have been my mother's domain after they were married, the pretty living room transformed into her bedroom? (Already on their honeymoon, my parents, both wretched sleepers, admitted they would have problems sharing a room.) Doors in the silvery foyer opened onto the ruins of a once-luxurious bathroom and a space that might have been a boudoir.

Now it was her young self who might at any moment appear, a reflection in the cloudy silvered mirror, having stepped out of the portrait by Sorine, done the year she met my father, that also hung in the living rooms of my childhood. My twenty-one-year-old mother has milk-white skin, rounded pink cheeks, a delicate rosy mouth, a strong, straight nose (the profile Beaton adored), and honey-colored hair parted in the middle, done up in a French knot—"madonna hair," my father called it, and was cross when, during their courtship, she had had it shingled. Her eyes are light blue, the color of an early-morning sky, and have a dreamy, slightly off-center look (one of them wanders), and this would always be so until those eyes suddenly focused in interest, amusement, or anger. She is plumper than she ever will be again; the twenty extra pounds will melt away without dieting between the time she meets my father and elopes with him nineteen months later—nineteen months in which unfolds "the great American love story," as breathlessly covered, month by month, in the pages of the stately *New York Times* as in the *American Weekly* and the *New York Graphic*.

By the time I first remember my mother, she was thin and exquisitely pretty. "Pale and ethereal," old friends recall the Ellin Berlin of the 1930s. The Ellin Mackay my father fell in love with was not ethereal, though she had a certain whimsy about her, an unexpected sharp wit, too sharp sometimes, that she called her "Irish sense of humor."

It is all history now, ancient history, the celebrated romance of the Catholic golden girl, born to millions, and the immigrant cantor's son from the Lower East Side who became America's greatest songwriter—the story that caught the world's imagination, Abie's Irish Rose in diamonds and waltz time, and canopied my childhood, matching any fairy tale or novel I might read. But in this haunted place, so soon after my father's death, that ancient story—our family's beginning—seems close enough to touch.

2

IT IS THROUGH my mother that I and my younger sisters know the beginning, before any of us came onto the scene; she was generous with those memories; she delighted, after all, in that beginning. Our father told wonderful stories, too, but not on demand, only when the spirit struck him; and you had better listen hard, for with a few notable exceptions he did not repeat himself; mostly he preferred listening to you, asking you questions. But our mother loved to reminisce. And time and again, as I pieced the story together, I found her memories confirmed, in family documents, in letters, in the written or spoken recollections of relatives and friends, though not always in the newspapers, which, she would say, was obvious: Newspapers inevitably got things wrong.

They met on the evening of May 23, 1924, at a New York dinner party, by the merest chance, my mother always liked to note, for my father was a last-minute replacement.

The hostess was Frances Wellman, Mrs. Allen G. Wellman (later Mrs. Harold Brooks), a society woman with ties to the Long Island crowd—the crowd of my grandfather Clarence Mackay—and a taste for the newer, livelier company of theater people. My mother, the postdebutante, was a friend, a charming younger addition to any evening—and my father, the songwriter, such a good friend that Mrs. Wellman could call him the very day of a party and ask if he could fill in for someone who had unexpectedly dropped out. He could and would. As anyone who knew him knew, he liked nothing more than a last-minute plan—or less than a commitment made weeks ahead.

So except for some unknown fellow's indisposition or whim, those two might never have met, though there were other links: Alice Duer Miller, the novelist, an Algonquin Round Table regular and first cousin to my mother's mother; Cole Porter, a well-liked colleague of my father's whose wife, Linda, in earlier days, had been a Mackay family friend. There were other houses where they might have sat next to each other, a stylish young woman, a handsome older man. It was a time in New York for smart, intimate dinners that crossed lines.

But the meeting almost took place too late.

For my mother, in the spring of 1924, was engaged, though still unofficially, to a Washington diplomat. Engaged, not because she was really in love but because it was time—twenty-one was old for a girl who had made her debut, as her father wanted, instead of going to college—because she was bored and too bright for the idle life she was leading. An honor student at a difficult boarding school, St. Timothy's, she had tried for a while taking classes at Barnard, alma mater of Cousin Alice, sister college to Columbia, where her great-great-grandfather William Duer had been president. (The Duers and Traverses, her mother's side of the family, were a brainy as well as an aristocratic lot.) But Barnard in the twenties was a hotbed of reverse snobbery, she'd say. No matter that she wore her plainest clothes and had the family car deposit her blocks away, unlike her friend Consuelo Vanderbilt, who wore furs and jewelry to class and had the chauffeur drop her off in front of Milbank Hall. "They hated me not one bit less," my mother would say, and tell of naively inviting her class in Renaissance art to lunch at Harbor Hill, the fifty-room Mackay mansion in Roslyn, to view her father's famous collection: the Botticelli, the Mantegna, the Verrocchios, the Sassettas, the tapestries and armor. No one accepted. The professor was said to have mounted the snub. After a term she quit. So much for higher learning.

Four months on a grand tour of Europe, in the summer and fall of 1923, had killed more time. In Paris, Ian Campbell, the future duke of Argyll, was her escort. "Robbing the cradle," she called it (he was six months younger), but he was fun to be with, and more accessible than most upper-class British men. Then, back in New York, there was the diplomat (she never would tell his name), attractive, slightly older, solid, someone she was fond of, someone her father approved of. She had accepted a ring, though wasn't ready, not quite yet, to make a formal announcement.

As for my thirty-six-year-old father, who knows what the composer-in-residence and part owner of the Music Box Theatre was up to in May 1924 as he put on his dinner jacket, brushed down his hair to slick perfection, and walked out with that brisk, jaunty stride. He certainly was not engaged to anyone, "except Sam Harris," as he liked to say, the man who produced the *Music Box Revue*s. On his mind, if anything, this springtime night, would have been the fourth in the annual series, coming up soon. The third edition, though it had run eight months and made a star of the unknown Grace Moore, had been a letdown, so the critics said, nothing in a pleasant score that compared to "Everybody Step," "Say It with Music," "Pack Up Your Sins and Go to the Devil,"

"Lady of the Evening," and "Crinoline Days." The charmed show in its fresh, beautiful theater, the show that ushered in the Jazz Age musical, Follies razzle-dazzle gone smart and small-scale, had lost some of its drive. And the composer was fretting, for the Music Box was something he cared about deeply—more deeply, certainly, than any lady in his life.

There was, to be sure, his friend Elsie Janis, the "Doughboy's Sweetheart" of the First World War, a singer and songwriter both; the Janis house near Tarrytown, presided over by Elsie's ever-present mother, was a favorite weekend destination; but there was no indication that this friendship was finally changing into something more. There was Neysa McMein the artist, recently wed to the dashing mining engineer Jack Baragwanath, the woman all the talented young men of New York fell for, my father's type, spirited, witty, with a certain hauteur; but there was no hint that he was carrying a torch for Neysa. He was a man with women friends: Anita Loos, Dorothy Parker, Alice Miller. If he had an occasional "girl"—one of those lush young women in a *Ziegfeld Follies* or *Music Box Revue* lineup—this was the best-kept secret in New York.

All people knew for certain was that he had been in love with Constance Talmadge, sparkling, seductive Constance, the movie queen, leading lady of Douglas Fairbanks and Ronald Colman. But Constance married a Greek millionaire. People also vaguely remembered that there was something tragic in his background: that he had married as a very young man, and his bride had caught typhoid fever on their Cuban honeymoon and died a few months later. He had poured out his grief in a ballad, his first to make a mark and one of his best, "When I Lost You," and tried to forget himself in work. That had been long ago, 1912, but something clung to him, made him elusive, different from the average attractive man about town.

But then there was something from the past that clung to her, too, the girl with the blond madonna hair arriving at the party. Something she never talked about, would have liked to bury, but that gave her an edge, an elusiveness of her own. The miserable old business of her mother: Katherine Duer Mackay, mistress of Harbor Hill, style setter, loving maternal presence, who, when my mother was ten years old, had gone off with her husband's good friend, given up her three children as the price of her divorce. Loss was compounded by scandal, the kind of headline scandal that causes a ten-year-old child to pause before ringing the doorbell of a friend's house, in a cold sweat, knowing that when she enters there will be a sudden silence. People will stop talking because they have been talking about her, her family—poor Clarie, shameless Katherine. But she doesn't turn and run away; she walks into the house, holding her head high, smiling and daring them to feel sorry for her.

So there he was, eligible but elusive, and there she was, semi-engaged but still at liberty. And she faced him—during cocktails, over the soup, between the roast and the salad when the hostess turned the table?—and said in the soft, clear fluting, slightly affected accents of old New York, "Oh, Mr. Berlin, I do so like your song 'What Shall I Do?' "

Mr. Berlin gave her a look, told her the title—"What'll I Do?"—as it appeared on the sheet music, already having sold into the hundreds of thousands, and accepted her correction. "Where grammar is concerned, I can always use a little help," he said. His voice was also soft, clear, and of New York, a newer, blunter New York with a bit of the street about it, a bit of show business and totally unaffected. She was embarrassed but not too. He was amused. A spark was struck. She was a great heiress, a spoiled, stuck-up darling; he was a world-famous composer with the pride and assurance of a self-made man. But both had lifesaving senses of humor, and their humors matched—fast, playful, sometimes a little rough on others.

The rest of the conversation is lost, but it continued briskly, no doubt, interrupted by an occasional lighting by him of her Turkish cigarette, fitted into a long quill holder, the badge of a young sophisticate.

What my mother wore on this memorable night is not recorded, but you can assume the dress was soft in fabric and color—rose or dusty blue or cloth of silver, most likely French, and flattering to a slightly plump figure, showing off the pretty arms and neck and throat, bringing out the creamy coloring— and that it caught a gentleman's eye, pointed a gentleman's eye to the girl within, her skin, her eyes, her hair. A dress that was becoming first, fashionable second. Once, when my mother was quite old, I told her in my father's presence that she looked wonderful, and he said, "Haven't you noticed, your mother has the prettiest clothes around. She always did." On another occasion, in the middle years, I remember my father putting his hand on her shoulder, smooth, ivory colored, barely tanned (she was wearing a bathing suit), and saying, "Have you ever noticed that your mother has the loveliest shoulders," and she bending her face toward his hand. When I recalled the episode—unusual, for they were rarely demonstrative in public—she said, "Oh, you know, he *liked* me."

The liking and the admiration were mutual and probably immediate, though she never said it was love at first sight, only that it had happened before they realized it.

When the dinner broke up, Mr. Berlin invited Miss Mackay to accompany him to Jimmy Kelly's in Greenwich Village, a cabaret where, in its earlier Union Square quarters, he'd once worked as a singing waiter. She accepted gladly; she hated to turn in early, didn't he? Another look: one night owl taking in another. Later, Kelly would tell people they'd met at his place, and my parents, with typical forbearance, didn't correct the story, which gave him such pleasure. After all, it was the same evening. And being alone in a nightclub surely constituted more of an introduction than being table partners at an uptown dinner party.

The next time they met, not entirely accidentally, at another dinner (host or hostess unknown), he offered to drive her home in his Minerva—silver and gray and a block long—as elegant a car as any in the Harbor Hill carriage house where twenty-five years of cars and broughams were lined up shining and unused, as in a museum. At the wheel was Jack MacKenzie, tall, burly, red-haired, a tank driver in the war and since 1919 chauffeur to Irving Berlin, who did not drive and never should be permitted to drive, this same Jack would tell me later with a shake of his handsome head. This night, no sooner were they on their way than they were overtaken by fire engines. "Can we follow them?"

asked my mother, who delighted in making young men escort her to three-alarm fires. "Why not?" said my father, not all that young but no less accommodating to this impulsive, captivating creature.

Their first real date was at the Astor roof, a favorite haunt of New Yorkers for warm-weather dining and dancing where the orchestra played Berlin songs, as orchestras would wherever they went. Next it was Coney Island with Frances Wellman and Cole Porter: the scenic railway, the Ferris wheel and the chute-the-chutes, my mother's favorite, one she would ride with her children and grandchildren, shrieking at the single downward plunge.

One night late, after an evening on the town, they went to 29 West Forty-sixth Street and climbed to the roof. A view that looked west, not across the trees of Central Park but across low buildings to the lights of Broadway, which in those days spread out like the lights of Coney Island from the Ferris wheel.

After that, Forty-sixth Street became a meeting place, an alternative to a hotel roof or a nightclub or Child's for early-morning pancakes, because perhaps by then they had been seen together too much and worried about gossip and her father's disapproval.

Much later to college-age daughters, this once-daring young person, now a middle-aged mother, like all the others, would lay down the law: "Never, never go to a boy's apartment alone." This was different. She did not hesitate to tell us about these secret meetings, even when we were at the most impressionable age. It was assumed (correctly) that nothing untoward happened between a properly brought up Catholic young lady (however lively her interest in the opposite sex) and a man of serious stripe, even at the height of the Jazz Age.

"Where else could we go," she would say, "where we wouldn't be seen and talked about? It seemed the simplest thing to do." Besides, it was a different time, a different kind of man, extremely attractive and not unsusceptible, but older, cautious, responsible, quite unlike these immature, irresponsible boys we kept company with. Besides, there was a chaperone, Ivan the butler, who cooked, though sometimes Irving made scrambled eggs, his specialty, with sautéed onions and tomatoes. She was interested that he could cook, for she herself couldn't so much as boil an egg or make a piece of toast. (A generation later he would still be making those late-night scrambled eggs—for me and my sisters now and whatever untrustworthy youths had escorted us home from a party—and toast would still be defeating her.)

Letters harking back to those early, carefree days record that he played and sang his songs for her. *Music Box Revue* songs: "Say It with Music," "Lady of the Evening," and some of the earlier songs, "Alexander's Ragtime Band," "I Love a Piano." It is easy to summon up that man at the piano singing in a high, wispy, always true voice, hunched over the keyboard, head cocked a little, faking the accompaniment, hands off the keyboard when the notes were too hard, harmonies sketched in with thirds, a single finger in the bass, everything about him pressing out the music— hands, mouth, shoulders, head, eyes. The girl listening is more mysterious, for she isn't in the least musical, but nonetheless transfixed; popular songs are part of life's fabric, hers and everyone else's. It would be one of the ironies later that our mother, the songwriter's wife, could not carry a tune, admitted she was tone deaf (like her own mother), and made a big point of this always, exaggerating for effect and in self-defense. Whenever she did sing, in her high, girlish, off-key voice, with a dreamy little expression on her face, one of those ballads of the twenties, the songs she considered hers, she got teased by her musical daughters and eventually gave up singing entirely, although they were still *her* songs.

And what of the vast gap between where he and she came from? Letters also record that he told her a bit about himself— memories stirred up because of the book Alexander Woollcott, the author and theater critic, was writing about him, memories of a four-year-old in Russia watching his home go up in flames, of a five-year-old coming to America in a ship's hold; of life on the Lower East Side in a crowded tenement, the youngest of eight children; of his father, Moses Baline, the cantor, who died when he was a boy, a stern, bearded man in a yarmulke with the gift of music; and his gallant, practical mother, Leah, who had died just two summers ago, who, no matter how little money there was, fed and clothed her brood. (In America his mother's name had become the less poetic Lena, but Leah was how he thought and spoke of her.)

There were closer memories of Israel Baline, known as Izzy, a rest-less, skinny fourteen-year-old who escaped from all those women to become a busker on the Bowery and then a singing waiter at Mike Salter's Chinatown café, Nigger Mike's; who, with another waiter, wrote "Marie from Sunny Italy" and signed it I. Berlin—the first stage in the transition to Irving Berlin.

And she, finding common ground where there might seem to be none, told him about her grandfather John Mackay, who had been an immigrant, too, a poverty-stricken nine-year-old boy from Dublin who sailed steerage with his family to New York and went west with the forty-niners. Working the gold fields of California first, as a pick-and-shovel miner, he had moved on to the silver mines of Nevada, to Virginia City where, with his two partners, he had discovered the famous Comstock Lode. Overnight Mackay be-came a millionaire, the richest man west of the Hudson, some said. Later, he founded the Postal Telegraph Cable Company, breaking Western Union's monopoly.

Like Irving Berlin, her grandfather was an American legend; and his wife was almost as remarkable—an impecunious young Nevada widow, who took her family abroad when New York society snubbed the newly rich Irish Mackays and became a leader of London and Paris society. Mrs. John Mackay, indeed, was still very much alive, in residence at Harbor Hill, just turned eighty, a pres-ence to contend with and love.

They were so good at conversation, the two of them later, the stories and one-liners and opinions flying across the dinner table, especially when there were guests, that I picture them at it from the start, she especially, words her music, her songs; exchanging bits and pieces of their histories, gossiping about mutual friends and acquaintances, sparring about politics. (It is election summer, and she, a Republican, supports Calvin Coolidge, while he, a Dem-ocrat, has high hopes for Al Smith.) Though perhaps I have it wrong and they were both quiet when alone, talking in stops and starts just about themselves, trying to figure out why they felt the way they did and what they should do about each other.

He attempts to keep things light, calls them a couple of idiots suffering from a bad but fortunately temporary attack of spring fever. But she one night, it being leap year, proposes. Joking, of course. Not joking at all.

"I'm in love with Irving Berlin," my mother confesses to my future godmother, Nellie Livingston, a friend from Southampton, where my grandfather rents a summer house. Nellie's parents, the Goodhue Livingstons, are old New York, back to a signer of the Declaration of Independence and beyond, and very Protestant old guard. But in 1924, Southampton is a place where old-guard Protestants and new-guard Catholics—Mackays, O'Briens—belong to the same beach, tennis, and golf clubs, where their children travel in the same jolly gang and seem to have erased those long-standing lines between the masters' and the servants' religion. Jews were something else, of course, alien people who didn't figure in the equation and were not welcome.

But forthright Nellie knows who and what Irving Berlin is. She has been to all the *Music Box Revues* and loved them. "Funny, I must have wax in my ears," says Nellie. "I thought I heard you say you were in love with Irving Berlin." "I am," says my mother. Nellie puts her hand on Ellin's forehead but finds it quite cool.

Nellie, my mother knows, is "the grave" where secrets are concerned. But there are others who are not.

3 _____

ENTER MY GRANDFATHER, mouth a tight, thin line under his brush mustache, blue eyes blazing, indignant in every portion of his small, tidy, imperious frame.

When I begin to remember this curious and complicated personage, in the 1930s, he is a nice old gentleman to me—the very model of a proper grandfather with a gray mustache I like to pull, calling it fake, and a buttonhole carnation I like to smell and eyes that twinkle at me no matter how fresh I am. And when I think of him in that earlier period, I also think of him as old—how could he have acted as he did if he weren't old? In fact, in 1924, at fifty, there is nothing old or grim about him, though pompous he can be. He is still in full middle age; there is auburn in his hair and mustache and zip in his demeanor; he shoots, he rides, he plays tennis and squash; by day he runs Postal Telegraph, the family business set up by his father (not too well, for he is not a businessman at heart); at night he entertains, at Harbor Hill or at the New York house on Seventy-fifth Street, dines out, or escorts to the opera socially prominent ladies who would like to be Mrs. Mackay (though they should know as a faithful Catholic he won't remarry). And there is one lady he really cares about, the opera and concert singer Anna Case (a choice that cannot be called stuffy). In other words he is a character. A character when he is good, a character when he is awful—and he is, no question, about to be awful. Though one can understand why, on this August day, the eyes are blazing and the generally quiet voice is thundering.

For finally she has gone too far, this middle child he has guided from high-strung girlhood to healthy young womanhood. Not single-handedly exactly, there have been helpers in the raising of his three motherless children: Mary Finnerty, the nurse; Josephine Noel, the chaperone; Pat Thompson, the housekeeper; tutors and coaches without number; the mother superior and nuns at the Convent of the Holy Child; the headmistress and teachers at St. Timothy's boarding school; and for the past four years his own widowed mother, the formidable Mrs. John William Mackay. But he has been there in command, what would be called nowadays a hands-on father, who has provided good times as well as discipline; and has imagined the job nearly done: his bright, too bright for her own good, impulsive "angel child" (as she signs her letters to him, quoting him), almost ready to settle down with a man who will care for her as he has. If he secretly suspects the man of the right class and religion isn't quite up to her intellect and spirit, he suppresses that thought; she could do a lot worse. Indeed.

So now—it is sometime in August—the dismaying word has reached him about a romance between his beloved angel child and Broadway's darling, Irving Berlin. Not by way of his friends the Livingstons, for staunch Nellie has not told. It is Frances Wellman, cupid, coconspirator, stricken with her responsibility, who has ratted. *Irving Berlin!* Mr. Mackay's fury is divided between the messenger, who is given no quarter for corrupting and then betraying his daughter, and the message itself.

My mother never gave the place of confrontation, but I expect it was at Harbor Hill, where my grandfather was overseeing preparations for the grandest party this house of parties had ever known, the ball he was giving in early September in honor of the Prince of Wales. The cozy study, away from the old masters and suits of armor, was where confrontations generally took place, after dinner, if my mother had her way, when my grandfather was just finishing his cigar and in a mellow mood—scenes about money, the bills she was running up, or the life she was leading, too many parties, too many late nights, occasionally and more importantly about the company she kept. But never a scene quite like this one, not so much because of what he said as the way it ended. He was possibly in this first discussion relatively restrained. He would not even comment on the way she had been sneaking about, on that poor besotted gentleman who hoped to marry her, on the talk being caused; he spoke merely of the unsuitability, the *impossibility,* of this man fifteen years older, a Broadway songwriter, someone from a completely different background, of no education, no position, leading God knows what sort of life. It is doubtful at first that he even mentioned that Irving Berlin was a Jew. There was too much else to mention, and he had, after all, Jewish friends—the financier Otto Kahn, who served with him on the opera board; banker Jacob Schiff, his Long Island neighbor; and Bernard Berenson, who advised him on his art collection. The anti-Semitism, which had to be there, which was part of the texture of his world, was unadmitted, well submerged. He simply said that naturally Ellin must stop seeing this man, "You must give me your solemn word." And my mother looked him in the eye, two pairs of light blue eyes locked in an old battle, her eyes expected to give way first, and said, never flinching, "No. I won't promise."

"Father was quite surprised," my mother would say wryly. For it seemed that only a year earlier she had had another unsuitable admirer, Leopold Stokowski, conductor of the Philadelphia Orchestra, known as the "sun god" for his halo of golden hair, his royal ways, and his irresistible appeal to women. My mother had met Stokowski for tea on several occasions at the house of a mutual friend. My grandfather, having learned of the flirtation, told my mother she wouldn't have a shred of reputation left if she was seen with such a man and must see him no more. After a token protest, my mother said, "All right." It wasn't worth a struggle. "Your father will ruin your life," said the sun god. "I hope not," said my mother.

Now my grandfather recalled this earlier intelligent bowing to his wishes. Said my mother: "This is different. I like this one."

Once before, my mother had fought my grandfather about something and not given in: the right to see her mother. Fighting a father—or a husband—she would say later, should not be done lightly.

Given the bitterness of the divorce and the devastation of an abandoned ten-year-old, it would have been understandable had she let her mother go; her older sister Katherine, known as "K," had until recently done just that; their mother, after all, had let them go. Easy, too, to understand my grandfather's implacable resentment, his fight for total custody; the other man, Dr. Joseph Blake, had been his old friend, someone who dined at Harbor Hill, went shooting at the Mackay lodge in Deep River, South Carolina. Worse, Joe Blake had been Clarie Mackay's doctor, the surgeon who had operated on him for cancer of the throat. Blake saved Mackay's life—and while he was doing it, stole his wife.

But the child Ellin remembered the fighting even before Dr. Blake came on the scene, fighting between the parents so bad sometimes that on an outing the children were removed to a second car (where some friendly retainer rode) and returned home—fights over religion (Katherine was a Protestant; Clarie was a Catholic), over politics (she was a bluestocking suffragette; he was a conservative businessman and philanthropist), the fights of two married people who find they have little in common, though once they were crazy about each other, seductive to each other, she with her beauty and impeccable New York background, he with his European education, his millions. Ellin, who adored her mother, saw the shadings and fought; for permission during the war, when the Blakes lived in Paris (Dr. Blake was head of the American Red

Cross hospital), to write her mother and receive her letters; and when her mother returned to New York in 1919, to see her, though always without her husband. The loyal Ellin refused to meet Dr. Blake.

It must have surprised my mother, on that August day, almost as much as it surprised my grandfather, that she was ready to defy him for a man named Irving Berlin as she had once defied him for her mother. Until that moment she hadn't known; now she knew. She loved this man and would have her way.

My grandfather put detectives on the case, a twenty-four-hour-a-day watch on Mr. Berlin to catch him out—in bed with a chorus girl, in an opium den, misbehaving in some sinister downtown way. My father, hard at work on the fourth annual *Music Box Revue*, was beginning to wonder where exactly his bad case of spring fever was leading. One night my mother called him up in the middle of a dinner party, not one to which she'd been invited, and asked whether or not she should return a watch her abandoned fiancé, the suitable one, had given her. "Return it, keep it. Whatever you want to do, dear, is fine with me," he said a bit nervously.

At least a couple of songs get done in August: a novelty number, "The Call of the South," a clever, syncopated countermelody to "Swanee River" that would be a hit of the revue and soon forgotten; and a successor to "What'll I Do?" called "All Alone," a poignant ballad that would not be forgotten, the first of three clearly written for my mother during the courtship (however often the composer might try, self-consciously, to deny this).

She, meanwhile, yanked back to her own world, is about to create a little incident of her own, the first but not the last, demonstrating her attachment to him.

It is the night of the great party. Harbor Hill, the Louis XIV style château by way of Stanford White, poised on one of Long Island's highest points, is lighted and decorated like a castle from Perrault for the visiting Prince of Wales. My mother is wearing a new ball gown and her grandmother's pearls. Mrs. Mackay the dowager, friend in bygone days of the prince's own regal grandmother Queen Alexandra, plays no favorites among her three

Mackay grandchildren. She loves them all: "K," the oldest, vivacious and dark-haired, married two years earlier to Kenneth
O'Brien of the Southampton O'Briens, a rising young lawyer who in
the 1930s will be appointed a judge of the state supreme court;
young Willie, seventeen, still in school, the heir, a sportsman like
his father; and clever, affectionate Ellin, the middle child, the
handful. But she and Ellin, who spends the most time with her,
have a special bond. "Granny" perhaps had a fantasy that night, as
had all the other grannys and mothers at the party. Then, again,
perhaps not, for certainly by then Granny knew of the problem.

Everyone is watching as the prince, the world's most eligible
bachelor, dances with the daughter of the house, one of the world's
great heiresses, to the music of Paul Whiteman, the king of jazz.
What on earth are they talking about, sleek Prince Edward with
the turned-up nose and hair like scratched gold and the saucy,
angel-faced girl? Now she has made him laugh! They are striking a
bargain: If Ellin would keep her father from giving the prince a
boring tour of the Mackay art collection, the prince would distract
her father at supper so she could steal away and phone her young
man—the composer, it so happens, of the very song they are dancing to. (Mr. Mackay had warned the men on guard not to admit one
Irving Berlin, on the highly unlikely chance that he might try to
crash the party; but how could he order Paul Whiteman not to play
that song—"What'll I do / When you are far away / And I am
blue . . .")

Miss Mackay was the only American girl, so the prince later
recalled, who talked to him about another man, let alone left him to
make a surreptitious phone call. "I found it refreshing," he said.

The big party over, my grandfather returns to the problem and
makes a deal: Ellin will go abroad for six months, and if at the
trip's end she still feels the same way about Irving Berlin, father
and daughter will discuss things. Whether or not Mr. Berlin will
feel the same about Ellin after six months does not seem to be the
issue.

In fact it *is* the issue. She has made up her mind. She is in
love and wants to get married. But my father, though also in love,
way beyond spring fever—it's nearly autumn now—has not made

up his mind. He worries about many of the same things her father worries about. About the difference in age, in backgrounds—his world and hers may meet at New York dinner parties, but they still retreat into sternly separate compounds. About religion—Jew and Catholic. My mother has broached the subject of being married by a priest. She herself, though she goes to mass, keeps up appearances, doesn't believe in all that anymore, she assures him. She has had such a strange religious upbringing: a Protestant like her mother till the divorce, a Catholic since. But a priest might help soften up her father. Irving, however, the cantor's son, doesn't see himself being married by a priest. Though he is not a religious person, doesn't even keep up appearances of being an observant Jew, he does not forget who his people are. And then, all the serious stuff aside, there is the simple reluctance of a longtime single man to give up his freedom.

In my father's mocking slang of the day, it was now a situation "with a beard," meaning something heavy, emotional; the beard was long sometimes, longer than Rip van Winkle's grandfather's, he said.

4 _____

SO, IN LATE SEPTEMBER, my grandfather and my mother sailed for England on the SS *Aquitania,* along with the minimum number of retainers: Hermine Tripet, my mother's diminutive, ferociously loyal French maid; William Mundy, my grandfather's genial gentleman's gentleman, and Mary Finnerty, known as Finny, once nurse to Willie Mackay, now companion to old Mrs. Mackay and sometime chaperone of Ellin's. Pretty to look at, with her wavy auburn hair and violet eyes, pleasant to listen to, all-round family counselor and peacemaker, Finny helped set the tone. In London, then Paris, my grandfather was sweetness itself, the debonair and loving father intent on showing his daughter a

good time—galleries, museums, shops, restaurants—the kind of
good time he and she could have together—not realizing at first
that though Angel Child had agreed to come away for six months,
she hadn't said anything about letters.

Almost daily Ellin wrote the person she called "my young
man," pages and pages in her narrow, curvy, untidy but legible (in
those days) hand, a girl in love who was also a born writer, an un-
musical girl whose prose is marvelously musical; observant, intelligent, ardent letters that delivered a clear message along with all
the gossipy details of what she was doing: that she was not about to
forget or be forgotten. Three or four letters to his one. But he was
working day and night now, doing "nothing but grind out music"
for the 1924 *Music Box Revue.* Comedy songs for Fanny Brice.
Sweet songs for Grace Moore. Airy, mostly forgotten, show tunes
like "Listening," "Tell Her in the Springtime," "Alice in Wonderland," "Where Is My Little Old New York?" "I really am delighted
with a good deal of my stuff," he wrote, "then again as I told you so
many times, the thrill of the Music Box has gone and now it has become a job that I love most when it's finished." Even if he weren't
dead tired from the show—the last, he thought; it was too expensive, too hard, to keep up the quality—he wouldn't be much of a
correspondent. Still, what he wrote, in his own wry, humorous
shorthand, in a fast, jaggedy, legible (always) script—a shy man
who couldn't bring himself to wax sentimental—told her he was
not about to forget, either, or be forgotten; that once the show had
opened, he was going to give his full attention to "us," what to do
about "us." In the meantime, he missed her—more, perhaps, than
he had expected—loved her, and was without question rising to
the bait of her own charming importunings.

Between letters, there were wires, sent naturally by Western
Union, Postal Telegraph's competition, with a code cable address
for him (eyebee) and various go-betweens for her—all the secrecy
a nuisance but not unromantic.

From Paris my grandfather went home. Then Finny de-
camped, leaving my mother in the care of other chaperones: first,
to supervise her autumn in Rome, Mrs. Laurence Townsend, an
impecunious socialite intent on finding her charge a titled Italian
husband; next, for the second half of the trip, back to Paris, then

Egypt and the Holy Land, there was her regular at-home chaperone, Miss Josephine Noel, likable, forceful, dispatched to scuttle Ellin's unsuitable romance with sheer nagging.

Wherever my mother went, she was more than welcome. Even without her secret life, to be the rich and pretty Miss Mackay was entrée enough. In Nice, the opera star Mary Garden (who once sang at her father's musicales) called on her at the Negresco. In Florence the William Actons were her hosts at the magnificent Villa La Pietra. In Rome there was tea with the Berensons, a tour of the Colonna galleries with Prince Colonna (a relative by marriage), a private audience with the pope, a ball at Princess di San Faustino's.

But the offbeat, out-of-bounds life was there, too: a get-together with Ray Goetz, the Broadway producer, Irving's early song partner and brother of poor Dorothy Goetz, the wife who died (would they like each other, Irving fretted; but they did, they did!); a lunch with Cole Porter to celebrate long-distance the opening of the *Music Box Revue*. Later, a letter enclosed a batch of great notices, the best since the first revue. "Weren't there any bad ones?" wrote Irving. "Answer, yes, a few, but what a fool I'd be to let you see them." He was glad she'd seen Cole. "I heard he took the outcome of . . . *Greenwich Village Follies* to heart, and I feel very sorry for him. [Follies knocked out all of Porter's songs.] I hope it won't stop him from going right ahead and working harder than ever. He really has much more than 'a nice little talent' " (quoting back a quote from a mutual friend).

And everywhere she went, orchestras played "What'll I Do?," and foolish young men danced with her to "their" song. True, one of the young men, Ian Campbell, back again, was not foolish, was a clear and highly suitable alternative. (The poor Washington diplomat by now had dropped out of sight.) But even with Ian, dancing till three in the morning, the song was her chaperone.

The stories would tumble out later for daughters, and even later for granddaughters, about this miserable trip that had its riveting moments. Her shock at the decadence of Roman society where everyone cheated, at cards and at love. A glimpse of Mussolini, head of the Fascist party but not yet dictator of all Italy, in a restaurant filled with these decadent types. "He was a man among paper dolls, powerful as a bull," she said. "You knew nothing, certainly not those Roman princes, would stop him." A shivery tale of an invitation from a young Italian aviator to fly with him one Sunday morning; another time she'd love to, said my mother, but she had to go to mass; before she could collect her rain check, the aviator crashed and was killed.

But in the Holy Land there was no socializing, only sightseeing, terrible hotels that put Miss Mackay in a snit, and the first stirrings, in a girl who had never given the matter much thought, of what it was like to be a Jew. In Jerusalem she told a rabbi, "My young man is Jewish, you know" (while a crusty Miss Noel commented in a Jerusalem church, "What a curious picture! [It] makes Christ look *Jewish!*"). How it pleased her, she wrote my father, to think that three or four thousand years ago, while her ancestors were still "swinging by their tails in some Irish forest," his ancestors were living in this enchanted city, civilized, educated people.

Random glimpses of our mother abroad, killing time in an interesting way till the six months were up, carrying with her, along with her guidebooks, a copy of Gilbert Seldes's *Seven Lively Arts,* which included, unknown to her snoopy chaperones, a photograph of Irving Berlin. There was never a doubt in her mind. And though all she seemed to hear were reasons why they shouldn't marry (even the sympathetic, high-stepping Linda Porter had said she was not a "big enough person"), the romance by now had acquired a couple of major backers.

The first was Joseph Schenck, my father's best friend, my future godfather. In January he had come to Paris bearing greetings and a message. An odd sort of cupid's messenger, this broad-faced, plainspoken Mr. Schenck, the Hollywood producer, whose friendship with Irving Berlin went back to Chinatown, when Joe was the neighborhood druggist and Izzy Baline a waiter at Nigger Mike's; whose movie-star wife, Norma Talmadge, was sister to Constance, Irving's old love. But he had charm, the sort that often goes with an ugly face; he admired and loved the man she admired and loved; and best of all, he approved of her. Irving wanted to come in February, he told her in private, to talk things over; and he, Joe, personally thought it would be fine for them to marry—the first to say as much—making himself her friend for life. Though the message she sent in return was that Irving must wait the full six months; she had promised her father and must keep her promise.

The second and more surprising backer was my grandmother, Katherine Duer Mackay Blake.

She had made her entrance via the transatlantic mails, which is as good a way as any for that intriguing character to get into the act. For Katherine Blake was not only a highborn beauty whose hauteur no scandal could diminish, she was also a lady with a pen: the author in her youth of two slight but well-received novels, neomedieval romances, and a passionate correspondent. "From you I've not yet heard what absorbed you from May to September!" she wrote her daughter in December in Rome. "Even now I don't really know why you're abroad. . . . Various people have told me that you had rather an admiration for Irving Berlin . . . and when I found out who he was and what he came from I could hardly think you could possibly be seriously interested . . . of course for all I know he may be an acquaintance of yours, so try to take the time to write me all you can about the clever musician Mr. Baline born in Odessa [the first of several misapprehensions], father Moses Baline, mother Lena Lipkin, charmingly written up by Alexander Woollcott in his *Enchanted Aisles*."

"As for Irving Berlin, he is a friend of mine," my mother replied cautiously. "I consider him a very great person [and] he makes no pretense, so anyone who knows him at all well knows that he was originally called Israel Baline. . . . As I have a bad habit of standing up for my friends, what I say of the charm, the real niceness of this new and to you strange friend will not sound unprejudiced. . . . There is a certain quality that distinguishes gentle folks from those who aren't and that quality Irving possesses. . . . " She finished by suggesting that her mother ask their cousin Alice, who knew Irving well, for reassurance.

"She will probably descend in purple and gold like the well known Assyrian upon the Miller household," wrote my mother to my father. "Of course the thing I should love . . . would be for you to meet mother. I think you might get on amazingly well. . . ."

To read Katherine's next letter is to hear her, almost see her, purple and gold indeed. "Of course . . . if you come back at the end of your probation & tell me you are going to marry Berlin because you love him more than anything else in the world," wrote this mother who herself gave up all, more than all, for love, "I shall say, my darling, it's your life & your choice & may your marriage bring you all that's best in love. You see I never approved of the Land Graf's treatment of Elizabeth. I should have said, 'My dear, if you want Tannhaüser, if you feel you can make him forget Venus in your arms, why God bless you!'" And then: "Joking apart, remember no matter what your choice I'll stand by you and hope for the best. . . . And I'll ask him to dine with you & will call on his mother & invite her & his father & we'll have a private room at the Colony Club and we'll all get acquainted." (Is she being funny? Probably not; she was said to have wit but little sense of humor. How would she know that her proposed guests were both dead?)

Now comes a note of caution: "Everyone tells me Mr. Berlin has wonderful appealing aspects, that he's a lamb, a charmer . . . [but] nobody has ever met his father & mother who are I am told Orthodox Jews & I'm wondering if they will ever give their consent. . . . [I]n the long run, Berlin would hate you for letting him go against the traditions of his race . . . so if you are to be happily married and to make him happy . . . you will have to consider traditions to which the children of Israel have been loyal through their long, long history."

That said (and though based on a false premise, amazingly prophetic), the mother's manifesto concludes on a quieter note. "You see every line you wrote showed your love & loyalty & as I read I realized it was up to me to make you feel that if this is to be your marriage I will never go back on you. I have a box for the matinee of the Music Box Revue for January 3rd & I shall go prepared to take a friendly pleasure in the work of a man who may some day be my son-in-law."

So my grandmother joined the fray, placing herself, with a side step or two, in clear opposition to her former husband.

The first meeting between future mother- and son-in-law was in midwinter, most likely at Alice Miller's, in New York. The two got on well indeed. "Your grandmother was beautiful, simply beautiful," my father would say to me. Beautiful was a word he used rarely, if ever, in speech or a lyric. But he said it of her. "And more important, very nice to me."

I can imagine her well, that Katherine Duer Blake of the mid-

1920s, who looks down at me from my dining-room wall, in a portrait by Howard Chandler Christy. My father would have registered the carriage, the cloud of dark hair, the fine features, the proud, slightly haunted expression, the deep lidded brown eyes that were much like his own. In the portrait she wears a filmy evening dress, peach silk with inserts of lace, a big jewel catching up the waist. That winter afternoon, I picture Katherine in a rich, dark color with pearls around her neck, the skirt longer than the fashion. (The famous beauty had piano legs.) Splendid in appearance and manner but direct in her conversation; instantly taken with the groomed look and quiet manner of Mr. Berlin; understanding that for all his fame and talent there was nothing flashy about him; getting quickly to the point of the interview: Ellin. How Ellin, once the six months were up, should be given the chance to make up her mind in the best possible circumstances, whether in Europe or back home (understanding no better than her former husband that it wasn't Ellin's mind that needed making up).

My father was impressed. He was less impressed when later, at the Blake house in Tarrytown, he met Mrs. Blake's husband, the noted surgeon, with his long, bony pirate's face and easy, genial manner. Whatever Mr. Berlin's feelings about Mr. Mackay, he could not take to any man who had stolen the wife of a friend. But that was beside the point. What mattered was that Mrs. Blake liked him, had written Ellin that she liked him, and should be glad to welcome him as her son-in-law. No doubt she approved in part because Mr. Mackay didn't. Annoying Clarie was still a pleasure. But that, too, was irrelevant.

Meantime, from Jerusalem, my mother had written my grandfather, to be on the up and up, that Irving was coming to Paris and had asked my father, Did he want to get married in Paris, or did he just want to "see"? She is writing, writing, all the time, it is a wonder she fits in any sightseeing at all. But the writing is finally bearing fruit.

Back in New York, my father has screwed up his courage at last and done the unexpected, the gentlemanly thing: He has asked my grandmother, since he obviously couldn't ask my grandfather, for her daughter's hand in marriage. Shortly thereafter, to my mother in Cairo comes a wire from my grandmother saying "he" has proposed and she has given her approval. Back goes a wire from my mother to my father in Palm Beach, accepting the proposal. The happy ending is at hand.

But wait. It is only March 1925. Everyone has been writing, wiring, meeting, organizing, but there is still my grandfather. After receiving my mother's letter about Paris, he sends a whopper in return. All stops pulled out: religion, future children of a mixed race, his own devotion, her youth, and much more. And my shaken mother writes Irving that she must try to make her father see, must be fair to the man who, after all, unlike her friendly mother, has brought her up. Irving must cancel his plans to sail. She is coming home.

Trying to please both sides, she almost lost the game.

5

NEARLY NINE MONTHS to go till that happy ending. Nobody talked much about those nine months. The stories dwindle and fade away. There are almost no letters to give a between-the-lines clue as to what is going on. Shortly after her return, my mother takes her grandmother to the *Music Box Revue.* Old Mrs. Mackay enjoys the show—Fanny Brice, Grace Moore, Bobby Clark, how can it miss; hears Ellin talk about Irving Berlin, listens to what must seem to her a fantasy, to match the ones on stage. But mostly it is not an amusing time in New York, in the huge Mackay house, like a fortress on Seventy-fifth Street, or in the bachelor apartment on West Forty-sixth Street. In May my mother has her tonsils out and comes out of the ether pathetically singing "What'll I Do?"; while she is convalescing, Finny, now won over, takes Mr. Berlin's contraband phone calls. But then my mother goes out too soon, in the Minerva, against doctor's orders. She talks too much; hemorrhages; my father is terrified.

Later, my father would often hark back to the *Music Box Revues,* the last of which old Mrs. Mackay attended with her granddaughter Ellin. They would take on deep nostalgic color for him, from the first one to the last; and he would vow to do another before he cooled. But he never talked about *The Cocoanuts*, the Marx Brothers show he worked on that summer and fall, except to say it wasn't the best score he ever wrote. Never talked about the actual writing of "Always," my mother's future wedding present, the song that didn't go into *The Cocoanuts* because the author of the book, George S. Kaufman (according to Kaufman biographers), made an unfortunate joke about the lyric. Nor did my mother talk about her second trip, the one in July and August, out west on the Canadian Pacific Railway to Vancouver, and then down the West Coast to California. She only said that at a certain point "the whole thing seemed hopeless, and we parted forever."

My grandfather seemed to have won. There is a single glimpse of his winning in a memo, preserved all these years, from my father's lawyer to my father, dated June 10, 1925.

In June there were many news stories, including a ridiculous one in the *New York Daily Mirror* that Clarence Mackay and Irving Berlin had actually met, Mackay threatening to cut off his daughter without a cent, Berlin saying that was no problem, he'd settle $2 million on her himself.

What certainly occurred, however, was a meeting between Clarence Mackay and Irving Berlin's lawyer, Dennis "Cap" O'Brien, at the home of Kenneth O'Brien (no relation), husband of my Aunt K. The immediate issue was Max Steuer. In later years the mere mention of Steuer's name—he was a famous trial lawyer often in the news, a hero to some, an immigrant Jew who, like my father, had risen from Lower East Side poverty to prominence— would cause my mother to tremble and my father to get a hard look on his face. Sent to track down stories told to Mr. Mackay by ill-wishing informants, Steuer reported that Irving Berlin was indeed a dope fiend, that indeed he had a dread disease, that indeed his relatives were mobsters. Cap O'Brien patiently disposed of each allegation.

But though convinced and appropriately apologetic, Mr. Mackay did not give up. On the contrary. He asked Mr. O'Brien to stay a bit and hear certain more subtle, more sensible, arguments against the match—that Mr. Berlin and Miss Mackay were both delicate, high-strung people. All credit was given, even in kindly terms, to Irving Berlin for his accomplishments, but Mr. Mackay worried that creating music put a strain on his health. Adding to that their separate backgrounds, the fact that all the fuss might have fanned the flames of romance artificially, he felt more time than usual should be given to a final decision; that it was Mr. Berlin's duty as an honorable person and a man of the world to insist on every reasonable test. Mr. Berlin would regard as very serious anything that would separate a father and daughter permanently, replied Cap O'Brien. "But he would not want Miss Mackay to think that he was any less in love with her than she believed him to be."

At the end of his account, my father's lawyer added this caveat: "Any reasonable suggestion that tended to prevent Miss Mackay and yourself from making any mistake and would aid in harmonizing Mr. Mackay with a decision is worthy of consideration."

On top of that there was a wire to Mr. Berlin from the young lady in question: "Had conversation last night. . . . Will tell you more fully when I see you . . . Meanwhile, nothing for you to worry about stop The situation better than ever before stop Postponement till autumn stop I go west in July for summer. . . . Will telephone tonight Do not call me." Not to worry?

Another witness, my grandmother, the sponsor of the romance, is heard from in a gallant letter to her friend Millicent Hearst describing her recent bout with cancer—cancer of the eye. "I have much to thank God for and anyhow I will not let a glass eye down me," writes Katherine in November 1925. "I went to a big dinner . . . last week and I got such an ovation I almost felt like a movie queen. . . . I see all the children often as . . . Clarie is not being difficult about their coming." And then, astute as always about others, "Ellin told me her engagement with Berlin was broken off in September and that it was all over. They occasionally see each other in New York and I think she is still in love with him and very unhappy."

Things lighten a bit in late November when an article appears in *The New Yorker*—"Why We Go to Cabarets; A post-debutante explains"—by Ellin Mackay. My writer-mother's first published piece. One of several clever, flippant pieces she'd written since her trip abroad that Alice Miller, on *The New Yorker*'s board, had shown to the editor, Harold Ross. He recognized a find: a member of the rich younger set (the readership he hoped to attract) who was willing to write of what she knew. Twitting the older generation, the piece recommended the democratic, frowned-on cabaret over the approved of, exclusive deb ball—though for scarcely democratic reasons. Party stag lines nowadays, explained Miss Mackay, included all sorts of undesirables, young men who lived far up on the West Side, or in Brooklyn even, while at a nightclub you danced with the escort of your choice. No matter that among the press notices was an editorial suggesting that Miss Mackay might have lost her father's Postal Telegraph Cable Company a few Brooklyn customers. The literary debut caused a minor sensation, the struggling magazine's circulation soared, and a grateful Harold Ross gave Miss Mackay a lifetime subscription.

And then, in December, my parents began appearing in public together, the mature approach, slow immunization. My mother attended the opening of *The Cocoanuts* and a party afterward at the home of Herbert Bayard Swope. Swope, editor of the *New York World*, the great pontificator who knew everybody there was to know, including Clarence Mackay, had declared himself a friend of the romance. At other parties, however, people were not so friendly. A few years ago I was given a glimpse of these home-stretch days by Helen Hayes, my parents' old friend, who was actually there—not yet the theater's great lady, merely a charming ingenue brought to these same parties by Charles MacArthur, golden boy of the Algonquin set, future coauthor of *The Front Page*, and her husband-to-be. "I wanted to take Ellin under my wing," recalled Miss Hayes, a lively, lovely lady of ninety who spoke of the twenties as if they were just last week. "Those clever friends of Irving's and Charlie's were so mean to newcomers. Woollcott, Neysa McMein, Dorothy Parker, Heywood Broun, George and Beatrice Kaufman—later many of them would become Ellin's friends, too, and I had to laugh when they discovered she was as clever and dynamic as any of them. Then they only wanted to pounce on this society belle whose overbearing father disapproved of their Irving, their God. She seemed very fragile. Both of them seemed fragile, two fragile beings."

My mother herself would only sniff when speaking of her first exposure to the group (Miss Hayes excepted) and recalled overhearing one lady telling another, "Well, she won't be twenty-two forever."

For Christmas of 1925 my father gave my mother a gold cigarette case, a present with a certain solidity. But on New Year's Eve, a Thursday, yet again they parted. He was planning to leave for Europe on Saturday; as far as she knew, he had sailed. In fact, he had not, and on Saturday night he was playing poker with Franklin P. Adams and some of the Algonquin gang; and though ordinarily he won, this night he kept losing and seemed, wrote F.P.A., New York's own Samuel Pepys, in his diary, unusually inept.

Obviously his mind was elsewhere.

6

ON MONDAY MORNING, January 4, 1926, the date honored above all others in our family calendar, and heaven help you if you forgot, my father telephoned my mother. He hadn't sailed for Europe. He could stand it no longer. He had the ring. Would she get married that morning? Could she come right now to his apartment and from there they would go to city hall?

She was wearing a gray dress that needed to go to the cleaners, because she was only on her way to the hairdresser. In the closet was a beautiful dress she'd bought much earlier to be married in . . . if. But not for city hall. She didn't bother to change even into a nicer city hall dress. She ran.

Next scene is a subway ride, the first for Miss Mackay. Then a cash window at city hall where my father, who had no money on him, asked my mother for two dollars to pay for the license. She held on to her purse and said she didn't have any money, either. "It seemed to me a poor way to start married life, paying for my wedding license." Benny Bloom, office manager of Irving Berlin Inc., who was there for support, came up with the necessary cash.

The witnesses were Max and Tillie Winslow. Not scary people. Familiar, cozy people. A blunt-featured man with high, wavy gray hair, one of my father's two business partners, Max Winslow was the smart Tin Pan Alley song plugger who had discovered one Izzy Baline singing at Nigger Mike's his parody lyrics of the day's popular songs and encouraged the impudent youth to write his own. Max was still the day-to-day encourager, sounding board, occasional critic—a kind of home base. Tillie was a fetching red-haired lady whose ebullience masked a hidden sadness: She and Max were childless. They would be Uncle Max and Aunt Tillie to me and given a special place, always, in the galaxy of friends. They were there, after all, on *the* day.

My father was nervous, the nervousness compounded by the confusion at city hall—the city clerk on his way out to an early lunch called back to perform the ceremony, the gathering crowd tipped off to who they were. My mother was serene. She was about to get her heart's desire. So was he, but that didn't keep him from being nervous.

"Did you never have a doubt?" I asked my mother once. "Of course," she replied in that flip way she had of distancing herself from a serious question. "Who doesn't? I remember once catching this sudden glimpse of him standing under a street lamp. He had a hat on I didn't much like, and he was chewing gum. As he chewed, his hat moved. I thought, Is he really what I am ready to give up all for, this funny little man chewing gum with his funny hat that moves as he chews, up and down, up and down on his head?"

He was.

As a child I liked to hear about the first calls she made from a phone booth. At Seventy-fifth Street she reached Finny, who promptly fainted. Mundy, my grandfather's valet, picked up the phone, asked what on earth she had said to Finny, and when told, said briskly he would call Mr. Mackay at his office. (Later in the day my grandfather went into his mother's room. "Now Mammy," he said, "Everyone's fine, the boy is fine, but I have some bad news." "Are you trying to tell me, Clarie," said Granny, "that Ellin has finally married Irving Berlin?")

Next my mother phoned my grandmother and suggested she sit down, worried she too might faint. Upon hearing the news, my grandmother conveyed delight in her own nonchalant way. On her way into Manhattan to meet friends, Mr. and Mrs. George Blumenthal, she said, "Well, hurry along, my girl, or you'll be late to lunch." Mr. and Mrs. Blumenthal would break out the champagne and give the wedding breakfast.

My father made his own family call, to his sister Gussie in New York, asking her to tell the others: his sisters Ruth and Sarah; his brother Ben; his Robinson nieces, children of his sister Ethel, who had died a dozen years earlier; his niece Sadie Liebster, daughter of his sister Sophie, who had also died young. Ruth's children still remember the reporters who swarmed around their house in Montclair, New Jersey, causing their mother to close the blinds for privacy.

Later that week my mother would meet Gussie, the Baline, after my father's brother, Ben, who would figure most directly in our family life. It was my upper-class Gentile mother's first exposure to my father's middle-class Jewish family: Gussie, who worked for Jewish charities and translated books into Braille; Ben, a furrier in New London; Ruth, who, with her husband, Abe Kahn, owned a paper route and a variety store in Montclair; the five Robinson sisters—Minnie, Martha, and Syd, who worked as secretaries in Manhattan; Lilyan, still in school; and Sophie, who had a beautiful voice and was studying with Grace Moore's teacher. My mother had met many of my father's Jewish friends and would meet many more. But his sister was a broadening experience of a different sort.

Gussie wasn't a Hollywood producer or a Broadway playwright or a writer for *Vanity Fair*. She was an intelligent, attractive thirty-nine-year-old woman from a completely different background; someone who, in her youth, had worked in a sweatshop and gone to night school; the unmarried daughter who had stayed home with her mother (and was said thereby to have lost some good matrimonial prospects); the one who saw Irving every Friday night when he came for dinner. Dark and handsome, with my father's nose and big brown eyes, bosomy, well dressed (in maroon, most likely, and wearing a modish hat), Gussie was now the one who took care of Baline family business for her famous younger brother, handed out the allowances, reported on crises; the one he fretted about and wished would find a good life for herself; the woman in the family, now that Leah was dead, who had a hold on him, though they could bicker like children. Now she was the first to meet his bride.

To the sister, the fair and aristocratic bride might be an alien creature, but she was pleasantly shy and eager to make friends. To the bride, the sister might be an alien creature—the dark Semitic looks, the nasal accent with its flavor of those outer boroughs, the working-girl stamp—but she had style, and more important, she was welcoming, opened her arms wide to this *shiksa* bride—might her mother, who took to her bed when Irving married the first *shiksa* bride, rest in peace. Each had gained a sister-in-law, one who would be with her, more in the mails and over the phone than in person, but still with her, barring a few years when nobody is speaking, for the next half century. Both women must have been relieved that they liked each other, as was the anxious man making the introduction.

"Dear Gussie, It was so sweet of you to send us the lovely basket and the wire," writes the bride from the honeymoon boat, the SS *Leviathan,* a few days after their meeting. "I wish I could have talked with you longer that one hectic day that I saw you, but there was no peace or quiet for anything in those days. I can never tell you how touched I was by your sweetness to me. I know how close you and Irving have always been to each other and how fond of you he is and it means a great deal to me to have had you welcome me as his wife with such kindness. . . ."

Every day that January week, from the Monday they were married till they sailed on Saturday for England, the hounded newly-weds stayed on the front page. And afterward, in London and Paris, before making their getaway to Madeira, they were followed about, with the same question always being shouted at them: "Have you heard from Mr. Mackay?" Those first days, reporters pursued and wrote, and if the bride and groom wouldn't talk, they made it up. They followed them to the Ritz Hotel in Atlantic City, where they spent their wedding night and the next day and night ("Some honeymoon," said the bride), then back to New York, printing things they hadn't said till finally the hounded pair issued a statement: "We have never said one word for publication except that we are very happy, and beyond that we have nothing to say." They did like to recall later the night when a storm cleared the block of reporters except for one drenched young man, under orders from his editor to stick it out no matter what. The newlyweds took pity on him, invited him up, gave him dry clothes and a drink; and though he had himself a scoop, an eyewitness account of the love birds in their elopement nest, he kept his promise not to write anything.

In the meantime, no answer from Clarence Mackay to the special delivery letter sent asking him to come to Atlantic City to give them his blessing, only a story (true) that Mr. Mackay had written a new will disinheriting Ellin; ten million bucks down the drain (though she still had a substantial trust set up by her father that he could not revoke—a pleasant surprise, she'd say, having believed she was indeed giving up all for love.)

I'm not sure when I first heard the part about Grandpa—the Grandpa with the brush mustache and bright blue eyes I knew and loved—the disagreeable part that made the elopement and every turn and twist of the early years of marriage, including my own birth, headline news. However and whenever the word came to me, it would have been dismissed by my parents, certainly until after this jolly Grandpa died. Oh, Grandpa, he was old-fashioned, you know that, they'd say, he thought anyone connected to the theater had to be wild and wicked . . . and then he was mad at us for running off like that, making him look foolish. . . . "From the day he and your father made up," my mother said, "they got on like a house on fire. Well, you know, you've seen them."

But even later the matter was still dismissed, especially by my mother. She rationalized the snobbery (you have to see it in context, class distinctions mattered to people back then), played down the anti-Semitism (look at your grandfather's many Jewish friends, it was a religious thing, he would have been the same about a Protestant—though we both knew this was simply not so). It was his world. His world, which was my world, was funny about Jews. He saw complications for me. As for my father, even he emphasized the sensible reasons to disapprove, especially the older-man bit, so that he would actually say to me, "I would have done the same; well, probably handled it differently, but felt just as upset." Though he said it with an edge, a laugh, hiding his feelings behind a joke, wanting more than anything for me to shut up and stop upsetting my mother.

The real heavy, as the years went by, became less and less Clarence Mackay, more and more people on the sidelines—the press, the friends with an ax to grind, the scandalized family, blowing things up, never letting up.

But none of this was in my child's perception. When I was little, the story leaped from the wedding day to the honeymoon on the island of Madeira. Pictures of Madeira opened my album, the one my mother made for me later that recorded my babyhood and childhood. I imagined them taking the boat the afternoon of their marriage, my mother sailing away in that same gray-dress-on-its-way-to-the-cleaners she was wearing when she got the miraculous call.

There were just those two people on board ship and then happy in a sunlit foreign land, sitting on a waterside rock in almost matching maillots and almost-matching haircuts; or on their balcony at the Palace Hotel in Funchal, she in a pleated chemise reading *The New Yorker*, he in flannels and a blazer, gazing into space; they look young and not that far apart in age. Nearly thirty-eight, my father shows nothing in his face except in the eyes, tired, even when he smiles. But in many of these snapshots the eyes are smiling, too; he looks pleased with himself. Why not?

Contentment prompts a honeymoon song, "At Peace with the World," another one of those romantic waltzes that had become his trademark, his first 1926 hit, better than anything written for *The Cocoanuts*—except for "Always," which had been released as a single song and was now my mother's: her wedding present. A rich gift indeed. The song would remain the biggest seller in the Berlin catalogue till overtaken by "White Christmas."

"I am well and happier than I have ever been in my life," he wrote Gussie from Funchal. "Ellin is wonderful and we are having a fine time together. Please tell the kids and the rest that you have heard from me and that I will write them all soon."

When the month was over and it was time to leave, my mother

sat on her trunk to close it and began to weep. "Don't cry, we'll come back," he said, though in fact they never did.

Oh, yes, I almost forgot: Hermine was along on the honeymoon. It went without saying that wherever my mother went, there, too, went the ladies' maid she had hired when she was still in her teens. "My first entirely adult action," she liked to say. Hermine loved that honeymoon, too, and all the trips that followed and would tell me travel stories; describe how she packed my mother's dresses in layers and layers of tissue paper so that they unfolded without a wrinkle; enumerate the luggage, the wardrobe trunk, the steamer trunk, the valises, the jewel case, the hat box, the book box, complain that my traveling mother's room was *"une vrais salade,"* messy as it was at home; and add the interesting detail that wherever my mother went, Hermine packed a complete set of mourning—just in case.

Back from Madeira, in London first, then Paris, my father returned to work; his musical secretary, Arthur Johnston, arrived to take down the honeymoon song and some new numbers for the summer edition of *The Cocoanuts.* Meanwhile, my mother felt sick. When the doctor confirmed that she was indeed in a family way, my father went off to Cartier's and bought her a bracelet, an inch-wide band of pavé diamonds. He was happy; she was happy, when she wasn't sick, that is, which was a lot of the time. But not so sick that she wasn't able to handle the reporter from the *Tribune* who telephoned her at the Crillon and said he understood she was expecting a baby in June (an alternate explanation, he was hoping, for the romantic elopement).

"I was married in January," said my mother. "Do you wish to deny it, then?" said the reporter. "I have no comment," she said. "But surely, Mrs. Berlin, you want to deny . . ." "No comment," she repeated. "But if you print the rumor, I will sue you and the paper for everything you have."

The rumor wasn't printed. (Though stories did appear in the tabloids that the Berlins were expecting the stork that summer, along with the inevitable speculations: Would a baby, even a premature one, soften up the obdurate Mr. Mackay?)

From Paris my mother wrote her grandmother. "Dear Granny . . . I wanted you to know but please don't tell anyone, that

I'm going to have a baby at the end of November or December. The only other person I've written . . . is Mother. . . . I'm awfully excited and so happy. Irving is an angel to me. I hope I have a girl. I'd like her with light curly hair and big brown eyes, I'd rather have twins. I shall stay abroad to have the baby. It will be more peaceful for me. The newspapers in America are so awful." She wonders if Granny got the letter she wrote from Madeira, the flowers she sent for Easter. She had heard Granny was sick and was worried. "I don't know if you want to hear from me," she ends, "but I miss you so much that I have to write you what I am doing. You were the one person at home I always told everything to."

From Paris my father wrote Alexander Woollcott, a silly, boyish letter. "Dear Pretty [a nickname the rotund Woollcott coined for himself] . . . First, it's none of your damn business why I haven't written before this (not that you've asked) and now that we have settled that, answer the following twenty questions.

1. How are you?
2. What have you been doing?
3. Are you still interested in the theater?
4. How many times have you seen *The Cocoanuts?*
5. Who wrote that funny speech you made at Princeton?
6. Have you visited the Samuels at my house?
7. Is anything missing there?
8. Do you know I was secretly married on Jan. 4?
9. Did you hear we were well and "hamly" [sic] happy?
10. Do you know we are going to be in London all summer?
11. That I am writing a musical show with Lonsdale?
12. And numbers for a summer edition of *Cocoanuts?*
13. And songs for Winslow?
14. When are you coming abroad?
15. Will you dine with us the night you arrive and from then on?
16. Do you know we will be glad to see you?
17. Do you care
18. Will you accept my love
19. And Ellin's
20. Do you still wear that funny hat?

Izzy Baline

But in August, when the Lonsdale show fell through, my parents decided to come home. For my father the London summer had been a professional washout—though just before it began he'd written a top-drawer song, "How Many Times?" a premarriage sort of song, jazzy, kicking up its heels, with lyrics indicating that the songwriter's sense of humor was still in working order ("I'd hate to think that you kissed too many / But I'd feel worse if you hadn't kissed any / Please tell me how many times"). He would need that sense of humor in the months to come.

They sailed home, not to New York but up the St. Lawrence to Quebec City, hoping to slip in unnoticed. The reporters were there, anyhow, all the way from Manhattan. My mother, six months pregnant, threw a fit, screaming and swearing, remembering nothing afterward of what she had said—and just as well, my father would tell her, it was pretty bad. Much later, a poised Ellin Berlin would meet one of those reporters. He recalled his side of things, how he had told the group assembled, "If we don't let that woman alone, she'll lose her baby." He had covered waterfront saloons and longshoremen's strikes, said this newsman to my mother, but never in his life had he heard such language as issued forth from the pretty mouth of Mrs. Berlin. "Put it there, Mackay," said he, an Irishman himself.

The pack had moved back and let her pass to the waiting Minerva, Jack MacKenzie at the wheel, ready to drive the boss and Mrs. B to Alexandria Bay, four hundred miles downriver, where Max and Tillie Winslow had a summer camp.

The four days' reunion with the Winslows was a continuation and preview of what was to come. To this day, people of Alexandria Bay and nearby Watertown remember the story of the Berlin visitation: the cameramen and reporters, kept back by the burly chauffeur who doubled as bodyguard; the visits paid by the Berlins and Winslows to the village, Mrs. Berlin in pink from head to toe, pink hat, pink dress, pink stockings, Mr. Berlin in plus fours (he and Mr. Winslow had been on the golf course); the sending of a telegram (by Western Union) to a New York florist ordering flowers for Rudolph Valentino, lying in state at Frank Campbell's ("They [the Berlins] were close friends of the late movie star," reported the *Watertown Times*); the departure, a would-be secret, to catch the train for New York.

In Grand Central Station another mob awaited. But if my mother lost control again, she never said. Never said anything about that New York homecoming; the reality behind the continuing tabloid stories, the rumors of a reconciliation between Mr. Mackay and his songwriter son-in-law, the rumors that the expected baby would be raised a Catholic, that to placate Mr. Mackay, Ellin and Irving Berlin would be remarried by a priest before the baby was born.

Not bloody likely.

7

I M A D E M Y E N T R A N C E into the world and this unquiet family at York House, a small, private Manhattan nursing home, on November 25, 1926 Thanksgiving Day, around two in the afternoon, interrupting the doctor's turkey dinner. This fact for some reason charmed my parents, for never a year went by when they didn't mention it.

What they noticed about me first, they said, was that I had eyebrows, perfectly defined black eyebrows like my father's, and his dark hair. But I didn't look like him, or her, though my grandmother said I resembled my mother as a baby, with her blue eyes. (Mine turned hazel soon.) From the start my parents said there was no one else in the world who looked like me, and when a baby appeared on the front page of the *Daily Mirror,* claimed to be me but not me, my mother called her lawyer to file a suit immediately. Her lawyer said she couldn't sue, if the baby was deformed in some way, yes, but this was a perfectly nice looking baby. "It's not Mary Ellin," my mother said indignantly. So though they had sworn to give out no photographs, they relented and summoned Edward Steichen, photographer of Garbo and Gloria Swanson, to take pictures, one of them for publication, of the new mother and child.

In the extensive coverage of what is, after all, a fairly ordinary occurrence—a couple has a baby—there is one notice I treasure. A wire-service editorial that was picked up by smaller papers around the country—the *Bridgeport Times,* the *St. Paul Herald,* the *Elmira Advertiser.* Slugged "Hideous Handicap," it read:

> The name of Ellin Mackay who before she married Irving Berlin, America's foremost songwriter, was herself America's foremost heiress, has been stricken from the chaste sheets of New York's Social Register.
>
> Strangely enough, the latest edition of the Register made its annual debut on almost the very day that the Berlins' latest edition in the person of a blue-eyed seven-pound daughter was born.
>
> The infant therefore faces life with the hideous handicap of neither its mother nor its own small self being given a paragraph, a sentence, even a period or comma in that arbiter of human destinies, the Social Register.
>
> Perhaps the fact that Dad Irving is one of the best known men in America, that his face looks down from the sheet music on millions of pianos, that his lilting tunes give joy to millions of people the world over, may compensate a bit.
>
> Perhaps, too, the fact that the names of the impeccably correct Social Register are put there for reasons of pedigree rather than of achievement may compensate the young lady, too.
>
> Here's hoping that young Miss Berlin has no colic brought on by worry at the grave omission.

My grandfather apparently sent no word. Aunt K, who wanted to see the baby but refused to meet or acknowledge in any way the baby's father, was told not to bother to come. Uncle Willie is unaccounted for. But the sense, in the middle of a happy time, of being shut off is only too clear from the Christmas note my mother wrote her grandmother, on monogrammed notepaper with a new address: 29 West Forty-sixth Street. "I can't let today go by without sending you my love. Try to think kindly of me, but however you think, I shall always think of you as you used to be to me: kind and loving."

The bachelor apartment is now a family home. There are new curtains, slipcovers, window-seat cushions, new pieces of bedroom and living-room furniture, along with the crib, the baby wardrobe, clothes tree, rocker; evidence abounds in an old Altman's bill that there was a fully equipped nursery and that one of the rooms was indeed transformed into my mother's bedroom. An old florist bill leads me to believe that a week before Christmas there probably were red roses everywhere—the American Beauty roses my father always sent my mother for holidays and anniversaries and a Christmas arrangement for the dining-room table. There must have been flowers from friends as well—welcome to the baby, welcome home, Merry Christmas—and somewhere a tree with presents underneath. In the bachelor apartment a newborn child is crying, and the former bachelor is working on a song—as if to counteract any sad feelings his wife might be having about her disagreeable family.

The song is "Blue Skies." The one my father always said was written to celebrate my arrival.

There is a different story, of course, to be found in that compendium of popular musical lore Max Wilk's *They're Playing Our Song:* that "Blue Skies" was written for my father's old friend Belle Baker, the husky-voiced, belt-'em-out singer who popularized "When I Lost You," "That International Rag," and "Cohen Owes Me Ninety-Seven Dollars." On December 28, three days after Christmas, Belle was opening in *Betsy*, a new Ziegfeld show with a Rodgers and Hart score. On December 27, she called Irving Berlin. There wasn't a "Belle Baker song" in the show, she wailed; could he help? According to Baker's son Herbie, then six years old, Wilk's source for this tale, Irving Berlin arrived after dinner with the first eight bars of a song he had "in the trunk." All through the night, keeping little Herbie from sleep, he hammered out the rest on Belle's piano.

The next evening, run into *Betsy* by Ziegfeld without Rodgers and Hart's knowledge, "Blue Skies" stopped the show, encore after encore, till finally the spotlight found Irving Berlin, in the front row, who stood up and took a bow. A mean trick, you might say, on Larry Hart and twenty-four-year-old Dick Rodgers, whose account of the evening in his autobiography *Musical Stages* is remarkably even-tempered: "It really didn't take a trained ear to appreciate that the Berlin contribution 'Blue Skies' was a great piece of songwriting, easily superior to anything Larry and I had written for the production, but at the time I was crushed . . . particularly since Ziegfeld had insisted he wouldn't think of doing the show with anyone else. A few words in advance might have eased our wounded pride, but Ziegfeld could never be accused of having the human touch."

A call to Max Wilk compounded my frustration. Had he confirmed the Belle Baker story with the central figure? Yes, indeed, said Max. In the winter of 1973 he had talked to Mr. B, who said, "You believe what Herbie told you, what does a six-year-old know?" And then, without denying the basic facts, "It's a much better story than that." Asked to elucidate, he said, "I have a lot of stories. I'm saving them for my biography." Maddening. But then my father, even before he was eighty-five and cantankerous, hadn't liked to be pressed.

The answer, however, was quite simply found in one of the treasures of the Irving Berlin office, the file of copyright cards—a card for every song with every song's history, when it was first registered (the title, the lyric, the music, in stages sometimes), when it was published.

"Blue Skies" had been registered the week before Christmas. It had been in the trunk less than a fortnight. Belle's song, but mine, too, there in my Irving Berlin songbook, on the "Blue Skies" sheet music with the fluttering bluebirds, in my father's strong, jaggedy hand: *For Mary Ellin, her song.* Christmas 1926:

> *Blue days all of them gone*
> *Nothing but blue skies from now on.*

Ten days later, on January 4, 1927, my parents celebrated their first wedding anniversary. It was the end of the beginning and the beginning of a strange, mixed-up time, part high life in the late twenties—Palm Beach, Palm Springs, Hollywood, songs for the 1927 *Ziegfeld Follies*, for the new talking pictures—part period of adjustment (now that you've done it, how do you make a life?). At its heart was a tragedy, out of the blue sky, the blow you can't anticipate; the sort of tragedy that can pull apart a relationship or, as happened in this case, cement it forever.

PART TWO

HARD
TIMES

Father and daughter, French Lick, Indiana, 1930.

8

O N E   D A Y , in the winter of 1937 when I was ten years old, I was rummaging where I had no business rummaging, in an old desk, temporarily displaced, available for rummaging because things in our apartment were being rearranged. In one of the drawers was a clipping. A yellowing tabloid front page with a headline—"Irving Berlin Son Dies"—and a baby picture of me.

More indignant than upset, I brought the clipping to my governess. "Look at this stupid newspaper," I said, "saying that I am dead . . . calling me a boy."

My governess was French-Swiss, soft-spoken and trustworthy, a center of calm in our sometimes overstimulated household. Her name was Gabrielle Amuat, a name that seemed to suit her repose, her slightly melancholy charm. You couldn't call her a soft brown winter bird, she was too angular and erect for that, but she dressed like one, enveloped you in the warmth of woolens and chenilles. Neither young nor old, not quite pretty, she had crimped brown hair, held in place by an invisible net, round brown eyes, a softly rouged triangular face, a gentle voice; she made French lessons a game, and nothing much except matters of safety and health caused her agitation. But now she was extremely agitated, pale behind her rouge, a hand flying to her mouth before reaching for what I held. Where had I found that? What was I doing, poking in places that were private? Why wasn't I practicing or doing my homework? A brief attempt to bluster her way out of the spot I had put her in.

And then: "Your mother would kill me, never, never, tell her that you heard it from me. Look at the date; that is not your birthdate. The newspaper just used an old picture of you. Look, it even says, 'A picture of an earlier Berlin baby.' "

So she told me what the world knew, though most likely had forgotten, but I did not know, the pitiful tale: that there had indeed been a son, Irving Berlin, Jr., born just two years after me, who lived only three weeks. It was something to do with his breathing, Mademoiselle said. His little heart just stopped, no one understood why. The tragedy had broken my parents' hearts, and they simply could not speak about it, and I must never speak about it to them.

I didn't believe her at first, though there it was, staring at me from the old clipping, not a mistake after all. I didn't want to believe her. How could they not have told me when they told me so much? How could I not know such a terrible and important thing? But then she added the final harsh detail, the final underscoring of why I must say nothing: that the baby had died on Christmas Day—in our family life the most spectacular holiday of the year. That made no sense, either, except that there was something nudging me about Christmas Eve, the day before the most spectacular day. Something odd. That every Christmas Eve my parents went somewhere. They wouldn't say where they were going. My mother acted peculiar when I asked and brushed me away, implying it had something to do with last-minute preparations, surprises. Only she didn't look the way she did when she was up to some surprise.

"Where does my mother go on Christmas Eve?" I asked my governess now.

"She goes to the cemetery," my governess said. "To put flowers on the grave."

That was what this old newspaper clipping meant, she said, taking it from me, crumpling it in her hand. I didn't need to look at it again. It would be printed on my mind for all time.

It was at the end of a restful, near-idyllic winter at the Desert Inn in Palm Springs—the winter of 1928—that my mother became pregnant for the second time.

Palm Springs was the latest, though not the last, in a series of places we lived when I was a baby and small child, for my parents moved restlessly about, following the dictates of my father's work, my mother's health (worrisome since my birth), looking for somewhere to land—a shadowy period always, talked about only sporadically, out of context, scattered bits like the pieces of the jigsaw puzzles set up on a card table wherever we lived.

The previous winter it had been a house in Palm Beach, my

bachelor father's favorite vacation place. "I know you've been here and hated it," he wrote my mother from Palm Beach before they were married. "I do too when the mob is here but tonight it's really grand—clear sky, moon, stars, palms waving, quiet outside of the birds and above all warm."

As a young married woman my mother presumably no longer hated Palm Beach. "Nobody ever had as much fun as your father and me when we were young," she would say in later days when life was slowing down and less jolly, and did not exempt Palm Beach from that generalization. Within the mob—the rich, social, party-ing crowd—were free spirits like Marjorie Oelrichs, the future Mrs. Eddy Duchin; Anita Loos, author of the current best-seller *Gentlemen Prefer Blondes* (who according to the press joined my mother in "black bottom" lessons at the local dance parlor); Nellie Livingston, my newly appointed godmother, who charmed my fa-ther with her lack of airs, her scrubbed, fresh-faced looks, her un-stinting approval of her best friend's new husband. There were offbeat characters like the Mizners; Addison, the architect of Palm Beach; Wilson, the con man and wit, nearing the end of their Florida reign (1926 was the year the land bubble burst), both chums of my father since the 1910s.

But there were also the friends and relatives by marriage of Clarence Mackay who didn't speak to Mr. and Mrs. Berlin, and there were the customs of the place, customs my Jewish father could shrug off as a bachelor, customs my mother might have de-rided when she visited as Miss Mackay but had done nothing about; customs they now confronted together.

It was no longer a question of her not choosing to go to the Gentiles-only Everglades Club, the center of Palm Beach social life, because it was filled with snobby talk and lightweight peo-ple. Now she couldn't go even if she wanted to. And if her friends told her it was nonsense, that Irving was "different," her response was a firm refusal and a countering condescension of her own: poor them, their loss, no big deal (or at least not one she would admit). My father's attitude was what it always had been—that shrug—he didn't like clubs, period, professional clubs excepted, preferring a place where you paid your money and got what you paid for.

However much fun that winter might have been, my parents did not return to Palm Beach as a couple for many years (though my father occasionally went there to work), and never with us children. It wasn't our sort of place, they said, and let it go at that.

In the Palm Beach of 1927 my father seems to have written just one song—a great one—"Russian Lullaby." Was I its inspiration? He never said so, and I never thought to ask, not associating that minor-keyed, Slavic lament with my own childish self (though when I was old enough to be aware of my roots, I never missed an opportunity to boast of being "half Russian"). Certainly there is scant connection between that "lonely Russian Rose" gazing upon her brown-eyed babe, yearning for a land that's free, and my mother, gazing at me in my perambulator under Florida palms, yearning for who knows what—for things to be simple, she might have said, for events and Irving to do her bidding.

Next, after a spring at Forty-sixth Street, comes the experiment in suburban living—my father's decision to leave Manhattan and live in the country. It would be good for my mother, good for his work, good for baby. So up the Hudson we went to Dobbs Ferry, to healthy fresh air, chirping birds, and sweet smells; to a turn-of-the-century stone house set on a sloping lawn, with woods at the edge and a swimming pool. For the rented house in Dobbs Ferry my mother bought her first set of china. She established accounts at village stores and dutifully kept a ledger of household expenses. In the leafy quiet of Dobbs Ferry, my father wrote part of the score for the 1927 *Ziegfeld Follies* (and possibly the first draft of "Puttin' On the Ritz" for a show he and Anita Loos were talking about doing—a twenties-style *Upstairs, Downstairs*). A little Dobbs Ferry photo album commemorates bucolic summer days, my father in a bathing suit with me in his lap, my mother in a white cambric linen dress and T-strap sandals, wheeling my carriage.

There was only one hitch to charming Dobbs Ferry. As my mother would recall, "*I* lived with *you* in the green country, in the good fresh air, while Daddy dear soon resumed his regular life in town, joining us on weekends." With a mid-August opening, this was predictable. But once the *Follies* opened, there were other excuses. She could see how it would go in the fall and winter. She was young and gregarious, unwilling to be cooped up in a country fortress, living for Fridays, when her dashing husband would return, a reluctant illustration of his 1909 hit "My Wife's Gone to the Country, Hurrah! Hurrah!"

By October we were back in Manhattan, at the Warwick Hotel, a favorite of theater people, conveniently located at Fifty-fourth and Sixth Avenue, just a few blocks from my father's office. Pigeons and pavement replacing tree-shaded lawns, robins, and a river view.

And what about the 1927 *Follies,* which starred Eddie Cantor, gorgeous girls, Joseph Urban scenery, and introduced a new singer from Chicago, Ruth Etting. "Peacock splendour" . . . "Immense for both eye and ear," critics wrote of the show, but the score did not command raves. Only "Shaking the Blues Away" has survived as a standard; sung by Etting, with her spirited twang and her rhinestone shimmy, it broke loose from the prettiness of the rest and stopped the show. "I don't know that any one of the songs is outstanding but you will hear a lot of them this winter," wrote Burns Mantle in the *News.* "[The Berlin] sense of melody is as perfect as any can be . . ."

"The First Minstrel's verse and music are naive as in the past," wrote Percy Hammond in the *Tribune,* "and the hits that are already Rotarian were entitled 'It All Belongs to Me,' 'Shaking the Blues Away,' and 'Ooh, Maybe It's You.' One ventures to suspect that the last named has been sounded before upon Mr. Berlin's guitar, a suspicion that in no way distracts from the ballad's popularity." (The last named is in fact a lightly disguised "Blue Skies," some sort of speed record for that kind of musical recycling in which even the best of songwriters occasionally indulge.)

The reviews—the first my parents pored over as a married couple—were friendly but not sensational. They undoubtedly hit a nerve, then were brushed aside in the high spirits of that summer of 1927 that included the Southampton wedding of Nellie Livingston and Frederick Cromwell, a favorite tale. How Nellie's mother, Mrs. Goodhue Livingston, Clarence Mackay's dear friend, had said that naturally Ellin Berlin could not take part in the wedding. No change, summer of 1927, on that front. "Well, that's all right," said

Nellie, the only Livingston daughter. "I don't need bridesmaids, ushers, all that. Freddie and I can just go down to city hall, and Ellie will be my witness." Mrs. Livingston gave in. Ellin was matron of honor, a vision, most certainly, in lavender chiffon and a picture hat. Irving Berlin, her husband, was one of the two hundred guests at the Livingston house who attended the ceremony and the wedding breakfast afterward. (Southampton opening its arms to the wayward couple? Not quite. My parents did not attend the bridal dinner, given by the groom's parents at the Meadow Club, which made it clear that Irving Berlin would not be welcome.)

After the busy summer, New York was quiet that fall. One song was sent off "for Winslow" to boost the publishing-house list, "The Song Is Ended," an instant hit, sheet music on every piano in the land, a melodious waltz with a haunting lyric, a song no one could say had been sounded on Mr. Berlin's guitar before. And though no new show was immediately in the offing (the Anita Loos project seems to have died), Mr. Berlin had another idea—a musical about a minstrel man, dramatic in story line, different from anything he'd done before, a halfway station, maybe, between musical comedy and that jazz opera he had always said someday he would write.

Then, in December, we were off again, headed west for California. Partly on doctor's orders: My mother, underweight and anemic, was told she should not spend the winter in New York. Partly to take a look at Hollywood. My father had been at the New York opening of *The Jazz Singer* (thought of always as the first talking picture though there had been a few other early experiments). He had listened to Al Jolson sing "Blue Skies," and he was intrigued by the new movie possibilities for a songwriter and also, it seems, by the notion that Jolson might make the ideal minstrel man.

So there we were in Palm Springs, still an end-of-the-world sort of place in the winter of 1928, a tiny hamlet set under jagged mountains, pink in the morning, purple at night, where people went for their health, to get away from it all. Everywhere was desert, a lot of desert in those days, and few houses. Our house was attached to the Desert Inn, Palm Springs's first hotel. It had a white-pillared veranda where my playpen, carriage, and toy piano were kept and where my mother read. At the sunny end was my father's striped canvas deck chair.

It was the best thing that could happen to a young married couple, my mother would say later, to be away together in some foreign or outlandish place, thrown in on each other, alone. In Palm Springs they celebrated their second anniversary. They rode. They played with me. They took picnics into the desert, Jack MacKenzie at the wheel of the olive-green Rolls-Royce that had replaced the Minerva. "Alone," their version, dependent as always on a retinue. Jack, the ever-present Hermine, Marian, my bossy, no-nonsense Scottish nanny.

Eventually, during the week my father began going up to Hollywood, staying at the Roosevelt or the Ambassador, talking about songs for the new talkies with Joe Schenck, chief of United Artists, and Sam Goldwyn, who had recently joined forces with Schenck; with Jack and Harry Warner, producers of *The Jazz Singer;* with Harry Cohn, head of Columbia Pictures, who had once been a song plugger for Irving Berlin and Max Winslow and was married to Tillie Winslow's sister Rose. Friends, and fellow poker players, from the days when movies had been made back East, in Astoria, New York, and Fort Lee, New Jersey, telling their old pal Irving he should get in on the great new gamble.

Meanwhile, on her Palm Springs veranda, my mother picked up her pen and wrote my father about this and that: about what she was reading (*Of Human Bondage,* "a swell book") and eating ("chicken and chocolate ice cream for your peace of mind"); about an instructive visit from Rose Cohn, who told the story of how she had dumped her stuffy lawyer-husband, the Cromwell of Sullivan and Cromwell, for the colorful Harry Cohn ("Mr. Cromwell found his pleasure in palling about with William Taft, Elihu Root, and such. And Mrs. Cromwell thought that was fine," but show business was better); about me, how cute I look in the clothes he had bought ("probably my feeling against rompers only needs your excellent taste in choosing some to disappear"), how I could say my name, more or less, when asked and "how do you do" while shaking hands. "She has rare charm," my mother wrote, "and I give you all the credit."

At the very end of March, about to leave Palm Springs for Beverly Hills, she notes I am a perfect child—but certainly hopes they haven't another on the way. They do.

Only two songs came out of that time in Palm Springs—"Sunshine," a cheerful ditty that nonetheless prompted morose news stories that Mrs. Irving Berlin was gravely ill (tuberculosis implied), that the Berlins were moving to Arizona. What other explanation, pondered the *New York Telegram,* for the latest Berlin lyric, "Pay your doctor bills / Throw away his pills / You can cure your ills / With sunshine." And as always, the old question: Would Clarence Mackay come West to see his sick daughter and be reconciled? Whether or not the song and the attendant publicity did the trick, it is a fact that by winter's end my mother was in touch by telephone and mail with my grandfather. The beginning of a long softening up; of nothing, really. (Whatever those first approaches, they did not include my father.)

The other song was a tender little waltz, "I Can't Do Without You," finished in March, shortly before my mother's twenty-fifth birthday.

April and May are spent in Santa Monica, in a house on Adelaide Drive, a street with dazzling views of mountains and sea. Pregnant, apprehensive—the California doctor has told her she is too frail to have a baby and should end the pregnancy—feeling none too well, my mother spends time with a new friend, Frances Goldwyn. She has met other Hollywood wives—Rose Cohn; Norma Shearer, bride of Irving Thalberg; Diana Fitzmaurice, whose husband, George, is Sam Goldwyn's favorite director. But Frances, with her springy dark red hair, her brilliant smile, her edge under the sweet demeanor, is more than a fellow wife; she is a potential pal. She has a little boy just my age; she has lived in New York and, like my mother, looks upon Hollywood with a cool eye; she, too, is a former Catholic married to a Jew, an important older man. She is also very smart, a reader and a talker, eager to learn what Ellin Berlin can teach her about literature and languages and to teach in exchange all she knows about life in movieland. Each thinks she is the other's mentor, a happy balance.

Meanwhile, my father is making his deals: to write the theme for *The Awakening,* an early Goldwyn sound picture, starring Vilma Banky (the song will be "Marie," not the swinging Tommy Dorsey interpretation that was a 1938 hit but a slow-paced waltz); the theme for *Lady of the Pavements,* D. W. Griffith's first movie with sound ("Where is the Song of Songs for Me," which decades later would resurface in *Mr. President* as "Is She the Only Girl in the World?"); and the title song of Mary Pickford's first talkie, *Coquette* (the very last of those whispery 1920s Berlin waltzes). He is also going ahead with that minstrel-man show. He has a title, *Mr. Bones,* and a writer, the actor and playwright James Gleason, to do the book; Jolson is interested. After a getaway winter, he is "pepped up again," as my mother puts it, ready for a summer of hard work, back East, in a rented house in Port Washington.

On May 11, 1928, my father celebrated his fortieth birthday. In photographs from that spring he is still amazingly young looking; he gives his wife loving young husband glances, his baby loving young father glances; snapped stepping out to a Hollywood premiere, there is boyish mischief in the half-smiling lips. Appearances are deceiving. Forty is not young. Forty is ancient if you hit the streets at fourteen. Forty, of course, is a mere boy if you are going to end up living till 101. But my father evidently had no such premonition. Rather, during this period he would exasperate my mother by saying, "I hope I live long enough to buy Mary Ellin her first ice cream cone," or, a bit later, "I hope I live long enough to see her in her first long evening dress."

Port Washington was only twenty minutes from Harbor Hill. Circling in on my grandfather? Not exactly. Port Washington was an even shorter ride to Great Neck, where Herbert and Margaret Swope lived. Long Island was a divided yet shared enclave in those days. There was the Long Island my mother had grown up in, the territory of the Mackays, Whitneys, Vanderbilts, Morgans, Hitchcocks, Harrimans, etc. High society, Piping Rock Club Long Island, almost all Christian, with that smattering of permissible German Jews—the Schiffs, Warburgs, Guggenheims—to make it seem not quite what it was; and then there was theatrical and movie Long Island, home of Adolph Zukor, Nick Schenck, George and Beatrice Kaufman, Howard Dietz, Harpo Marx, etc. At the

Swopes', the two Long Islands met. No reason for my parents *not* to rent a place where my father had been weekending for years.

Whether the move was also strategic, I cannot say. Whether or not the phones buzzed between the summer rental and the castle on the hill, I have no knowledge, only an indication of movement in an undated 1928 letter from Finny to my mother. "Do write a line to your Granny," writes Finny, "full of affection as she needs that and does not always get it from the others, needs it more than she needs her money. More than anything else she has your affection for her, she tells me so often."

But my pregnant mother didn't stay put even for the whole summer. In August she took me to the Adirondacks, to Loon Lake, where her father had dragged her as a girl to put roses in her cheeks—partly for the fresh air that made her less queasy but mostly to give my father, who stayed on in Port Washington, space to work on *Mr. Bones*. "I realize very clearly that with me and my friends and the baby and my constant demands . . . it is impossible for you to do good work in the house," she wrote from Loon Lake. And she expressed a wish, after the baby was born, after the show opened, to go abroad so he could study music and work on "something different"—and posed a tantalizing question: Had he "given up" his opera entirely, "the short one for Robeson?" (meaning certainly Paul Robeson, the triumphant young star of Eugene O'Neill's *Emperor Jones* and currently of the London production of *Show Boat*).

All of a sudden, letters are beginning to reflect concern, little shivers of uncertainty about the future. Not their personal future. No matter how ill-tempered she gets, he remains "good," "gentle," "the sweetest person"; no matter how uncommunicative he gets, she keeps battering away at his reserve; love surmounts all. It is his songwriter's future she's fretting about. His *composer's* future. Where he might, and should be, heading. "I'm not belittling what you have done," she writes. "But while talent and facility withers with years, genius matures. And I don't think you've ever stopped long enough to listen to that maturing genius."

Then, on September 4, back in Port Washington, my mother took a call from Finny. Granny, who had a bad heart, had had a heart attack. Finny had called Mr. Mackay in London, "K" in Southampton, and was now calling Ellin. That meeting at Louise

Mackay's bedside, emotionally charged as it must have been, is described with the greatest reticence in my mother's fictionalized biography of her grandmother, *Silver Platter*. On the day Mrs. Mackay took ill, Willie stayed home, and the married granddaughters came to see her. "The grandchildren when they went into her room tried to hide their anxiety," my mother wrote. "But Louise saw it. It pleased her that as she talked to them in her accustomed way their strained young faces relaxed." Reassured, they went away. At five o'clock Louise asked for tea and her paper, the Paris *Herald*. A few hours later, Willie called Ellin back, along with the priest. But before the priest or Ellin could arrive, "Louise's heart stopped beating and without pain, without even realizing it, she died."

I thought it a beautifully understated last page of a remarkable book. I understood the book's limits: meticulously researched, richly detailed in all aspects of Louise Mackay's history, accepting uncritically her social values, it contains no mention whatsoever of the battle over my mother's marriage, only a casually charming allusion to the fact it took place. Nor for that matter is there any mention beyond the bare fact of Clarie and Katherine's divorce. And so, out of a delicacy she herself dictated, I never asked my mother, was that the first time you had been back to Harbor Hill? That you had seen your grandmother? Nor did I try to learn about the funeral at St. Mary's Church in Roslyn, where my mother, six months pregnant, had sat in the front pew with her father, between Willie and K. It was sensitive material always, not to be poked at.

Anyhow, in September 1928, the year was heading to its end—the birth and early death of my brother—to the sealed-off time when questions and stories would stop entirely.

9

IRVING BERLIN, JR., was born on December 1, 1928, after a difficult birth. Mine had been difficult also. My mother did not have children easily, though new, improved anesthetics would make the births of my younger sisters "a relative breeze," she would say. The second birth must have been even more frightening because of her health. She was sufficiently scared in the final weeks of pregnancy to write a new will and a letter to my father explaining the elaborate instructions regarding him, me, and the baby to come and the disposition of her money and jewels.

Then, suddenly, the ordeal was over. She had survived. She had given my father a son. To celebrate, my father gave my mother a sapphire ring, 17 carats, deep in color, simply set, just one big gleaming stone that she wore always. I can see it now, a blue square against the whiteness of her long-fingered hand.

There was also "My Little Feller." When I first came across this unpublished 1928 song, I assumed it was written for the baby, one more excruciating detail. In fact, it was written the previous May for Al Jolson's second movie, *The Singing Fool*, a sentimental tale of a father and his small son. Jolson wanted changes. A dispute followed, and the song was withdrawn, replaced by the more emphatic, though similar, "Sonny Boy." So there it was in December, not wasted after all, ready to be published in celebration of Irving, Jr.'s arrival—"*Sweet as can be / Climbing my knee / Wait'll you see—my little feller . . .*"

They brought the infant home in time for Christmas. We were in a house now, with a garden and an East River view, 9 Sutton Place. A proper home at last for the proper family we now were— mother, father, sister, brother. And then, around five o'clock on the morning of Christmas Day, Irving, Jr., was found dead in his bassinet by the nurse. Much later, long after I was grown up, when my mother could finally bring herself to say a few words about the tragedy, she blamed the nurse for not being vigilant enough— maybe. The term crib death was not yet used, but that was what it was, she said, and even the most alert nurse might have been helpless.

Among the first people to arrive at the house was Nellie Cromwell. She was the one, she told me later, who had answered the doorbell and opened the door to my grandfather. "Ellin is waiting for you, Mr. Mackay," Nellie said, watching him hurry, grim-faced, upstairs.

Already, after the death of old Mrs. Mackay, my grandfather
had made certain gestures of goodwill toward my mother. He had
sent her books and furs, laces and a handkerchief, that belonged to
Granny; he had sent a pair of diamond combs, a diamond chain,
and three strands of the family pearls. (The other three strands
went to K.) My mother had written thank-you letters that are
painful to read—such an uncorking of relief, of desire to be reconciled. "Thank you with all my heart. . . . I shall use [the laces] on
some very beautiful dresses. The loveliest I shall keep for Mary
Ellin's wedding. I am so happy that you gave me a handkerchief of
Granny's. So intimate and personal a possession of hers will be
dearer to me than anything . . ." And again, "I know she would
want you not to be too unhappy but rather to find consolation in the
knowledge that you gave her more happiness than mothers expect
from sons." And still again, after thanking him for "my beautiful
pearls," "But, do you know, Daddy, what makes me the happiest?
It is to have you give me the hair pins and the diamond chain that
you gave Granny. . . . I want so much to see you soon."

The first recorded meeting between father and son-in-law is
upstairs at 9 Sutton Place, Christmas, 1928: an unimaginable confrontation. What words could have been exchanged between the
heartbroken husband and the grieving, still disapproving father?
Condolences gravely offered and accepted; the formality desper-
ate, under cover of a shared, overwhelming concern for Ellin.

Irving Berlin, Jr., was buried in a flat, featureless plot at
Woodlawn, cemetery of the Duers. (The Mackays were in a spectacular mausoleum at Greenwood, overlooking the spires of lower
Manhattan; the Balines were down below in Brooklyn, in the endless, crowded fields of Washington Cemetery.) The service was private. Small black-edged cards were ordered on which my mother
could respond to flowers and letters with the fewest possible
words. One of them, to Gussie, survives. "There is nothing I can
say but I want you and all the family to know how grateful I am for
the sympathy and kindness you have all shown me."

And what, of any of this, did I, aged two, register? I must have
seen the baby, at the hospital, in the house when he came home, in

his bassinet and long white clothes. I must have talked to him, said, "Baby boy, oh, oh"; my favorite doll that year was one I called "baby boy." Then, suddenly, baby boy was gone. My mother and father would have said the angels had taken him and he was in heaven. I knew about angels. I said my prayers. My parents might be nonbelievers and have put my religious upbringing on hold; they might have had their first bad fight when my mother suggested raising me as a Catholic, such a terrible fight, she would say later, such rage on both sides, that she did not ask again; but prayers were comforting to a small child, my mother insisted. And so she recited the Lord's Prayer and taught me to say, "Now I Lay Me Down to Sleep," and, "God Bless Mamma and Daddy" and everyone else I could think of. Maybe I put the baby in my prayers for a while. But the memory would have disappeared, along with the new nursery. And we left the house in the spring and never returned.

After New Year's my father took my mother to Miami. They lived on a houseboat or a moored yacht—or so remembers my aunt Gwen Mackay. It is her voice now, recalling this piece of the history to me not long ago. Widow of my Uncle Willie, she is the last of that generation of relatives, a good-looking, vigorous eighty-six-year-old with the snapping blue eyes, great grin, and tennis player's figure I remember from my youth. In the family lineup, she and Uncle Willie were the young, "with it" ones who stayed up late and danced and dashed about and wisecracked in a way that made children laugh. Never a businessman (the year he turned twenty-one my grandfather sold Postal Telegraph), Uncle Willie was a gifted photographer, a sportsman by avocation, and for fun he played the saxophone. (In his later years he had a combo that he took to hospitals and old folks' homes all over Long Island, playing tunes from the 1920s and 1930s—a fair share of them by his brother-in-law.) Aunt Gwen, who liked to rough it, to fish and shoot, also enjoyed nightclubs and Broadway openings, dressing up in the latest Paris fashions.

So Aunt Gwen and Uncle Willie were in Miami that winter of 1929, on the first stage of an extended honeymoon, partly to be with my parents but also because Miami was dashing—a resort for theater people where, after the beach all day, you could go out on the town, just like in New York.

Would my parents have been at Willie and Gwen's February wedding if they hadn't been in mourning? Aunt Gwen isn't sure. Already present at the wedding was my grandmother, a dramatic figure in a fur-trimmed coat and cloche hat, sitting, head high, in the front pew of the church next to her former husband, my grandfather. She was even more dramatic at the reception when she took off her coat and hat, revealing silk and pearls, a huge head of dark hair, lightly streaked with gray, and those deep-set eyes. There was something grand and slightly melancholy about her appearance at this festive occasion, with 1929 splashed all over it—ushers in traditional morning coats, bridesmaids, shingle-haired and slouching, in dresses that were long in back but barely grazed the knees in front.

Behind the surprising presence was yet another miserable episode in the running melodrama that was the life of Katherine Duer Mackay Blake. Once again she was in the midst of divorce proceedings. The great romance, begun during my grandfather's convalescence from cancer, the scandalous marriage for which she had given up her three Mackay children, the apparently happy marriage, which had produced four more children, was at an end. Finished, because while my grandmother was convalescing from *her* cancer (one of those deep-set eyes was glass), Dr. Blake had begun an affair with the nurse. For a while the romance was a secret, but by autumn of 1927, Dr. Blake had moved out. Now my grandmother was preparing to divorce him, in New York State, for adultery, naming Miss Drake, the nurse, as corespondent. As my mother would say, "Mother did not enjoy doing things quietly."

But Katherine could almost forget Joseph Blake, sitting beside Clarie as Willie and Gwen said, "I do," watching later the happy pair do a Charleston that cleared the floor. Afterward she wrote Gwen's mother, Josephine Rose, thanking her for making "our children's wedding a happy day for me. . . . I must tell you," she continued, "how I admired you for the way you carried off a situation which might have been difficult. Of course, I think Clarie behaved to me like a Christian & a gentleman & so his was the hardest part, to him goes the greatest credit."

With Clarie and Katherine on her hands, it seems unlikely that even the gracious Mrs. Rose could have managed an invitation to Ellin and Irving. Aunt Gwen's first meeting with her brother-in-law, in any event, was in Florida. "Irving was delightful; comfortable, relaxed, and so attractive. That black hair, those bright eyes. He whipped us off on a boat for the day, but I think they also lived on a boat. We had a perfectly lovely time. Ellin was sweet and very quiet. I had the feeling she didn't want to see anyone much; and she didn't talk about the baby, not one word. You were not there. I'd remember if you had been, because as a little thing you never stopped talking."

It's a glimpse, no more, of life on that Florida boat: Uncle Willie, with his sunny, handsome face, his all-American grin, his rapid-fire delivery, my mother's sporty kid brother and his pretty, high-spirited bride who enjoyed nightlife—the young honeymooners, he twenty-two, she twenty, wanting to cheer up the couple in mourning; my father, deeply tanned, the tan covering a lot, putting the guests at ease, wanting it to work for Ellin; and my grief-stricken mother, under a kerchief, making a huge effort, talking lightly above her feelings.

"Ellin is a little better," my father wrote his sister Gussie in a long letter mostly about Gussie's problems, poor health, a depression, hard times he wants her to pull out of. "Her nights are not so good. As for myself, the sunshine here has really done me some good and I feel much better. I am looking forward to getting back to work. It seems so long since I've done any."

The last good work stretch had been the previous summer and early fall. Movie songs. Single numbers, a funny novelty, "Yascha Michaeloffsky's Melody," and two ballads, "Roses of Yesterday," which became a fall hit, as old-fashioned as its title, and "How About Me?," ignored at the time, a cabaret singer's favorite later, with a real 1930s sound to it. And at least two songs clearly intended for *Mr. Bones*—"Swanee Shuffle," a minstrel-style jig, and "Let Me Sing and I'm Happy," the ultimate troubadour's signature song. An August letter from his collaborator indicates they have a first act.

But now, in March of 1929, my father returns to Hollywood to write songs for *Hallelujah!*, King Vidor's all-black saga of the South. Into *Hallelujah!* goes "Swanee Shuffle" along with the brand-new "Waiting at the End of the Road." What has happened to *Mr. Bones* (not to mention the long-term opera plan)? From New York my mother writes of her anxiety for Irving to have "a big success." She has this "horrible feeling" he hasn't "done so well" since they've been married, and now that she's strong again, she wants to help him. "It's simply grand about *Mr. Bones*," she writes in April. "I feel you are going to do wonderful work for it. . . . You sound ambitious again for the first time in months and I'm so happy I could cry." What has happened (maybe grand, maybe not) is that *Mr. Bones*, the exciting, different show, has become yet another Jolson movie (to be retitled *Mammy*). "Please make it very good," my mother writes. She'll do anything, go anywhere—Honolulu, Rapallo, Venice—for the sake of his work, short-term, long-term, and wonders if they should take me abroad with them. Taking me, my father decides, is too complicated. My mother agrees. They can have a fine time alone.

There was even more uncertainty in those springtime letters from New York to the Roosevelt Hotel in Hollywood than in the Adirondacks letters of the previous summer. Intimations of something going on, unadmitted so far, that from the distance of years seems mysterious, how a time that included the writing of so many major songs could be "not doing well." But close up, the big songs are far apart and not attached to the excitement of a score, a show, just single releases and movie scatter shots that seem to be going nowhere.

It was Aunt K who supervised my summer while my parents were away: my O'Brien cousins—Marie Louise, Katherine, and Morgan—were my summer playmates. Peace had been made between the sisters. I knew Aunt K now, with her high, laughing, sugary voice and her glinting, long-lashed brown eyes, as I knew my grandfather, the natty gentleman with the bristle mustache. He had been to see me on Sutton Place. A whole parade of relatives came that spring to view me—Mackays, O'Briens, Balines. Uncle Ben, down from New London, a grayer version of my father, with a crumpled, quizzical face and a long cigar; Aunt Gussie, bringing cousin Mildred Kahn, an exceptionally pretty brunette who left with a door prize, a boxful of my mother's brand-new, apparently never worn clothes.

When summer came, my nanny and I moved to the Irving hotel, in the village of Southampton, just a walk away from Aunt K's blue-turreted Normandy château with a joke name. "What should we call the house?" Mr. and Mrs. Kenneth O'Brien had asked Mercer, the Mackay butler, a deadpan sort of fellow who was known to shoot craps with gentlemen houseguests to augment his tips. "Why not call it Chateaubrien?" he quipped (as in the wine or steak). They thought it a splendid idea, and so the house was named. Just another minute from Aunt K's was the Spanish-style beach club, with its tiled roof and turquoise swimming pool. How to explain that picture of me in an old rotogravure, in my white piqué hat and rompers, leaving this place where one-half of me was unwelcome (where most of the world, if the truth were known, was unwelcome)? My parents had obviously decreed that at two years old I was not going to be corrupted or snubbed.

Every few days postcards came to the Irving from my mother and father—long since lost but fixed in my memory, part of a packet that I would play with as an older child, imagining myself in the picture, too: scenes of Venice and the Lido; of Munich and Baden-Baden and the Black Forest; of Paris and London. But snapshots survive: my mother on the Lido beach in a floppy hat and pajamas, looking adorable, flirtatious, only a little sad at the edges; my father in a beach robe, stylish, a little cryptic; my mother and father with a tall, elegant white-haired woman, Princess Jane di San Faustino, American-born, merrily widowed, who, with Cole and Linda Porter, for much of the twenties, had presided over Venetian party society, moving from palazzo to ever bigger palazzo. (The Porters' last Venice summer at the sumptuous Palazzo Rezzonica was 1927, a holiday with a story attached, which my father told to the musical-theater historian Robert Kimball, who told it to me. In 1927 Ray Goetz had asked Irving to write a show around Ray's wife, the very French musical-comedy star Irene Bordoni, to be called *Paris*. I.B. turned him down, saying the person to write such a score was Cole Porter. "You can find him in Venice," said Irving. Goetz persuaded Porter to do the show, which opened at the Music Box in October 1928. The score included

"Let's Do It" and according to Kimball was the turning point in Porter's Broadway career.)

In Venice my mother is recovering; she is entertaining her husband. Later, she will say it was one of the great trips, the great times, that last summer before the Crash, with only one discordant note: that all the important older European men she met, men like Count Volpi, Italy's minister of finance, were already talking war; not *prophesying* the next war, taking it for granted.

What's up with my father is less clear. A piano must have followed him, that special piano with the transposing keyboard that went wherever he went, to a hotel, on a cruise ship or ocean liner. The trip was planned as a working holiday. But the songs for *Mr. Bones* (aka *Mammy*), the ones used at least, were written before they left; no songs whatsoever seem to have been written that summer. Was he thinking about the secret opera? In a springtime letter my mother was still pushing—"Someday you'll write something for the Metropolitan"—the last mention of the matter in any surviving letter. Did the opera die that summer? Or before it ever began?

What I know of this is only what my father told me years later, when I was studying music at Barnard. How as a young man, before the First World War, he had wanted to get some formal music education and write a ragtime opera. Instead, he had done his first Broadway musical, *Watch Your Step*, a milestone in itself, and it had been shows from then on. But the opera idea nagged at him. In the mid-1920s, Otto Kahn had approached him on behalf of the Metropolitan Opera, and my father had said that Jerome Kern or George Gershwin, with their training, would be better bets. Still, he had started thinking about it again and actually tried something. "But it didn't work," he said. "I decided to give the whole matter up, once and for all, and stick to what I knew how to do—do pretty well—which was writing songs." "And that was that?" I asked. "That was that," he said.

When my parents' trip abroad was over, my father left for California. A few weeks later, my mother and I joined him. It wasn't a fishing expedition this time. He had entered the movie business. My mother was about to become a Hollywood wife. And I was about to acquire that treasured possession, my first memory.

10 _____

M E M O R Y   B E G I N S with a pink wall. I am three years old, playing ball on emerald-green grass in front of the wall with my California friend Sammy Goldwyn. Though not very good at catching, I am determined to learn; the little boy must not escape till he has taught me. At another time we are playing with balloons, batting them against the pinkness till they burst, but not sad at the loss, gleeful.

Not long ago I went looking for my wall, and other ancient landmarks, in the company of that same Sammy Goldwyn, a producer like his father and a first citizen of present-day Hollywood, otherwise known as L.A. The wall might or might not exist, he said, depending on whether it had been my wall or his, for my house was gone. But his was still standing. I would be able to imagine quite clearly what life was like, in the fall of 1929, when my parents established themselves a block away from his parents, in a house that belonged to Joseph Schenck, on the corner of Camino Palmero and Hollywood Boulevard.

In the heart of Hollywood, within easy distance of downtown and a short ride to most of the studios: that was where upper-echelon movie people lived in those days, said Sam as we drove inland from Beverly Hills toward our old neighborhood. In the summer they "went out" to the beach, to Santa Monica (the chieftains and stars) or Malibu (the writers and directors). Beverly Hills was still open country, crisscrossed with bridle paths, a place where people looking for land and privacy had begun to build. The heart of the old residential community was here, where he was parking the car—this steeply rising block of low-slung brick-and-beam apartment houses with handsome plantings where once Joe Schenck's house had stood, and next to it, Sam and Frances Goldwyn's first house. By 1929, the Goldwyns had moved to larger quarters a block north on Camino Palmero, and that was the house that survived in my memory, in reality, which we now peered at through an ironwork fence, a gracious gray mansion, Edwardian in style, with a lawn at the south end and a brick retaining wall—about the height of a three-year-old.

To the north end of the gray mansion, hidden among large trees, was a playhouse for grown-ups—the place where the men had their poker games, though sometimes they played a half dozen blocks down Hollywood Boulevard, in Sid Grauman's office above the Chinese Theater. "That was my first memory of your father," said Sam. "When did he ever have time to write songs? As a kid I imagined him a man living by his wits, playing cards with my father and someone you called 'Uncle Joe.'"

When I was growing up, the high-stakes poker games were part of a mysterious, fabled past. The father I knew played gin rummy, a more sedate game (though the stakes weren't peanuts). But that poker-playing father, with his poker face, dealing out the cards, raking in the chips, was out of reach, like the vanished house down the street, of which no photographs exist. "It could have been pink with green trim," said Sam. "And I remember that the house had a bad history."

Then I remembered, too. One of my mother's stories. Of a house in Hollywood that Frances Goldwyn warned her about. A man had blown his brains out in it, and bloodstains were still on the wall; scrubbing and repainting could not erase them. Then Joe Schenck bought the house, and shortly thereafter his marriage broke up. Then Emil Jannings, the silent-film star, lived there, and his career had been ruined by the talkies (though later he would make an inspired appearance as the doomed professor besotted with the young Marlene Dietrich in *The Blue Angel*). When my father insisted it was the best house for us, my mother agreed to live in it if he would have it exorcised. Frances arranged for a priest to perform the exorcism, and shortly thereafter we moved in.

"There was a loneliness about your mother," said Sam. We were now in a booth at Musso and Frank's, a few blocks east on Hollywood Boulevard, the neighborhood restaurant then and now. "I remember your father as a happy person and accessible, one of the most accessible adults I ever knew. This was later, of course, when I was older than three. Your mother was elegant and composed. My earliest memory of her was that she talked funny. Her voice was totally different from other voices. More than just an eastern voice, a very, very refined voice. In those early days I have a picture of our mothers sitting outside, gossiping, while the men played cards all day, all night, until it was time to go back to the studio. My father was almost compulsive about gambling. Your father wasn't compulsive. I'm not sure why he did it. Maybe because he liked to be with the guys."

But there must have been parties, premieres, a social life, I said to my old friend. "Wives still sat outside. Wives did a lot of reading. In the old days wives felt out of place because there were so many beautiful women around. As a woman you were an actress, a writer, or nobody. At the parties, men talked business at one end of the room, women talked their talk at the other—wives, that is. The women in the business—Frances Marion, Sonya Levien, Anita Loos—were free to roam. Put Ellin Berlin in that and imagine."

By the time I observed my parents' Hollywood life firsthand, things were different. Friends from New York had arrived— Harold Arlen, Harpo Marx, the Gershwins, Oscar Levant, Jerome Kern, Fred and Phyllis Astaire. The Hollywood structure loosened. In this earlier period it must have been a balancing act, nerve-racking. My pale, ethereal mother, with her funny voice, frighteningly polite in public, scathing in private, a New York golden girl making mental notes, gathering material for a collection of stories she knew she would never write. My father, knowing what she was thinking, whom she was inwardly calling a fool, "common" or worse, trying himself to do the politic thing, which was to get on with these people who held the power. For instance, he had to reconcile his young wife's understandable desire to snub Marion Davies, William Randolph Hearst's mistress, because of her affection for Hearst's wife, Millicent, with the Hollywood reality: Hearst and Marion Davies ran the place; you didn't just turn down an invitation to their palatial retreat at San Simeon.

Though my parents did in fact—to be politic—visit the Hearst castle once, my father never changed my mother's attitude. This was made clear later in a letter from my mother when she and I were back in New York. "Mary Ellin has been charming . . . but listen my dear, Saturday in a shop she was singing. She has a way of singing that sounds like words but proves to be unintelligible syllables. Suddenly I realized she was singing over and over, 'Marion Davies, Marion Davies, Marion Davies.' I was horrified and made her stop—So I mildly suggest that if she must sing about moving picture actresses she pick a respectable one like Mary Pickford. Darling, promise me she *never* met that woman anywhere did she?"

From Musso and Frank's and the business district, past those other relics of the late 1920s, the Ambassador and Roosevelt hotels, tall buildings for those days, still marking the skyline, it was another short ride to the working town, the bungalows where the bit players and technicians lived and the studios. First came United Artists, studio of Sam Goldwyn and Joseph Schenck, where, in the fall of 1929, *Puttin' On the Ritz* (starring Harry Richman, Joan Bennett, and the title song) was being filmed and where, six months later, *Reaching for the Moon*, the third Irving Berlin movie of 1929–30 (starring Douglas Fairbanks and Bebe Daniels and featuring the young Bing Crosby), would be filmed. Another few blocks east on Melrose was RKO, a newcomer in 1929, small, white, and narrow, smack up against Adolph Zukor's great big Paramount; and then Columbia, Harry Cohn's domain, acquiring class by way of the recently hired Frank Capra.

Warner Brothers, where the Jolson movie *Mammy* was in production in September, was in Burbank, out of the enclave, as were M-G-M and Fox. But the geographic neatness of that old movie town was what struck me as we drove back up to Hollywood Boulevard on Gower, with the head-on view of the enormous HOLLYWOOD sign that the conquerors had planted on the bare brown hills. "Hollywood *was* very small in those days," said Sam. "With the Crash it rose and grew. The Depression made talkies, everyone's escape."

The first movie set I ever visited, aged not quite three, was *Puttin' On the Ritz*, during the filming of the "Alice in Wonderland" sequence, a number originally in the 1924 *Music Box Revue*. The memory is sharp, freestanding. I am making my way with my parents, my dark and dapper father, my pale, soignée mother, through a tangle of wires, being lifted over, held on to so I wouldn't get separated in the confusion, the rush of people taking their places, people in costumes representing playing cards, kings, queens, knaves, diamonds, hearts, clubs, and spades, cards come alive, hurrying about. Through the crowd I'm propelled to a central lighted place where a lady with long yellow hair wearing a blue dress pretends to be a child. "That's Alice," my mother says, "and she's in Wonderland." Now my father has disappeared into the confusion, is part of the confusion. Daddy has gone into Wonderland surrounded by all those ominous figures. I begin to howl. "Daddy will be back," says my mother, holding me fast. "Don't cry. If you cry, we can't take you to all these interesting places."

My wails were perhaps prophetic. The week in which they filmed the "Alice in Wonderland" sequence was the week of October 21, 1929—the week that ended in Black Thursday and even blacker Friday.

In a night my father lost a fortune—everything he had invested in the market—no sum ever given, but others have put the figure at $5 million (in today's market about $50 million). He lost virtually all his savings, whatever he'd cleared and not spent from twenty years of generous earnings. Afterward he brushed it off, made a joke. "Luckily I had a rich wife," he would say. My mother's trust, conservatively invested, did not go down the drain—"though your father never liked that, my having to help out," she'd say.

He would also admit he had been taking it easy since his marriage. Why not? He was a rich man. Then all of a sudden he wasn't. Taking it easy was no longer a possibility.

Only there seemed to be a problem.

I don't remember exactly when I first heard about "the dry spell," which had begun even before the crash. When my father first said, "You know, there was a time when I thought I'd gone dry and I lost my nerve." Certainly long after the fact, long after the story had been told, again and again, for there was no secret about it. Later, he would tell the whole world. To me, a teenager, he dropped it in a conversation about something else, to counter a complaint or correct some notion I'd expressed about things always being smooth sailing for him. But even when he mentioned "the dry spell," even when my mother called this low point "a depression," there were few details (and no details in her letters of the day, only allusions to Irving "looking badly," sounding "pathetic and exhausted" on the phone). No linkage to this Hollywood sojourn that I would later recall with such delight, my first real memories. The pink wall, the boy next door, the palm trees marching up the hill, my tricycle, a too fast descent, a crash, howls, though nothing like the howls when I fell off the swing and cut my forehead—origin of a permanent scar between my eyebrows that gave me a frowning aspect even when I wasn't frowning. (My father comforted me by pointing to the line on his own forehead; when only a little older than I, he had been in his berth in the ship's hold, sailing to America; and someone from above had dropped an open penknife on him, narrowly missing his eye.)

From "the dry spell," I remembered afterward Christmas lights on Hollywood Boulevard, though nothing of Christmas itself. It must have been grim for my parents, the first anniversary of the baby's death, yet lavish for me: the tree; the decorated table; a decision made that Christmas would be observed for me, later "the children," without stint, as if it weren't my parents' black day. Another kind of exorcism. We greeted the New Year by going to the Rose Bowl Parade. We had our picture taken on a soundstage by Cecil Beaton, who spent December and January in what he called "the funniest place in the world." The look in this photograph is that of the 1930s, my mother's hair grown out, slicked behind her ears, her long sleeved silk dress only a foot off the ground.

In the spring there was an Easter party, preserved in my album, photos of me, Sammy, and two other little girls with our egg-hunt baskets and stuffed bunnies as tall as we were; of me standing among giant eggs, some chocolate, some gaily painted cardboard with presents inside; my mother's Easter lavishness, second only to her Christmas lavishness.

Except at Eastertime, 1930, my mother wasn't there. My mother had not been in Hollywood since the beginning of February. At Eastertime back in New York, something sad and grown-up was happening. Mrs. Blake, my grandmother, was dying.

I wish I remembered her, this mother of my mother, who had been so fond of my father. I don't. I was only two the last time I saw her. I try to imagine her in an armchair, calling me to come and give her a hug; "You know how I love to be loved . . . to feel little hands and arms around my neck," she wrote my mother in a wistful letter around the time she was separating from Dr. Blake. But that day, while she and my mother were talking, I occupied myself by pushing her perfectly arranged books, every one I could reach, to the back of the shelves. The visits weren't all that many. She spent summers in Bar Harbor, winters in Tarrytown, later Irvington. She had her hands full with her own younger children, Katherine and Joan, now in their teens, Billy almost twelve, Mary, the baby, just five years older than me. With the breakup of her marriage she had moved back to New York. But we went to California.

And then, sometime in the fall of 1929, her cancer, thought to be cured, recurred in the liver, a death sentence in those days. My grandmother didn't know she was dying. The symptoms had to do with the stomach, or so she thought; and on the X rays, the stomach was clear. She didn't know, when my grandfather began visiting her, that she only had a few months to live.

My father always wanted me to write a book about my grandmother, one of those books I should do when everyone had "cooled." He would inevitably end these conversations by saying, "The ring. That business of the ring at the end."

Between my grandmother and grandfather was a bond, never quite broken. My mother liked to recall that after her sister K's wedding, my grandmother, who had neither participated nor been invited, got wedding announcements out—*Mrs. Joseph Blake takes pleasure in announcing the marriage of her daughter*—before my grandfather could get them out himself. "I *thought* that would annoy Clarie," my grandmother said when hearing of his fury.

And then, five years later, there they were at Willie's wedding, side by side, in near amity. Clarie kind; Katherine grateful. Who knows if a tiny thought entered her mind on that wedding day; entered it again, in the spring, when her divorce became final, and again in July, when Dr. Blake married Florence Drake, the nurse. Such a silly thought that nonetheless grew when she became ill and Clarie began paying her calls. And was suddenly not a thought but a reality when one day he arrived with a small box, within the box a ring. And said they would be remarried, or perhaps only implied it, as he put the ring on her thin finger.

My grandmother then made her own gesture; she took instruction and quietly joined the former enemy, the Catholic church, focus of her greatest battles with Clarie. Still feeling wretched, not quite understanding why, she made plans with bravado. "Our worries are over, girls," she told Joan and Katherine. "Before too long, we'll be back on easy street, back in the castle on the hill. We'll have a wonderful life again."

But then suddenly, having done what he had done, said what he had said, Clarie went on about his life and did not come again. "Where is Clarie?" my grandmother asked my mother at the end of March.

"Away on business, away shooting," my mother replied.

"Where is Clarie, why hasn't he come?" she asked again at the beginning of April, shortly before slipping into a coma.

"He is busy getting your room ready at Harbor Hill," said my mother. The words were her last to her mother, who never regained consciousness and died on April 21, a little less than three weeks short of her fifty-first birthday.

"How much she had of beauty and brilliance and glamour," my mother wrote my father a few months later from Bar Harbor, where she had taken me to visit the Blake children. "How lovable she was and how much courage she had and how little wisdom. And how quickly the years went by, bringing her only a little happiness and no peace at all."

The end of the story came a year and a few months later, in July of 1931, when my grandfather married his mistress of many years, the singer Anna Case. Both my parents were at the wedding in Roslyn and at the luncheon afterward at Harbor Hill. Though eventually things became smooth and affectionate between Anna and her younger stepdaughter, on that wedding day my mother was highly displeased and confessed later to having worn a green dress, considered bad luck. Whatever her displeasure, the marriage did at least help reconcile my father and grandfather. The exact moment when they looked each other in the eye, shook hands, and put the past behind them is not known to me. But my mother always said, somewhat dryly, that the final push came from my grandfather's friend and lawyer, Frank Polk, who when Clarie announced his matrimonial intentions, said, "You cannot marry Anna Case and not receive Irving Berlin. At least not unless you want to make yourself the laughingstock of New York." A questionable remark on several levels but apparently effective. (It was never quite clear whether he was referring to Anna's being in a branch of show business, so to speak, or to her humble origins: a blacksmith's daughter from New Jersey, she had been discovered by a Metropolitan Opera representative singing in Wanamaker's department store.)

It was a confused time that followed my grandmother's death. I have a dim memory of being back East in a big house with porches and many windows, giving onto blue water with boats. It is the house in Great Neck my mother has rented for the summer, thinking my father will be done with Hollywood. I remember my mother reading from *A Child's Garden of Verses* the poem about going to bed when it is not yet dark and hazy pink light filling my room as I went to sleep. I also remember her playing with me. I had a splendid doll's house, two stories with a kitchen wing and an attic, white with green trim. Later my mother told a story of this summer of our giving a wedding and a reception in the doll's house, everything very stately. Suddenly, I began breaking the legs off the chair and tables.

"What on earth are you doing?" asked my mother.

"Oh, I am just breaking up the party," I replied, already playing with words like everyone else in the family.

But of my father that summer there are no recollections whatsoever. Why would there be? Except for one brief visit to Great Neck in August he wasn't there.

Now I can trace the course of that spring and summer, never talked about later, because of letters my father wrote to my mother and Max Winslow, letters reflecting worry and uncertainty, indicating that the low period continued. How he had wanted, after my grandmother's death, to scrap the movie called *Love in a Cottage,* later *Reaching for the Moon,* and to bring his idea (a shipboard romance the week of the Crash), his songs, and himself back East to my mother and me. He then decided he couldn't do that to Joe Schenck or himself. "Even tho' Joe had people signed for the picture, he was agreeable to let me do it as a musical, knowing how badly I wanted to be with you at this time," my father wrote my mother. "But I feel that I should do one good thing for the movies after all the fuss—especially after the Richman and Jolson pictures which we know were not important as far as I personally was concerned."

Enthusiasm built for a while. "Have written a waltz for the picture called 'Reaching for the Moon,'" he wrote, "and it's the best waltz I've done since 'What'll I Do.'" But it was a different sort of waltz entirely, a dark, glamorous song, in a minor key, with a long chromatic line that said good-bye to sweet Jazz Age wistfulness—a song that was part of "breaking my neck to get a new sound" as he put it to Max Winslow—of trying to work his way out of the "dry spell." Then his enthusiasm flagged. The screenplay wasn't right; the director wasn't right. A two-week visit from my mother in July only reminded him of how lonely he was. In August there was a new director, one Edmund Goulding, "a genius [who] talks my language," he wrote. "However if it's the greatest movie that ever was it will not have been worth it and believe me never again. This separation is terrible and pointless."

Meanwhile, my mother was house hunting. Except for the five months at 9 Sutton Place our New York home had been the Warwick Hotel and seemed likely to be the Warwick forever. She had looked at houses in the East Eighties and Nineties; at apartments on the river, which she liked, and nearer the park, for me. Nothing was right, or the money wasn't right. Money came up a lot in the summer after the Crash. Even in the midst of this period of gloom and self-doubt my father could tease my mother out of a money fit, could write, "Am terribly upset that you should worry about discussing our financial difficulties via the Postal and let everyone know we are so poor we can only afford $16,000 a year rent."

In the late summer of 1930 they actually settled on buying a property on East Ninety-third Street, two small side-by-side houses that they planned to tear down and replace with a new five-story house (a plan scrapped by year's end). Though in New York business, including the music business, was shot, "the picture really looks great," my father wrote Max Winslow. He bet they would have one of the biggest hits of the new season. "Goulding is doing a great job on the story. The numbers are well placed."

And then, sometime in October, my father and the director who spoke his language had such a violent disagreement that my father walked out before the shooting was finished—so recalls a surviving witness, Mr. Maurice Kussell, choreographer of *Reaching for the Moon*. Every night after he left, Irving would telephone, talk to Kussell and Arthur Johnston, his musical secretary and arranger; but he did not return. The fight concerned Goulding's desire to turn the movie into a straight comedy, take out songs. By the time *Reaching for the Moon* opened the week after Christmas, all that was left of the score was the title song, not even sung, just played behind the credits and as mood music for a love scene, and a forgettable little dance number sung by Bing Crosby, "When the Folks High Up Do the Mean Low Down."

Into the dry spell had been inserted a total fiasco.

There is a photograph of my father and my own small self that always hung in my mother's bedroom, taken at French Lick, Indiana, the Baden-Baden of America, where my father went in November of 1930 to take the cure—to pull himself out of his funk. We are posed on a lawn sprinkled with fallen leaves, the vague outlines of a hotel veranda behind. I'm in a caped wool coat, leather leggings, and a cloche hat, miniature of what my mother might wear; from under the hat drop dark bangs right to my eyebrows. My father is in a golfing outfit, cap, jacket, sweater vest, plus fours. He looks thin, pensive, eyebrows slightly raised, lips curved up, nowhere near a smile, but a trace of humor in the eyes, as if to say, Look at where I have landed myself, and what am I going to do about it? He is not that sleek, romantic-looking man my mother married. He is careworn and sharp-edged, skeptical, and looks the way he will for the next ten years, the childhood father I remember. I come to his waist. We are holding hands, carefully, lightly, a little timorously. I am being good and know it. But not committing myself about this experience of being photographed. My round little face, in expression, is a mirror of his.

Somewhere along the way, in that year my father hit, for him, rock bottom, a bond had been forged between us as light and careful as those touching hands in the photograph, yet powerful. The mother-daughter bond had been forged much earlier. But there was a barrier between my father and the nursery, a barrier now broken down. Maybe it happened during those weeks we had been together, without my mother, on Hollywood Boulevard, when he might, or might not, have introduced me to Marion Davies; mediated weeks, certainly, by the nurse, the cook, the maid, Jack MacKenzie, but still there we had been, thrown in on each other, alone. After those weeks he had written my mother, "Really I'm crazy about that kid now that she's grown to be a person." I had chased after him from the time I could toddle, called after him from the time I could talk, bemoaned his absence when he was away, and had caught him at last—for the moment, anyhow.

_____ 11

T H E   Y E A R that followed, 1931, the year we lived at the Warwick Hotel, is dark in my struggling, emerging memory. A dark tunnel after the flat-out, shadowless sunshine of California. The darkness of a room that is gloomy, however much sun comes through the windows, with heavy hotel furniture and hangings and twin beds from which I jump, one to the other, when Marian isn't looking. On the other side of a living room or down the corridor are my parents' bedrooms, my mother's a perpetual mess of books, scattered tissue paper from the dress boxes she has unpacked, little piles of clothes she has dropped. Somewhere high above us is a room for Hermine, the picker-up of the mess. Downstairs, off the lobby, was a gloomy paneled dining room where we ate some meals, though many more were upstairs; for all of my childhood I took unreasonable delight in those room-service tables on wheels, the covered dishes with their dull, silvery color, the warmer, with its flickering blue flame and odor of Sterno. People must have been friendly to little Miss Berlin, with her nanny in tow, but too much fraternizing would have been frowned on. Come along, dear, don't bother the nice man, dear.

Beyond the hotel was Sixth Avenue, a shadowy thoroughfare, with the El just one block to the south, turning west off the avenue before it reached us. There was something intriguing, a little frightening, about that high-turning El that was so close, with its roaring, screeching train we never rode, calling us in vain.

There was my school on Seventy-ninth Street, Miss Hewitt's, a small, old-fashioned private school with a coziness that belied its exclusivity. Miss Hewitt's was not dark. I still have my first report, goods, very goods, an excellent in music. "Mary Ellin is a most enthusiastic little kindergartener who will develop into a splendid group leader"—which meant, no doubt, I was bossy. There was Central Park, afternoons and weekends, neither light nor dark, but gray mostly, with icy air, that "fresh air," before the days of pollution, that everyone was so crazy for children to breathe.

On most Saturdays there were birthday parties, the beginning of the ritual: excruciating excitement when getting dressed, whether as a Gypsy, a fairy, or simply oneself in lace-collared velvet; the determination, once arrived, to have fun; the games, the magician, the supper—creamed chicken in a ring of rice, ice cream on a bed of spun sugar, cake—with the nurses standing behind your chairs, adjusting your napkin, guiding your fork. Inevitably, excitement became disappointment because someone was mean, someone won and you lost, someone pulled a snapper in your face. And then, back home, your mother's questions: Did you have a good time, dear? Did you say thank you and curtsy to your hostess? And your assurance that it was all wonderful—your parents weren't the only ones with secrets.

On some Saturdays there were no doubt outings with my mother, who enjoyed taking me places—to visit a relative, to the Museum of Natural History, to a fairy-tale play given by the King-Coit Children's Theater, children in the audience, children on-stage in orange makeup and glittering costumes, talking in queer, exaggerated voices.

My father might on occasion have joined us. But the outings were often separate. My mother had a theory that girls never got to see their fathers alone and had been pushing me off with him since I was a toddler in Port Washington. "What will I do with her?" he asked. "Take her to the Village, buy her an ice cream cone," my mother answered. I had returned a mess and happy. He had pronounced the expedition a success. Maybe he walked me up Sixth Avenue to the Horn & Hardart on Fifty-seventh Street. Certainly one of my earliest memories is of the two of us at the Automat, he enjoying as much as I did putting in a nickel and extracting a piece of pie.

At the Automat was where *Face the Music* would begin.

Although my father's new show had no title yet, he and Moss Hart were beginning to write it. The dry spell was about to be over, though not in an instant. We returned to New York in December 1930. In mid-February 1932, *Face the Music* opened. Fourteen months. Nothing much happened till the spring of 1931 when Sam Harris introduced my father, fishing for a project, to twenty-nine-year-old Moss Hart, author, with George S. Kaufman, of *Once in a Lifetime*, the comedy hit of the 1930–31 season and Hart's Broadway debut. Hart had an idea for a new *Music Box Revue*. Over a Sardi's lunch, Hart would recall some years later in *Stage Magazine*, my father said he didn't want to do another revue, he wanted to do a show with a story. "He did, however, see a distinct possibility [that my] idea could be translated into the kind of musical story he wanted," Hart would write, "and suggested that I immediately pack a bag and move down to Long Island for two weeks. . . . I stayed for four months and then moved back to New York and lived with him for eight months more . . . you not only write a show with Irving Berlin, you live it, breathe it, eat it and were it not for the fact that he allows you to sleep not at all, I should also say sleep it."

My father's description of the ordeal immediately after the show opened, in an interview in the *New York Herald Tribune*, is a variation on the same theme. For nine months he and Moss Hart struggled. Two months of writing songs that were old hat, repetitious, "Tunes and lyrics that had been loafing around my head"; of doubts he could do it; seven more months of trying to get the book and the score right. At some point a team was assembled, Sam

Harris to produce, George S. Kaufman to direct, Hassard Short, designer of the *Music Box Revues*, to stage and direct the musical numbers.

Songs began to come—the ones, anyhow, that made their way into the show—in the summer, in July, August, and early September. "Let's Have Another Cup of Coffee," "Soft Lights and Sweet Music," "You Must Be Born with It," "On a Roof in Manhattan," "I Say It's Spinach," a stream of fresh-sounding, lilting, easy songs, some sprightly and mocking, others romantic, something uncorked, bubbling to the surface. The summer setting was another house by the water on the North Shore of Long Island. But who knows for sure if the stream of songs came in Sands Point, New York in the Warwick, or a hotel room in Atlantic City, only that they were coming, that the dry spell was over, as the script was coming, a high-spirited, outrageous tale, inspired by real-life New York City scandals and the Depression, of broke millionaires, cops on the take, a crooked police chief who decides to launder his money via show business.

And then all of a sudden we were out of the gloom of the Warwick Hotel and moved, in time for Christmas, into the sky-high apartment that would be our home for the next seven years. I remember that after the Warwick, that penthouse at the top of 130 East End Avenue was coming from the darkness into the light, a blaze of Manhattan light; and in my memory the disconnected flashes changed to an uninterrupted ribbon of time with todays, yesterdays, and tomorrows.

PART THREE

A ROOF IN MANHATTAN

Irving Berlin and Moss Hart, creators of *Face the Music* and *As Thousands Cheer.*

12

THE BEGINNING of the new time, in the light-flooded new apartment, is always the same. I am getting ready to go someplace with my father. He has not told me where. "A surprise," he has said, coming into my room, disappearing again. My father is quick and dark, quick as quicksilver, as dark as a wizard—now you see him, now you don't. When he opens the door, I'm excited. When he departs, there's a hole, though I'm happy playing alone in this first real room I've ever had. There is my doll's house, my little gray desk; there are my books and toys, which have traveled about as I have and are now arranged in neat rows on the shelves opposite my bed. The old bed, once my grandmother Blake's, is upholstered in a delightful new toile with colored-in scenes of a storybook town where flags fly from a red-roofed palace and people hurry along cobbled streets; a place to climb into and have adventures.

It's Washington's birthday, 1932, a day of no school and un-interrupted play, but now I'm being helped into my outdoor clothes by Mademoiselle, Marian's replacement, who has quickly won me over with her sympathetic ways. As she puts on my leggings, she chats to me in French, distracting me from the hated leggings by admiring my new velvet-trimmed coat and hat. *Voilà! Vous êtes prête.* Not quite. Where is my little pocketbook that would complete my costume? My father, back in his hat and over-coat, is impatient. I am having a small, self-contained fit. "Isn't there *some* pocketbook?" he asks Mademoiselle, who fetches one of hers. "Okay?" he says, hanging the outsized bag around my neck. We are off, a doting father, a spoiled little girl about to be-come less so.

Walking up East End Avenue, chattering, I ask my father what *is* the surprise. "If I told you, it wouldn't be a surprise," he says, walking faster. We turn into a large brick building with a

95

canopy; up an elevator, down a corridor into a big room filled with flowers. There, sitting up in a bed so high she can hardly reach to hug me, is my mother. I start to tell her about my morning, ask her to admire my hat and coat, my grown-up pocketbook. And then my father shows me the bassinet. "Well, well," he says as I peer at the tiny, live, pink-faced doll with dark fuzz on top, "how about that? You've been wanting a baby sister, and here she is." I continue to look. I nod. "So what do you think?" For once I am silent.

Memory can play tricks, I know, but recently I found confirmation of that long-ago February excursion in a family scrapbook: a newspaper photograph of my father and myself arriving at the hospital, accompanied by an interview obtained later by telephone. How did Mr. Berlin feel, a new show that opened just five days earlier, a new baby? asked the reporter. "Wonderful, wonderful." But how did Mr. Berlin feel about having another girl? "A girl was what we desired all along. What could be better than two girls?" replied Mr. B. "We are overjoyed." And what about me? What did big sister have to say? Not a lot, my father admitted. "Little Mary [Ellin] was very much surprised when she saw her sister. You see, she didn't know a thing about it."

By the time my mother and the baby, named Linda after my parents' longtime friend Linda Porter, came home, I had recovered my tongue. I had indeed wanted a sister, teased for a sister. If I was displeased, it was with my parents for springing it on me like that. Now curled up at one end of my mother's bed, looking at the tiny thing cradled in her arms, I asked where the baby had come from. "An angel brought her," my mother said. "From heaven."

I nodded. I saw the angel in my mind's eye, the golden wings, the halo, the sparkling dress. Saw her until one afternoon when I rushed into my mother's room to challenge her with her storytelling. She soothed and explained: She thought I had been too young to understand. Mothers translated things sometimes. Babies did come from heaven, in a way, like everything good in life. "Just blame it on me," she said, "your silly, old-fashioned mother."

"But you don't understand," I wailed. "At school I told them I'd *seen* the angel and exactly what she looked like."

The illusion, the reality: Life on East End Avenue had begun.

It's more than fifty years since we left that three-storied home in the sky, but I can travel through it still, room by room, in my mind, beginning with the lowest floor, where the bedrooms were. My mother's, on the corner, looked down to the toy brick houses of Henderson Place and on the other side to Carl Schurz Park, with the river beyond and the bridges that glittered in the sun, Hell Gate and the Triborough (still under construction the year we moved in). At the center of a room that seemed to me enormous was her big black chinoiserie bed, with its figures of fishermen, its bridges and pagodas. There was an accompanying chinoiserie desk, also black and gilded, a desk my mother never used. She did everything— telephoning, bills, letters—in bed or on the blue-and-white-striped chaise longue, where she also reclined when Miss Champney, the manicurist, came to do her nails. The chaise longue was where, on weekends or holidays, I sat while my mother finished her breakfast, waiting for the treat, the lump of sugar dipped in coffee, called, for some reason, a *canard,* the French word for a duck, a joke. When my mother was away, the chaise longue was where, dressed up in one of her bed jackets, I sat while Hermine brought me a breakfast tray or, pretending to be Miss Champney, did my nails.

Even more exciting than the bedroom was my mother's dress- ing room and bath, with its mirrored walls of closets that held her rows of shoes, her hat boxes, her suits, blouses, and dresses hid- den away in garment bags. At the far end was the big tub and the painted chair where I sat keeping her company while she had her bath, the whole room steamy, smelling of Mary Chess bath oil. Though proper, even prudish in many ways, my mother had no ret- icence about being naked in front of her daughters. But should my father knock at the bathroom door when I was present, she would cry, "Go away, I'm not dressed." How silly, I thought, till the day I accepted that for him to be with her naked, even seminaked in un- derclothes, was something too intimate to be shared with a child, an adult mystery beyond my grasping.

That, unlike other children's parents, mine had separate bed- rooms in no way detracted from a sense, acquired early, that on a private level they were not just happily married, they were two people who held each other in a particular and intense regard.

Next to my mother's pretty, fanciful bedroom was my father's more sober, more concentrated male domain, with the Chinese-red curtains and chair, the brown chiffonier brightened by silver brushes, the closet with his rows of shoes, the standing rack where Langley the butler set out the shirt, tie, and suit of the day, and the carved-wood bed my father said came from "the old country." On the bedside table was a tinted photograph of the dark-eyed, stiff-haired, determined-looking lady who had brought him from that old country as a little boy into a safe new land.

My father's stories about his mother were few but often repeated. How, thanks to her, even in deepest poverty, he had never been hungry or cold—only so hot in the summer that he slept on the fire escape. How later, when money was plentiful, she had had a chance to show off her cooking: the gefilte fish, made from scratch, that melted in your mouth, the wonderful roasts, the peach and apple pies. We would hear, too, about his first real son's present, bought with his first real earnings, a rocking chair, and how she would sit in no other, would rock back and forth in the window of her Bronx apartment (also a present from him), watching for his arrival on Friday evenings; and how she had a special place for him to smoke, on the Sabbath, a forbidden cigarette. How different she was, this plain-faced, homespun woman, from the other grandmother, the dazzling one whose picture was in my mother's bedroom. When my father once said I looked a little like *his* mother, my face fell. "That picture was taken when she was old, at least sixty," he said, rather hurt. (Years later he would tell my pretty sister, Linda, pink-cheeked, dark-browed, a kerchief around her dark, curly hair, "You remind me of my mother when she was young." Linda took it as a compliment.)

But no photograph seemed to exist of my father's father, who had led the exodus of wife and seven children to the New World. (The oldest brother had stayed behind in Russia.) My grandfather Moses, the cantor, the scholarly and musical one, was a shadowy figure always—as shadowy in my mind as my father's actual birthplace. Somewhere in Siberia, I had the impression as a child, though later I would hear that the rest of the Baline family came from the western part of Russia. It was all equally exotic to me.*

---

*Latter-day research by my sister Linda indicates that my father was probably born in western Siberia, in Tyumen (sometimes given as Tumen or Temun), which is what appears on documents from 1942 on. Confusion arose because the Baline *family* came from the village of Tolochin in Byelorussia. That was where

Most of the time, though, it was my father in my room, examining my toys, asking me about school, what my friends and I were up to, what I liked best and why, endlessly curious about his growing child, making an occasional amazed comparison between my childhood and his own. But I don't remember finding anything remarkable about the fact that I lived in a penthouse high above the river where many blocks lower on the same East Side my father taught himself to swim in the murky waters; where at eight years old he nearly drowned, clutching still, when rescued, the pennies he'd earned selling papers that day, which he would take home to his mother in the crowded tenement flat on Cherry Street. From tenement to penthouse: that was what could happen in this country if you were lucky; if you had a "little knack," as he referred to his talent, and knew how to use it.

Whatever else was going on in the world around us, in the winter of 1932, at 130 East End Avenue, the American dream persisted.

Beyond my room with the storybook toile was the nursery—white furniture, blue chintz curtains with rose-colored ties, and a shelf of stuffed animals I was told were for the baby, not for me. Crying came from the room. "The baby needs to cry," said the nurse, the authority, a dour presence in white, shooing me away when I wanted to know what was wrong. The nursery was a pure place, forbidding and forbidden; that was how Nanny Hughes would have it, and my parents tended not to interfere, saying (somewhat naively) that nurses knew best.

Then came Mademoiselle's room, a brown nest matching her soft, somber clothes, yet cheerful; her things neatly arranged, her tidy drawers smelling of rose sachets. A room in its sweet order that delivered a message to the mostly Anglo-Saxon staff, the Irish and Scottish maids, the English cook, the English butler: I may speak French, but I am not Hermine.

---

most of my father's siblings were born, where Moses and Leah returned after their house burned, and from where they set out to America. Tolochin was in the township of the larger and better known Mogilev—and Mogilev was what my grandparents wrote on their immigration papers and what my father put on his naturalization papers and his marriage license. Sometime between 1925 and 1942 he must have had confirmation that he himself was indeed born in Siberia, that his father, an itinerant cantor, had migrated to Tyumen.

For Hermine's room, next door, was the scandal of the household. Shoes and purses on the floor, clothes and stockings on the bed, tissue paper scattered everywhere; on the dresser a melancholy display of my mother's old perfume bottles, emptied to the dregs, never thrown out; in the center, an ironing board, always up. And then, floating above the hellish squalor, hung from a light fixture or high hook, would be a heaven of perfectly pressed clothes: ruffled silk blouses, sleeves held in shape with tissue, skirts, every pleat ruler sharp, rippling, wrinkleless dresses, spotless evening wraps—my mother's clothes, Hermine's sublimation.

Just past Hermine's room, behind a firmly closed door, were the maids' rooms and the servants' parlor, a place where I was told not to go, where "they" relaxed and got away from "us." A back stairs led up to the kitchen and pantry, also out of bounds ("they" had to get their work done), though on a rare weekend afternoon Mrs. Hauck, the cook, might invite me in to make fudge and molasses taffy.

As artful as any French chef and as demanding of her kitchen maid (frequently changed), Mrs. Hauck had pinned-up pepper-and-salt hair, brawny forearms, and a broad face filmed with perspiration. Long after she retired, my parents would recall her cooking, the fluffy purees, the velvety sauces, the beef you could cut with a fork, the green vegetables that were actually green, the apple charlotte, the Bavarian creams. Didn't I remember? And I would say yes, from Sunday lunch and special occasions, and remind them that at the children's level meals were sauce-free, iron-rich (I was anemic like my mother), recitable as a nursery rhyme: Monday hamburger, barely cooked; Tuesday liver with not enough bacon; and so on to Friday's fish, white and bland, garnished with mashed potatoes and stewed tomatoes that ran into the rest. "How you dwell on the negative," my mother would say tartly. "Blame me who made the menus, not our dear Mary."

Unlike many cooks, Mrs. Hauck was also good-natured. She had to be to put up with my teasing and the outbursts from the dining room, forgotten by my parents in their nostalgia, if things were less than perfect.

The dark green dining room, formal yet jolly, with its Venetian-glass cabinet, like a face on legs, its tapestry of a boy and girl gamboling in the woods, was where we children ate breakfast, lunch, and dinner. (There was no children's dining room.) It was a place of boredom, delight, or distress, depending. Boredom was sitting alone at the supper table with uneaten food congealing on the plate, everyone else finished and gone. Delight was watching my father carve the Sunday roast beef; was exchanging glances with my mother at his Sunday lunch routine, the announcement that he himself wanted nothing, he'd barely finished breakfast, then eating a full meal anyhow till the terminal groan of "my poor stomach." Delight was conversation with my parents and any friends or relatives who might be present, grown-up talk with me taking part. Despair was when, it being just us, my mother focused on my table manners or without warning burst into tears because the gravy was cold, the beef overdone; or, worst of all, fit a cigarette into one of her quill holders to annoy my father, who said, "Now, Ellin," which only made her puff harder, and who, when I put in my two cents' worth, turned to me and said, "Don't you start," in a voice I seldom heard but dreaded. Despair was compounded when I was sent to stand in the corner, facing inward, my back to the room, to think about my misdeeds. (There were no spankings in our family, only an assortment of noncorporal humiliations.) Delight was forgiveness when I said I was sorry and my mother said she was sorry, too, for as quick as she was to blow up, almost as quickly did the storm pass.

Equally challenging, though more serene, was the living room across the way, a gleaming, glamorous space anchored at one end by the black Steinway grand piano; at the other, the life-sized Sorine portrait of my mother, aged twenty, in a white blue-sashed dress. With its many windows and French doors leading onto the terrace, its white damask sofa and chairs, its Louis XVI pieces upholstered in deep-blue velvet, its midnight-blue rug that showed every speck of dirt, the living room was not for playing but not off limits, either. (If I wasn't to hang out backstairs with those friendly, chatty servants, I obviously had to hang out somewhere.) Toys were not missed in this place of charmed objects: the coffee table with the orange fish flickering in its silvered surface (which, unlike my real goldfish, did not die and float belly up in their bowl); the lamps with the ivory Chinese ladies and gentlemen that I imagined came alive when everyone had gone to bed.

In the living room I practiced daily and had my piano lessons

twice a week, lessons I had demanded shortly after my fifth birthday, proving I was not too young by picking out tunes by ear. No ordinary teacher arrived, but my parents' friend Pauline Chotzinoff,
sister and accompanist to Jascha Heifetz, wife of Samuel Chotzinoff, music critic of the *New York World,* later music director of
NBC. Chic, black-haired, and petite, Mrs. Chotzinoff did not "give
music lessons" but found the money my mother offered (twenty-
five dollars an hour in 1932) useful. In spite of her bossy ways (she
taught me not as if I were a friend's child who might have a small
talent but a future professional), I liked her; liked the sight of her
rounded fingers, the short red nails, on the keyboard when she
played for me, my reward for a good lesson. Less charming was
when I was dismissed and she stayed on for tea with my mother.
For I imagined that their laughter and low talk concerned me, my
shortcomings, how badly I had played.

The living room was also where sometimes, later in the day,
my strict seven o'clock bedtime stretched, I curtsied to guests and
was sometimes asked by my father to entertain them with my latest
piece. An apocryphal story, told in a gossip column, had my
mother suggest, when I stumbled badly, that I play with one hand,
or even one finger. "Oh, you mean like Daddy," I was quoted as
saying. Not likely. I was fresh, but not that fresh, and knew, besides, that Daddy played with all his fingers. But the performances
were a fact and continued throughout childhood. Whether playing
for Gershwin, for Oscar Levant, for Harold Arlen, or for my fans
from the back of the house, my small fingers flew willingly and un-
wittingly on, with, as time passed, fewer false notes.

"Are you musical, dear?" people would ask, people who
hadn't had the privilege of witnessing these performances, which
demonstrated a dogged love of music, if no great virtuosity. "Have
you inherited your father's musical talent?" Or later, "Are *any* of
you Berlin girls musical?" Or still later, "Are any of your *children*
musical?" Or recently, "Your grandchildren?" The answer was,
and is, yes . . . no. Yes, if loving music, all kinds, having an ear
and playing an instrument or having a pretty voice (the next generation), is what they mean by "musical." An emphatic no if they
mean any of us (so far at least) have approached my composer-
father's singular, inexplicable genius.

• • •

On the third and top floor was the best room of all, the two-storied library where, before my parents built floor-to-ceiling bookcases, there had been a musician's gallery, a bit of lore evoking Old King Cole that fascinated me. The furnishings and many of the books, I was told, came from Forty-sixth Street: the sofa and deep armchairs, upholstered in golden beige, the dark-wood tables, the Persian carpet. My father liked to show me the big Shakespeares, bound in red Moroccan leather, he had bought as a young man in London in the first flush of success and riches. Set inside each cover was a painted medallion of a heroine—Portia, Viola, Rosalind. The illustrations within told of romance, intrigue, great deeds. My mother would take me to thrilling performances of Shakespeare—Maurice Evans as Richard II, Helen Hayes as Viola—but these books were the original thrill.

The sturdily furnished library was where on a Saturday or Sunday afternoon I sometimes entertained friends; where I had my little-girl birthday parties and where we had Christmas. But, most important, the library was where the brown transposing upright piano was, the old one with the knob that moved the keyboard, at which, at odd hours of the day and night, my father worked. Though he only *played* in the key of F-sharp, the black note key that fell easily under his fingers, he needed to *hear* songs in different keys. Patiently, he explained the mechanism to me. One pull of the knob, and as he continued to play in F-sharp, out the notes would come in C or G or E-flat, or whatever key was right for singing that particular song.

Sometimes sounds would float down to the next floor, a faint sequence of notes, notes that thumped like a drum, or melancholy, slowed-down notes and mournful thirds; disconnected sounds that made no more sense than the blind man who came every third week to tune our pianos but would eventually order themselves into a finished song.

The library was the secret room at the top of the stairs that in dreams, in reality, I could not reach.

This, then, was the setting in which I seemed to awaken the winter Linda was born, look upon my surroundings and find them pleasing. The gypsy years, the dark days at the Warwick receded.

This was the way it was and always had been. And central to the way it was, beyond the enclosure of the apartment, beyond the small section of the city that was my territory, was a place called Broadway, my father's territory, where, playing that winter of 1932, was a show called *Face the Music*—though it was not playing at the "Music Box," my father's special theater built to house his shows, this dislocation causing a certain confusion, I remember, in my mind.

The Music Box had a tenant, a sensationally successful tenant, *Of Thee I Sing*, which had opened a bit earlier that same winter with music and lyrics by the Gershwins and a book by George S. Kaufman and Morrie Ryskind. *Face the Music* was at the New Amsterdam, a big hit in its own right—in the bleak winter of 1932 there was room for more than one musical satire, it seemed—launched by reviews of the sort my father had not seen since his courting days and the 1924 *Music Box Revue*.

"As brilliant a Broadway lampoon as ever laughed at trouble . . . the score is out of Irving Berlin's top shelf," wrote the *Tribune*'s Percy Hammond, who had been so condescending about the 1927 *Ziegfeld Follies*. "The best [tunes and lyrics] that Mr. Berlin has yet placed on display in a song and dance and guffaw extravaganza," wrote Robert Coleman in the *Mirror*. "Sharp, caustic, beautiful and beguiling . . . shook the town's superlatives," wrote Brooks Atkinson of the *Times*. Burns Mantle of the *News* was less impressed, and most critics had quarrels with the second act; but overall (and in the afternoon papers as well), it was generous praise: for the Moss Hart book—about broke millionaires, millionaire policemen—that took on Tammany Hall and hard times in New York, just as *Of Thee I Sing* took on the White House and the entire nation (though *Of Thee I Sing* would win a Pulitzer Prize and *Face the Music* would fade into obscurity); for the outrageous stars, in particular Mary Boland (as Mrs. Crooked Police Chief); for the dazzling Hassard Short staging, for director George Kaufman's nonstop pace, and always for Irving Berlin, back on Broadway after too long an absence.

When they read such notices, given the hard time just passed, what must my parents have felt and said, allowed themselves to say and feel? Relief, excitement, in spite of the inconvenient timing, my mother about to give birth, with other things on her mind. My father indicating with a small *humph* how pleased he was, how good it felt to be back in town with a hit; but subdued, exhausted, after too many disappointments and uncertainties. They are elusive, those two people behind a closed door in the wonderful new apartment, five days before Linda's birth, trying to take in what has happened. Whatever you guess at, they seem to be saying, you won't get it quite right.

Here is what I actually remember about *Face the Music*. That there were two songs on the radio, in the air, that winter and spring, songs my father had played and sung for me on the big black living-room piano that stood out in a special way from other current songs my five-year-old ears delighted in—"I've Told Ev'ry Little Star," "I Love Louisa," "Wintergreen for President." One of these special songs, "Let's Have Another Cup of Coffee," had words a child could see and taste and a simple, spirited tune a child could remember. (Years later it would be the first of their grandfather's songs I sang to my children.) The other, with "music" in the title, was an evening song, silvery, tantalizing, with a melody that began in a place you didn't expect and grown-up words—"soft lights and sweet music, and you in my arms"—vanished after it finished, blissful to hear again. Two songs that were an introduction to two musical sounds, with one source: my father.

But what stayed in my mind of the actual performance of *Face the Music*, was no musical number, no spectacle—the Automat opening, the dance in the hall of mirrors to "Soft Lights," the penthouse dissolving into a castle in Spain for "On a Roof in Manhattan"—but (what else at five years old!) the finale when the funny, plump lady, Mary Boland, in pink chiffon and a feathered headdress, rode a real-live elephant onto the stage. The excitement was unbearable. My father the wizard had outdone himself, for me, for the clapping, cheering audience.

But now, quite abruptly, the scene shifts. Broadway dissolves. The penthouse, with its awninged terrace, its pretty outdoor furnishings in place for warm-weather city living, dissolves. Summer plans, up in the air all spring, edged with a certain nervousness at the grown-up level, are set. We are not going back, after all, to that

Manhattan adjunct, the North Shore of Long Island, with all the friends and the easy commute to Broadway, but to secluded Loon Lake in the distant Adirondacks. The Berlin family is taking to the hills—who knows quite why. And a new character, my father the outdoorsman, makes his entrance.

13

MY ADIRONDACKS FATHER wore rough clothes, khakis, flannel shirts, hiking boots, and a yellow slicker when it rained. With no city hat or pomade to hold it down, his hair reverted to its own naturally curly state; he looked handsomer to me than the sleek gentleman I knew in New York, California, or Sands Point. Most charming of all, he was a regular part of my day. Somewhere, in one of those rustically furnished log cabins that descended in levels to the lake and composed our "camp," must have been his piano. He must have been working, though it's not clear on what; but if he was, in all this woodsy silence he was out of earshot. Mostly, he seemed to be taking the summer off. We swam; we went out in the motorboat; we walked through the woods on deep pine-needle paths, picking the tiny wild strawberries that grew everywhere. *Fraises des bois,* my father called them, exaggerating his poor French accent for my benefit, suggesting we save the ones we picked to surprise my mother, who was spending a lot of time resting and reading.

I remember the fishing expeditions to a nearby lake. What was wrong with the fish in Loon Lake? It must have been too easy to fish there. We drove over the bumpy back roads—my parents, me, Jack at the wheel. No Mademoiselle; that would have spoiled it. No Linda; she was only a baby. At the lake a boat waited, which Jack rowed till we reached the right spot. Then the wait, the silence, the first sight of shapes moving in the dark green water. Permission to hold my father's rod. The tug on the line. Rod and child almost into the water. Large hands circling mine and pulling the rod up hard. "Now it's hooked," my father says. "Now you can reel it in all by yourself." Back on shore my mother opened the big straw hamper and spread the picnic, averting her eyes when Jack cleaned the day's catch (she felt sorry for the fish), which my father cooked on a twig fire in an old iron pan, butter first, shaken till it sizzled, then the fish, flipped over like pancakes, just a few minutes. And it was delicious, crisp on the outside, sweet and firm inside, so different from the disgusting fish of winter Fridays.

There were expeditions to Ausable Chasm to ride the rapids; to a mink farm where I stuck my finger in a cage and was bitten. "Leave it to a Berlin to be bitten by a mink," said Aunt Gwen, visiting at the time. "Nothing less would do for Ellin and Irving's child." On the last day of August there was an eclipse. Getting up before dawn, driving many hours, a drive that seemed to take forever, to a place near the Canadian border, being given dark glasses and told not to look at the sun (why were we there?), especially not at the moment when the moon covered it entirely, for the flickering at the edge could make me blind. Then, suddenly, the witchcraft that justified the buildup, the animal noises and birdcalls as the sky darkened, the apprehension that gripped all of us, grown-ups too, when all at once early afternoon became night.

It was a spectacular finish to a magical summer, the first I remembered clearly, everything about it remaining as sharp and immediate as the small, hard pillow, stuffed with pine needles, that I kept on my bed all winter long.

The reality for the adults, as was often the case, was more complicated.

Behind the companionable, enthusiastic exterior of that Adirondacks father was a shaky, uncertain man. There were reasons, certainly, for him to be generally worn out, to be concerned about my mother, who was having her own hard time. But why he was still shaky professionally is puzzling, given *Face the Music*'s reception (though the expensive production barely broke even and could not survive Mary Boland's midsummer departure); given the enormous popularity of "Soft Lights and Sweet Music," and "Let's Have Another Cup of Coffee," which became a Depression theme song, the flip side of "Brother, Can You Spare a Dime." A fear perhaps, considering how hard that effortless-sounding score had come, that the dry spell, when everything he wrote seemed worthless, would return.

Except even in the dry spell not everything *was* worthless. Maybe the dry spell hadn't been so dry after all.

In August of the Adirondacks summer, Max Winslow, worried by the negative signals he was getting from the north woods, decided to take a chance, to go behind his friend and partner's back and send one of those "worthless" songs, "Say It Isn't So," to Rudy Vallee, the nation's number-one crooner. Vallee liked it and sang it on his Thursday night coast-to-coast broadcast. No matter that the mournful, pleading melody, with its half steps and wide leaps down, was hard to sing. Words and music were made for each other. The song was, as they said then and as it actually happened, an overnight hit, at least in part, the man who wrote it liked to explain, because people were tickled by a love song derived from such an incongruous source—"Shoeless" Joe Jackson and the notorious World Series of 1919, when a newsboy was supposed to have cried, "Say it ain't so, Joe," upon hearing that his hero's team had thrown the game.

Encouraged, my father took a look at another one of those discarded, no-good efforts from the dry spell, which would become an even bigger hit. I can see the sheet music still, with its wavering night sky, on the piano rack at East End Avenue and remember excited talk about this new song, "How Deep Is the Ocean?," which I tried unsuccessfully to pick out, though the words were easy to learn. The questions were ones a child asked, a whole song in questions, questions answering questions—"How much do I love you? / I'll tell you no lie, / How deep is the ocean, / How high is the sky?"

"Those two songs came at a critical time," my father would say later. "And they broke the ice."

At the end of the summer he returned to New York with an idea for a new show, a second collaboration with Moss Hart, something as topical as *Face the Music* but in the form, very simple this time, of a revue that would take its skits and songs off a newspaper's front page. A natural. Why hadn't someone thought of it before?

That show would be *As Thousands Cheer.*

• • •

As for my Adirondacks mother, spreading the picnics, receiving my woodland offerings, reading aloud tales from *The Green Fairy Book* that came alive in the flickering light and shade of the lakeside landscape—a long time afterward she would tell me what that summer had meant for her: how, the previous winter, just as things seemed to be taking a turn for the better, she came to a dead stop. Postpartum blues were a generation away; "a walking nervous breakdown," she called it. She couldn't read, couldn't concentrate even on a detective story. Faced with going out to dinner, she panicked. What would she say to Swope, to Woollcott? She had nothing to say. In the wonderful penthouse she had such vertigo, such fear of sleepwalking in those few hours she actually slept, that some nights she put furniture between herself and the window and ordered window bars for the bedroom floor—for the children, she said.

Concerned people came to visit her. My worried father even summoned Dr. Blake. *Dr. Blake?* But the archenemy was one of New York's great doctors. The great Dr. Blake suggested that Ellin see a psychiatrist. Wandering around her bedroom, he examined photographs and said, "Lovely of Katherine," and, "I always liked that one of Clarie," until she screamed at him that he was the one who needed a psychiatrist and to get out. But Dr. Damon, her obstetrician, also suggested a psychiatrist. She didn't want to see one, she insisted. She knew what was the matter. The death of the baby. The death of her mother. The cumulative strain of the estrangement with her father. His remarriage. Three pregnancies in five years, two of them very rough. She could cure herself. A few weeks away would do the trick. In April my father took her to Bermuda; but Bermuda did nothing. Worried about the effect on me and baby Linda, she talked to our pediatrician, Dr. Oscar Schloss, who didn't suggest a psychiatrist. He said, "Why don't you go away to some really quiet place for the summer, Mrs. Berlin, and stop trying to get well."

By August, when guests began coming, when Max Winslow pulled his midsummer surprise, she felt better. In the end, she said, it was my father who had helped her, not by telling her all the things she had to be cheerful about but by demonstrating it, being kind, making her laugh. Or perhaps just being more cheerful himself.

That second winter at East End Avenue was when I first noticed my mother working, caught her stretched out on her chaise longue writing on a yellow legal pad. She didn't want to be interrupted, you could tell. But she never made much of this activity; never told of how she began writing those romantic, slightly ironic short stories, set in the New York social world she knew so well— a debutante falls in love with an aging football hero, a misalliance leads to tragedy, an inept mother ruins her daughter's social life— the first of which appeared, in 1933, in the *Saturday Evening Post*. Whatever the struggle, it was behind closed doors. There was no sense of what happened between the first scribblings and crossings out (my mother did not type) and the eventual publication of a story with sleek illustrations, a man and woman embracing, two women in a grave exchange: boring stories to a child that my father told me were "*wonderful*." There was only the admission that as a writer she was completely dependent on her husband; read aloud to him all works in progress; might flare up at his advice but took it in the end, the advice the same as he gave himself. Something wasn't simple enough. "You don't need all that," he would say, putting a line through a cherished paragraph, a page, a series of pages. He, of course, said she didn't need help, she would have figured it out on her own. "She is a pro," he would say firmly, something my mother would never say of herself.

For she was of the generation and mind-set that insisted that a married woman's work be done on the side, never interrupting her first job—her husband, her children, her home. If you were a professional like Cousin Alice Miller, that was different, though not entirely. Edna Ferber *was* different, but who would want to be homely, unmarried, crotchety Edna? When, years later, after my mother had published her second novel, I said, "If you hadn't been Daddy's wife, you could have been Edna Ferber," she laughed and repeated the remark as a joke. "Not literally," I pressed, "but if you'd put yourself first more." She shook her head at the foolishness. Even after a dozen stories, four books, at least one of them a best-seller, she insisted on her amateur status, though who is to say how much this had to do with theories of wifeliness, how much with the respective caliber of his and her talents.

My mother never said that the writing was part of her rest cure that summer of 1932; but clearly it was.

A complete cure, of course, was something more. The unexpected anger and distress, the wounds from way back, that had caused the depression in the first place—these things were pushed back down, only to erupt when the pressure became too intense, in outbursts my mother regretted but apparently could do nothing about and called "the Irish in me." Outbursts the children would reduce to a question in code. "How's the weather this morning?" we would ask Hermine or our governess or nurse, and we weren't referring to the weather outside. Sometimes I wonder how it would have been if, instead of curing herself in that long-ago time, my mother had swallowed her pride and consulted a professional. The same, I suspect. The doctor, he or she, would have said something suddenly unacceptable, and my mother would have risen from couch or chair, never to return.

And what of my father and his problems in that long-ago time? Work had banished his melancholy, work that pleased both him and the public. He had no interest, either, apparently, in examining deeper causes than a writer's block, a fortieth birthday, big losses in the Crash. A mid-life crisis, he might have said ironically, had the term been around, before pushing his anger and distress back down, and keeping it down. Outbursts were not his style, at least not on the home front. In the family he was known as "a slow burn"—slow to anger, equally slow, once angry, to recover. "The Russian in him," my mother would say.

Decades later, in his sixties, when he suffered a far more serious depression, my father would say, "I should have gone to someone years ago. It's too late now." But years ago, he shared my mother's resistance to all that newfangled stuff. And there was always an edge, an irritating hint of mockery, when my parents spoke of a friend's analysis, even a friend as dear as Moss Hart.

But none of this did I know or think about as a little child or as a bigger one—my father's problems, my mother's sorrows. No more than I knew or thought about the depressed times in which we lived, the actuality behind the election talk that fall, behind the new name, Roosevelt, that was the center of so much argument among my parents and their friends. (Though by 1936 both my parents were ardent New Dealers, in 1932 my mother, the Republican, voted for Hoover, and I am uncertain about my father, the Democrat, who had voted for Al Smith in 1928.)

The Great Depression was there only at the very periphery of my vision: the allusions to those little girls and boys who would give anything for the food I called disgusting; the sight, from a car window, of bonfires in the street, of beggars and long lines of hungry-looking people waiting for a handout of food; of angry faces, men and women both, women sometimes holding up children, coming close to the car window at an intersection; the feeling of shrinking back in the car as if the grown-ups would prefer us not to be seen in our Rolls-Royce, under our fur lap robe, as if it would be better to be invisible.

So, at the very periphery of my vision, I had a childish sense, perhaps, that these people, my parents, although enormously privileged, were in some way doubly fragile, needing protection from themselves, from the world around them.

14

M Y   F A T H E R was a vivid presence that year I was six, the year of *As Thousands Cheer*. Home a lot. In and out of my room, curious about what I was listening to on the bedside radio that was my sixth birthday present, amused that I was now plugged into ordinary America, one more child listening to Uncle Don, Little Orphan Annie, Irene, the singing lady (not letting on that as far as he was concerned, Rudy Vallee notwithstanding, people listening to music on the radio had eroded a large segment of his business, the sheet music that for years had been sold by the thousands in stores across the land). In and out of the living room when I was practicing, letting me explain to him, the untutored one, notes, sharps and flats, symbols for rhythms and keys. (He was not quite as ignorant, however, as he pretended. Someone in this period, I note, had been giving *him* a few lessons. Among his papers is a music manuscript sheet with the thirty-two-bar melody of "Soft Lights and Sweet Music" and a line in his hand: "1st lead sheet ever taken down by Irving Berlin, Aug. 16, 1932.")

I remember my parents at the Miss Hewitt's Christmas pageant. I was an angel—not typecasting. There was an argument with the angel next to me, the whispering becoming audible. "He is." . . . "He isn't." . . . "Yes, he is." "Who was what?" my father asked afterward. "The baby's father," I answered. "She said Joseph, I said God." My father said that was my mother's department. She said, "You were both right," and let it go at that.

I remember my father taking me to *Alice in Wonderland*—Alice again—and to the dressing rooms afterward to meet Alice and the White Queen, Miss Eva Le Gallienne, an imposing presence, with her regal carriage and imperious glance. Then I was allowed to go on the stage itself, the empty theater in front of me, sit in Alice's chair by the fireplace, and climb up almost to the mantel, putting my hand through the gauze that was supposed to be a looking glass. I remember my mother taking me to *Hansel and Gretel* at the opera house and cheering when the children popped the witch into the oven. No illusion there, the real thing, wickedness worsted.

I remember a general feeling of busyness, holidays, visitors. Certainly this was the winter that my stepgrandmother, "Aunt Anna," our own resident prima donna, came into view on the arm of Grandpa, wearing one of her spectacular hats, the gold cockade, perhaps, and sang in her big, golden, just slightly sharp soprano voice Christmas carols and an operatic "Always."

But of the writing and mounting of *As Thousands Cheer*, the year's major and formidable accomplishment, I have almost no recollection other than the general impression of a faint tinkling behind the library door, idiot notes that would eventually arrange themselves into whichever of the songs were worked on at home, "Heat Wave," "How's Chances," "Easter Parade," "Not for All the Rice in China."

I knew later that my father "sweated blood" over a score because he told me so and my mother agreed. But I never saw him sweating blood, never heard him say he was having a helluva time with this song or that. "The reason Irving is so good," Sam Goldwyn, Sr., said once, "is that he never takes himself that seriously.

He just does it." It would be more accurate to say that he took himself entirely seriously when it came to work but still just did it.

We heard about other struggles, to be sure. We knew my father had a terrible time sleeping. The household revolved around his repose; my mother's, too. The hushing, the tiptoeing as we went up to breakfast. The carryings-on should my night-owl, night-working father have to wake up early to make a morning train or doctor's appointment. The evening before shot to hell. Early dinner. To bed at ten, though naturally not to sleep.

Sometimes we would hear about trouble at the office. My father's going to his office was part of daily life, though heaven forbid he should go there at eight or nine in the morning, like other children's fathers. Noon was early for his workday to begin. He didn't just publish his own songs, I soon found out, but those of many songwriters. He published "Who's Afraid of the Big Bad Wolf?" and all my favorites from *Snow White* and *Pinocchio,* and later a whole host of grown-up hits—"I'll Get By," "Yes, Sir, That's My Baby," "These Foolish Things," "All of Me"—materialized with the Irving Berlin imprint. In the office were his partners, Saul Bornstein, who was strictly business, not part of our home life, and Max Winslow, "Uncle Max," though sometime during 1933, Uncle Max departed for Hollywood, to work for Harry Cohn, his brother-in-law. There was the chief song-plugger, handsome, affable Dave Dreyer, who wrote his own hits ("Cecilia," "Love Letters in the Sand"). There were the office managers, Abe Schwartz and Benny Bloom; the arrangers, Arthur Johnston, and beginning with *Face the Music,* Helmy Kresa, who would take down the songs of Irving Berlin for the next forty-five years; there was my father's secretary, Mynna Granat, platinum blond, stylish, smart, the future second Mrs. Dreyer, who would be replaced in 1947 by the less conspicuous, no less smart, Hilda Schneider (who would be replaced by no one). As a child I marveled at the confusion in that cluster of small rooms that called itself an "office"—the cacophony of pianos and voices, singers trying out songs, songwriters demonstrating songs, people shouting on the telephone, the excitement and noise and laughter, the desks piled high with show business newspapers, the shipping room, with its stacks of sheet music. But that wasn't where the mystery lay. My father the businessman, who liked the hardheaded side of things, wasn't the father, however colorful, I was interested in.

But the creative father was more elusive. It wasn't just the songs, when and how they were written, but the shows of which they magically became a part. The whole process. The book. (My father not only wrote the score of *As Thousands Cheer;* he collaborated on the skits as well.) The casting. The costumes, choreography, sets, and lighting. He had the approval of everything. The rehearsals, rewrites, tryouts, the final "freezing" of a show (The moment when no more changes could be made)—he was there. But all those gritty, tinseled activities that would one day be laid out in the lyric of "There's No Business Like Show Business" had no part in my childhood. If now and then we got behind that curtain, there was no backstage aura to our family life. This was a deliberate decision on both my parents' part: that I, and later my two sisters, would be brought up offstage, out of the public eye, leading our own lives; and God forbid any of us should end up in show business. It was also a matter of style. It was like the Christmas tree in the library. Trimming the tree was not a family affair. The tree was trimmed behind closed doors and revealed to the children in full splendor, with all the presents beneath it, on Christmas morning. So it was with a show.

The most I would have known beforehand about *As Thousands Cheer,* besides the tinkling on the strange little piano in the library, was that in April my father and Moss Hart sailed for Bermuda to write "a new show." Mr. Hart was by now a familiar figure, a favorite among my parents' friends. A tall, dark-haired man, instantly recognizable for his spectacular widow's peak and soaring eyebrows, he had a way of talking to children, as he drew on his pipe, that was elaborate and funny at the same time. Mr. Hart was a very funny man. He and my father laughed a lot when they were together. From the way they laughed you would have thought writing a show was a lark.

So my Daddy and the funny Mr. Hart went to Bermuda to work, and my mother, pleased to hear that things were going well, decided to pay her husband a surprise visit on his forty-fifth birthday. Benny Bloom, who handled family travel arrangements and had been around show business a long time, sent his boss a wire: "She is coming to surprise you on May 11th." It became a family joke later, that warning wire giving the hardworking gentlemen "time to get the girls out," as my mother put it. That both my parents found it genuinely amusing was additional proof, if I needed it, that nobody considered straying. "When would I have had the time?" was the way my father put it.

Mr. Hart and Mr. Berlin had a wonderful time writing that show, and out of their two back-to-back shows came a friendship that lasted for the next twenty-eight years, till the sad day that Moss Hart, still young by my parents' and all his other friends' reckoning, died. "If Moss were around, I'd be working still," my father, aged ninety-six, said to Kitty Carlisle Hart, Moss's widow, in one of those latter-day phone calls that were his way, in old age, of keeping up with friends.

The Hart-Berlin enthusiasm carried over into the summer, such a different summer from the one before. We were in Montauk now, at the far end of Long Island, in one of the "seven sisters," those late-nineteenth-century shingled cottages built by McKim, Mead and White along a high ridge of moorland. Our house, second from the end, had a peaked roof, a glassed-in sun porch on the ocean side, and a huge chimney pointed like a hand at the sky. "The ugliest house I ever saw," Aunt Gwen would recall, but wonderfully comfortable and bright, a house in the full air, with sun streaming in, lighting up the heavy woodwork and dark corners.

A half mile beyond was the beach, a delightful new playground with a new set of equipment. I remember white beach hats, rubber beach shoes, wooden sand toys and little wooden folding chairs; Mademoiselle in a flowered bathing suit, halfway to her knees. It was a beach almost to ourselves, where I played with Linda, a toddler now in rompers or trunks, curls escaping from her floppy hat. We buried each other in the sand, scared each other with a horseshoe crab, till the nurse (still there, that annoying nurse) removed Linda with an expression of displeasure in my direction.

My father, working all week long on the show, came only on weekends to this charming place. During the week the only male presence in our female household was Jack, who was our swimming teacher, lifeguard, and chauffeur, who drove us fast along the old Montauk highway (then the only highway), the "roller-coaster road," with our stomachs left somewhere behind. There were trips with my mother to the lighthouse, to a dairy farm to pick up butter and thick cream, to Home Sweet Home, where another man who wrote songs had lived long ago. But I knew that all this was just killing time till Friday, that when my father arrived, there was a change. The car door slammed, and she was on her feet, running to meet him. It was no secret how she felt about him; the look on her face told you all.

On weekends it was hard for my father to simmer down. He drummed his fingers and annoyed my mother by molding the inside of dinner rolls into small, compact balls. He chewed too much gum, smoked too many cigarettes, jumped when the telephone rang, and fiddled at the piano. But his nerves were the healthy kind, the kind that ended up with a wonderful song, a hit show; the kind that didn't shut you out. I was still his devoted summer shadow who matched arms with him to see who was the brownest (he was, but I came close), who followed him into the surf, showing him my new trick of diving under the waves, astonishing my mother as well, who swam only on the calmest days.

Now there was deep-sea fishing: the smell of the boat, oil and gas, bait and salt water; the baking sun; the sea like crumpled tinfoil; the motion that made my mother, and later my sisters, seasick but which for some reason did not affect my father or me. Though I have a photograph of him with a sailfish twice his height ("Daddy is the one on the right," the inscription reads), I don't recall our having any such spectacular catches together that summer, or later. But there were some good-sized bass and blues and a great many blowfish. "Tickle their stomachs and they'll blow up and burst," my father would tell me, but I could never bring myself to do it. He was full of that kind of lore, adding to it by asking questions of the men who manned the boats, about weather and navigation and how business was that season, one professional to another. But there were silences, too, and in those silences, accompanied sometimes by the faintest whistle, I could tell that his mind was elsewhere, that the bright, broad, empty horizon was being filled. Some little phrase was running around his brain, invisible, yet ever-present, that had nothing to do with fishing or me.

All summer long we lived in the seclusion of Montauk, forty-five minutes to the east of Southampton, the old stomping ground, off limits by necessity and by choice. My parents were very selective about social activities. An opening at the John Drew Theatre. A few discreet visits to Aunt K's blue-turreted château so that I could play with my O'Brien cousins, with whom I had a hilarious time: Marie Louise, dark and curly-haired like her mother, a few years older but never condescending; Morgan, a year or so younger, a scamp, with Uncle Ken's narrow eyes and comical side-of-the-mouth delivery; blond skinny Katherine, my age, the ringleader. The visits rationed. Mrs. Berlin had not forgiven Southampton, and Southampton hadn't really changed its anti-Semitic ways. "Ellie dear"—I can hear Aunt K's voice, girlish, teasing, placating—"and these sweet little girls, such strangers . . ." In the social column of the *Southampton Press* it was noted that Mr. and Mrs. Clarence Mackay spent Fourth of July week with Judge and Mrs. Kenneth O'Brien and went to Gardiners Island, which my grandfather leased in those days as a shooting preserve. If Grandpa, in white flannels, blue blazer, and straw boater, Aunt Anna, in smart summer piqué, and their white dogs came to Montauk, the visit did not stay in my memory. But there was a party that was something to remember; a promise of what grown-up life held in store.

Staying in the house that weekend were Aunt Gwen, Uncle Willie, and another couple, a pretty woman with noticeably made up eyes and a man who looked enough like my father to be his brother, Mr. and Mrs. Thalberg. Aunt Gwen remembers that Mrs. Thalberg, the movie star Norma Shearer, gave her a bit of advice: "If you want to avoid wrinkles, my dear, you must not read at night, and you must not smile." My memory was only of the festivities Saturday night—peering through the railing of the upstairs landing at the white dinner jackets, the women in their long, clinging dresses with cap sleeves and low backs; following my mother's golden blond head as she moved among her guests. Somewhere at their center, more important than a movie queen and her genius husband, was a man with a shiny black face playing the piano. His playing was jumpy and fast, skittering up and down the keyboard in a way I'd never heard before, and he sang in a scratchy voice songs I would later put names to. "Honeysuckle Rose," "I'm Confessin' That I

Love You." At some point my father took me downstairs and introduced me to the man, Mr. Waller, someone who could really play the piano. "Listen to him, kid, you can learn a thing or two," my father said. Eventually, I went to sleep to the sound of that skittery, infectious playing, that voice that made fun of itself, of a world that wasn't nearly as hospitable as the evening might have implied.

Way out in Montauk, with Fats Waller to entertain, the unorthodox Mr. and Mrs. Berlin had given the best party of the Long Island summer season. And then, at summer's end, they went on their way, back to what mattered to them, what was really going on.

The Music Box opening of *As Thousands Cheer* was September 30, a Saturday, which meant an extra day and night to wait for the notices. Given the first-night ovation, the general rapture of the gold-plated audience (following raves in Philadelphia), the reviews surely had to be worth waiting for. I can imagine my parents doing some cautious celebrating at the party afterward at the Swopes'. Even Moss Hart, a nervous wreck all evening, sick to his stomach, was almost ready to believe they had a hit on their hands.

But nothing could have prepared them for the unreserved, unanimous cheering from the critics of New York. It is still extraordinary to read those notices, one after the other, so many different voices saying the same thing: that the show was brilliant, unimprovable; that the combination of Moss Hart and Irving Berlin was, in one critic's words, "a beautifully gloved sock on the jaw of the present day universe"; that the score was satin and the book spectacular in its irreverence. "Spectacular" is the word used again and again, for the stars—Clifton Webb, Marilyn Miller, Ethel Waters, Helen Broderick—for the production, for every item on the program. The critics, one and all, welcomed back the revue, a form thought dead and buried with the twenties, and gave thanks to Mr. Berlin and Mr. Sam Harris, composer and producer of the famed *Music Box Revues*, for "turning and returning the trick so well." Burns Mantle, who had reservations about *Face the Music*, abandoned all caution: "I agree with Sam Harris that Irving Berlin is a genius," he wrote. As for Brooks Atkinson, "Mr. Berlin has never written better tunes or more sparkling lyrics and Mr. Hart has never turned his wit with such economical precision. In these circumstances there is nothing a reviewer can do except cheer."

I wish I had a picture of my father reading those notices. I don't. But I have a telegram he sent that Monday morning to Max Winslow in Hollywood. It is picture enough. "Dear Max," he wired, "the notices for show this morning are better than they were for the first Music Box Revue. It is bigger hit than I ever hoped for. Stop. Best to everybody. Irving."

One afternoon during the Christmas holidays of 1933, my father took me to the Music Box to a matinee of *As Thousands Cheer.* I can still remember it, number by number: the opening like a Gilbert and Sullivan patter song—of newsboys hawking a story about a man biting a dog; Marilyn Miller and Clifton Webb singing "How's Chances" (the parody of heiress Barbara Hutton escaped me but not the beat of the tune); Ethel Waters, in a bandanna headdress singing the weather report "Heat Wave." Then the boredom when they talked, everybody laughing at what? Actors pretending to be the president and First Lady or John D. Rockefeller and son? Then the relief of a new headline, a change of scenery, another song. Marilyn Miller, surrounded by comic-strip characters, singing "The Funnies." "Easter Parade," the first-act finale with Miller, Webb, and a mob of children, all in old-fashioned dress, no colors, just rotogravure browns.

If I didn't understand completely—I had just turned seven—that the dark, dapper man beside me had written all those songs, along with his share of the boring talk, I understood enough; and even more when we went backstage and were surrounded by the rotogravure children with their corkscrew curls and pantaloons, some of them not much older than I. "Hello, Mr. Berlin," they called. And he was suddenly part of it, back there in his natural habitat. Then, before returning to our seats for the second act, he introduced me to the stars—the sleek man with the thin mustache, the pretty blonde, the sour-faced comedienne and my favorite, the tall, thin, dark-skinned lady who sang "Heat Wave."

Later, I would hear a story about those stars: how, in Philadelphia, Marilyn Miller, Clifton Webb, and Helen Broderick had refused to take a bow with Ethel Waters, she being black and they white. He would respect their feelings, of course, my father had said, only in that case there need be no bows at all. The next night, Mr. Webb, Miss Miller, and Miss Broderick took their bows with Miss Waters, who not only sang "Heat Wave" and "Harlem on My Mind" but "Supper Time," a harsh and eloquent song that made some people, as it was intended to, quite uncomfortable, including the critic John Mason Brown. He called the somber interlude, with its headline of a lynching, unsuitable and urged its removal from the show.

The curtain-call story had to do with color and color blindness. But I liked to give it another interpretation. "They must have been jealous," I said. "She was the best."

So I had a glimpse at last of my father in his world, that mysterious world beyond the limits of my horizon. A glimpse of glory.

Then the treat was over. I was home in my room, getting out of my party dress and into my pajamas, having supper on a tray; and presently, Mademoiselle approached with the blue bottle and spoon, the dreaded milk of magnesia, the price paid at the end of any day of unusual excitement that was assumed to have left a small stomach churning.

_____ 15

LATER, I WOULD HARK BACK to that December matinee as the moment when there was a click, small but definite. In our particular family I had reached the age of reason. And what my reason told me was that no matter how much my little-girl's life was said to be "just like everybody else's" or, anyhow, just like that of my schoolmates, it wasn't. Though everyone is "different," I was more "different." But at the time, if the truth were known, that memorable afternoon fell into place as yet another grand occasion in a childhood so filled with grand occasions, with "difference," that who and what my father was, in those early days, seemed simply the final icing on the cake—all this and Irving Berlin, too.

I think, for instance, of the whole holiday season that wrapped itself around that afternoon at the Music Box, of the Berlin Christmas, with its prelude the Berlin Hanukkah, and of the way my parents, the former Miss Mackay and the eminently Jewish Mr. Berlin, managed to fashion out of their differences a set of traditions and rituals that remain among my fondest childhood memories.

It is another way of viewing us, another piece of the picture.

My parents enjoyed holidays (and when they didn't, pretended they did). Unlike some of their more sophisticated friends, they seemed to understand the importance, particularly in childhood, of the special day, the same every year, the special stories, foods, and decorations and that special sense of well-being that accompanies a holiday. And, of course, the presents. We were particularly lucky, I thought, because we had a double set, Jewish and Christian, along with all the national and folk days shared with everybody.

But holidays were more than expressions of my mother's well-known lavishness, concerning which my father would remark, more than once, "I gave up trying to get your mother to economize. It was easier just to make more money." Holidays were a learning experience. Leave it to my mother, as clever as she was extravagant, to make them that: the occasion for addressing the delicate business of our having as parents two worldly people with fiercely held and opposing faiths not far behind them.

Both our parents would pass down to their children the moral and ethical values common to all great religions; give us a sense of what was right and what was wrong; raise us not to be good Jews or good Catholics or good whatever else you might care to cite, but to be good (or try to be) human beings. But it was our Catholic mother, though out of the church while I was growing up, who would handle the matter of explaining and recommending to us our double heritage. It required all her ingenuity, but she was up to the task.

Briefly, she considered becoming a Unitarian, the branch of Christianity most palatable to Jews, then abandoned the idea in favor of her own informal version of the Judeo-Christian tradition, acceptable to my father, interesting to her. She would teach her children the prayers she herself had said as a child and at Christmas tell them about the Infant Jesus, symbol of hope, sent to earth to look after little children, and skirt over the complications of Easter. She would also lead us through the Old Testament and later take us to Temple Emanu-El, New York's most fashionable synagogue, to seders and to services on Yom Kippur and *Succoth*. When we grew up, she said, we would be free to choose—if we knew what was best for us, the religion of our husband. It seemed to me later that, like the good sport she was, she gave the advantage to her own husband's religion. There was no taking us to St. Patrick's at Christmas or Easter. But then, she could not treat the Catholic church as "getting to know your heritage," and I learned not to tease about that, for her eyes flashed a warning to pursue it no further.

It wouldn't quite work out, when we "grew up," as my mother hoped. All three of us would share our father's agnosticism and sidestep our husbands' faiths. But as a child I *was* reassured, secure in the knowledge that there was God, with his white beard, the Infant Jesus, with his halo, and twelve-year-old Jesus, the boy preacher who grew up to be the greatest of the Jewish prophets and who, when the wicked Romans killed him, rose from the dead and went to heaven. Clear in my mind, always, was that Jesus was brother under the skin to Moses, that Mary was a Jewish mother. Somehow it all fit in. My Jewish father, who had written "Easter Parade." My non-Jewish mother, who, in our first at-home seders, read the children's questions from the Passover service, explained the symbolism of the unleavened bread and the lamb whose blood marked the doorways of Jewish houses—though it was tricky about the Angel of Death and those poor Egyptian baby boys who hadn't had a chance to do anything bad. Still, it made sense, because she wanted it to. Everything made sense—Jewish and Christian holidays, Jewish and Christian relatives, Jewish and Christian friends. And always, there was this dreamy emphasis on the romantic ancientness of the Jews that had first struck my mother, not yet married, in Jerusalem.

And the other side, the ugly, scary, or merely "unrealistic" side, quite apart from the theological side, how it really was out in the world between Christians and Jews, what the dangers as well as the virtues of "mixing" might be, we put off considering. Even when around nine I began to grasp why we did not buy toys marked

"Made in Germany," to half-grasp the meaning of my father's Russian village going up in flames, of the word "pogrom," I still didn't relate it to me, to us, to our life. I only thought that to be a "half," as I called myself, was to have the best of all possible worlds.

So, in December, out of the same enormous box that held the crèche, the Christmas books, came the branched candlestick and the Hanukkah books. The menorah was set up on a living room windowsill. Settled into the white damask sofa, my mother read the story of Judas Maccabaeus. We discussed what the story and the holiday meant and how, out of such a bloodthirsty history, could come peace and hope; we lit the first candle, and I opened my Hanukkah present, a mere token of what was coming on Christmas. If I can picture my father, the nonbeliever, it is listening to the reading, learning just like me, for he had long ago forgotten the story, pleased that this is what my mother and I are doing.

A few nights later, there she was again, on the same white sofa, reading the Gospel according to Luke. "And the angel said unto her, fear not, Mary, for thou hast found favor with God." A lot of Luke before we got to "The Night Before Christmas" and the hanging of our stockings on a bedroom chair, though there were two perfectly good chimneys.

But in our house even Santa did things differently; he found his way to the bedroom floor and had time not only to fill those enormous stockings but sew onto the exterior so many extra packages that none of the stocking itself was visible, only a crust of gold and silver paper. (Santa's—my mother's—secret was duplicate stockings, one for me to hang, one for her to stuff weeks ahead and shop for year round; thus the variety within, the costumed dolls, the wooden animals, miniature crockery, little pipes and bells picked up by my parents on this trip or that, mixed in with the more familiar puzzles, jokes, games, yo-yos, the soaps in animal shapes, the chocolate cigarettes and cigars, and in the toe a gold Cartier's charm, a book that opened, a car with moving wheels.)

If I picture my father on Christmas Eve . . . but I don't. He enters later, late the next morning, one reason for those incredible stockings, my mother would say, to keep the children busy so even on Christmas her husband could get his rest. He is seen first in

Linda's room, helping her open the last of her stocking, help she does not welcome; little and slow, she has slept late herself, is savoring every present. "Merry Christmas, Daddy, I see you're up finally," I say. "Is it time for the tree? Why are you opening Linda's packages?" "Yes, let's go see the tree now," responds Daddy, clapping his hands briskly. "Come on, everybody, it's late," as if he were not the one who has kept everybody waiting.

Tall as the ceiling of the double-storied library, second in my eyes only to Radio City's, our tree is silver and blue, with big frosted baubles, blue lights, and a blue angel at the top; an overwhelming yet cool and elegant tree rising above the packages and toys beneath which are every color of the rainbow. So many packages, so many toys, my mother rushing about with pencil and pad, crying, "Wait, not so fast, what was that, who was that from?" as my father settles down to some object that takes his fancy—a toy bathroom that he plays with till the mechanism reverses itself and water pours over the carpet, a toy swimming pool (the same), a make-your-own-perfume set, even more disastrous. (My parents open their own presents later, except the ones from us—bookmarks, cross-stitched towels, crocheted doilies, needlepoint pincushions, handiwork frantically finished up Christmas Eve by nurse or governess.)

Such a surfeit prepared for by the annual rite of giving away large numbers of old toys to the New York Foundling Hospital. This ritual, designed not only to make room for the new but to make us think of children less fortunate than ourselves, was given the *coup de grâce* by Linda, the nursery wit, who asked when our sister Elizabeth arrived on the scene, "Now that you have a new baby, are you going to keep your old children?"

At some point on Christmas Day my father never failed to tell the story of himself, a naughty, undevout little boy sneaking out of his Orthodox Jewish household to visit the Irish family across the street, gape at their Christmas tree, and share in their nonkosher holiday food. In spirit, on Christmas Day, the future composer of "White Christmas" was still a naughty visitor, appreciative of the way my mother had knocked herself out but a little quizzical, as if to say, We don't need all this, I know that, you know that, let's keep our heads.

Presently, relatives arrived for Christmas dinner, which was another form of learning experience. There was a boisterous contingent from my mother's family: Aunt K and Uncle Ken and the very noisy O'Brien cousins; Grandpapa and the very dressy Aunt Anna (the Willie Mackays and little Michael Mackay, Linda's friend, had Christmas on Long Island with Aunt Gwen's family), plus the somewhat more dignified Balines: Uncle Ben, a grayer version of my father, with the same amused brown glance, down from New London for Christmas week, a good time to close up the shop and visit the New York relatives; Aunt Nettie, fair and stately, unruffled by strangers or confusion; my Baline cousins, Milton and Russell, big boys with thick fierce eyebrows like my father's, who were good-natured about getting down on the floor and playing with a couple of kids.

In the unfolding family landscape I knew Uncle Ben was the relative my father loved best, or at least had no difficulties with, as he had with Aunt Gussie (not visible at Christmas). Like Gussie, Ben took family business off my father's hands and had a caretaking attitude toward his famous younger brother. He stayed in my mind between visits (there were two or three a year) because he gave me every Christmas a fancy wrapper, satin or velveteen, as sumptuous as one of those fur coats he designed for rich Connecticut ladies. I knew my mother also loved him, his laconic manner, his sense of self (everything but his cigars, which he finally gave up smoking in her presence). Even in the Depression, Uncle Ben's business kept afloat. At the end of every summer, my father lent him the money to buy pelts and every winter said, "Forget it," and Ben said, "Forget it," and repaid the loan. The boys got large checks for Christmas from Uncle Irving. Otherwise, my parents would say, "Ben won't let you do anything." Like my father he was a fisherman and had made, in his basement carpentry shop, a fishing boat, seaworthy, of course; when Ben did something, he knew how to do it right.

The sight of my father and uncle together gave me a good feeling always, but then so did my father and grandfather, another trim pair, of a height, both smartly dressed in dark blue suits, men of the world being hearty with each other, talking about Europe, Long Island, mutual friends like Otto Kahn and Herbert Swope, my grandfather, who sometimes dropped his "g"s calling my father

Irvin or Irwin, my father calling my grandfather Mr. Mackay. Not by a flicker was anything betrayed. Long afterward my mother once said, "Your father probably never forgave your grandfather." But she was rarely that frank. "Such a droll pair," she was more likely to say, and tell of the time my grandfather, taking my father around Harbor Hill, reminisced about the party for the Prince of Wales and said, "Irwin my boy, I wish you could have been there." Could he have forgotten his admonition to the guards that night? Completely forgotten?

Perhaps it was Aunt Anna, who wasn't at the party, either, who made him forget. Sumptuous Anna, with her jewels, her hats, her décolletage, her spunky story: the poor New Jersey girl with the exciting voice who refused to change her name from good old Dutch-American Anna Case to Anna de la Casa and got hired by the Met, anyhow; who sang Sophie in the American premiere of *Der Rosenkavalier*, recorded for Edison, and after a fight with the opera house management over roles, became a leading concert star of the 1920s. My father liked to recall wanting Anna for a *Music Box Revue*. She was lovely looking, with porcelain skin, a high-bridged nose, but she turned him down, saying once you sang popular music you could never go back to the other (though Grace Moore proved her wrong). It was also said that along with the voice went a prima donna temper, a shrewish tongue—poor Grandpa—though no sign of this at Christmas.

As for Grandpa himself, nothing colored my enjoyment of this amiable gentleman who produced five-dollar bills from a fold in the curtain and, though old, was entirely recognizable as the six-year-old boy with the fake mustache and admiral's costume in the portrait in my mother's bedroom. And when, as the senior member of the holiday gathering, he took his place on my mother's right at our gleaming candlelit Christmas table and looked about him at the family scene, you would have thought this union, thriving on its differences, had had his approval always.

Many years later, when Christmas was celebrated irregularly in my parents' house, if at all, my mother said, almost casually, "Oh, you know, I hated Christmas, we both hated Christmas. We only did it for you children."

The implication was that for them the happiness had drained

out of Christmas on December 25, 1928, the day my brother died. But there it remains in my memory, a glorious simulation, their gift to us, the single most beautiful and exciting day of the year.

16 _____

S O I C O M E to Easter, 1934; an Easter to end all Easters, with a new Berlin hit, "Easter Parade," to celebrate it for the first time and every Easter from then on; followed, in May, by a five-part radio cavalcade of Irving Berlin songs on the "Gulf Oil Program," an Irving Berlin *Time* cover story (his first), and an editorial in the *Washington Post,* pegged on the broadcasts, that finally said it: Irving Berlin was "Songwriter for the American Nation."

But there was trouble that Easter in our nursery paradise. Though Linda, two, was getting cuter with every passing month, at seven, going on eight, fresh and gawky, with a perpetual scowl on my face, I had lost the last of my little-girl cuteness and had become a problem at home and abroad. Cozy Miss Hewitt's, which did not prepare for college, had been replaced now by big, noisy, competitive Brearley, just a few blocks up East End Avenue, the school for brains, a scary but stimulating place. At the hard, new school the first reports were as good as at the old, easy school. I had brought proud offerings of homework marked "very good" to my parents, who cared—how they cared—especially my father, who made no distinction, where school was concerned, between a girl and boy. You would have thought he had plans for me to conquer the world, the way he pushed and praised. In every class, as if my father were there behind my shoulder, I was the first with the waving hand, the correct answer, the uncomfortable question, but I had made no friends.

Who can say why? It was something more than being a new girl or terrible in gym, the place where shining counts with other children. Something, maybe, to do with all those differences, not just the glamorous sparkling ones but others less delightful—my

Aunt Gussie, Grandmother Leah, and Uncle Ben on a Connecticut holiday, sometime in the early 1910s.

My grandmother Leah in *the* rocking chair, the one my father bought her with the first real money he made.

Mr. and Mrs. Benjamin Baline—"Uncle Ben" and "Aunt Nettie"—at home in New London, in the 1940s.

UNLESS OTHERWISE STATED, PHOTOS ARE FROM THE BERLIN FAMILY COLLECTION.

Right, Mrs. John W. Mackay—
"Granny" to my mother—in 1928,
the year of her death.

Below, my beautiful grandmother
Katherine Duer Mackay, later Mrs.
Joseph Blake.

Grandpa Mackay with Uncle Willie,
Aunt K, and my mother.

My mother, Ellin Mackay, around the time she met my father.

My father, Irving Berlin, around the time he met my mother.

Mr. and Mrs. Berlin in Atlantic City, a favorite resort, in 1927.

The Berlins in Palm Springs, winter of 1928.

On the way to a big surprise, February 1932.

With biographer and longtime comrade Alexander Woollcott (probably at Woollcott's "Island" in Vermont).

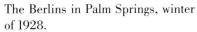

On a Hollywood soundstage in 1930, the year of the now-forgotten early Berlin movies: *Puttin' On the Ritz, Mammy,* and *Reaching for the Moon.*

Alaska, 1937. Taking time out from the movie *Alexander's Ragtime Band*, with me, Sammy Goldwyn, my mother, and Linda in front.

"The three little Berlin girls"—Elizabeth *(left)*, Linda *(right)*, and I—Lew Beach, early 1940s.

FRED A. PARRISH

With Joseph Schenck—"Uncle Joe" —in Los Angeles in 1936 at the Silver Jubilee of "Alexander's Rag-time Band," the song that brought Irving Berlin to fame.

Arriving at a Hollywood premiere circa 1930 with Norma Shearer and Irving Thalberg, who later the summer of *Top Hat* were our Santa Monica neighbors.

George Gershwin's time exposure of himself and his old friend Irving Berlin, taken in California in 1937, a few months before Gershwin died.

PHOTO BY GEORGE GERSHWIN

IRVING BERLIN AND
THIS IS THE ARMY

IB with Noël Coward backstage at the London Palladium, the first overseas stop, November 1943.

Meeting the royal family on the same tour: *left to right,* IB, Princess Elizabeth, Queen Elizabeth, Princess Margaret Rose, King George VI.

With Marlene Dietrich, entertaining the U.S. Fifth Army "somewhere in Italy," May 1944.

With Eleanor Roosevelt, backstage after the show, 1942.

The Berlin Christmas, 1942, in Detroit where the show was playing.

With *(left to right)* W. C. Handy, Shelton Brooks ("The Darktown Strutters' Ball"), and Harold Arlen, at the 1940 ASCAP convention, shortly before the broadcasting boycott.

With Dorothy and Richard Rodgers in 1946, the year of *Annie Get Your Gun*.

With Cole Porter and Audrey Hepburn, sometime in the fifties in Hollywood.

Right, father and daughter take off for Europe shortly after the opening of *Call Me Madam,* October 1950.

Below, Marvin Barrett and I, just married, October 15, 1952.

TWO PHOTOS: RENE BATIGNE

With Pablo Picasso at his Vallauris studio, 1951.

Lunching with Marc Chagall in Vence, on the same trip as above: *left to right,*
Chagall's daughter Ida, my father, me, and Chagall.

My parents' silver wedding anniversary, Hawaii, January 4, 1951.

The Ball of the Roses, New York, 1953: *left to right,* Linda, my father, me, my mother (who has taken the Mackay emeralds out of the vault).

"For Granny from Grandpa and Elizabeth Esther," March 22, 1954.

With Irving Hoffman in Lew Beach, circa 1960.

Beekman Place Christmas, 1963:
Granny and Grandpa.

Marvin and I, eleven years married.

The growing family: *clockwise*,
Elizabeth Barrett, Grandpa, Granny,
Marvin, Linda, Baby Caroline,
Edouard; *on the floor*, Irving,
Katherine, and Mary Ellin Barrett.

Beekman Place, September 1974. The last photo session:
above, at the drawing table; *below*, at the piano.

seven o'clock bedtime, earliest in the class, the funny clothes my mother put me in, like high shoes laced up to mid-ankle (so I wouldn't have piano legs like my beautiful grandmother), and old-fashioned underclothes with buttons (no explanations deemed necessary) and too-fancy French party dresses with babyish short skirts; plus all those things I wasn't "allowed" to do, like fraternizing after school on weekdays or going to movies (though the other side of that was how many books I read, or had read to me, how much theater I went to). Maybe it related to being more at ease with grown-ups than with other children or the secret conviction that, however much I might chafe at my mother's rules, I had the most interesting, charming parents and the most fun life any child could have. And my classmates set out to humble me.

This naturally was not something I brought home: the snubs, the whispering, the cliques in blue gym suits that wouldn't invite me in.

Instead, what I did bring home from school one day was a Mickey Mouse watch that did not belong to me. For some time I had been teasing for this popular item. Never mind all the other riches—the books and toys and costumes, the radio and Victrola, the string of pearls with the sapphire clasp, the coral beads, the golden charm bracelet. Inexpensive, omnipresent Mickey was what I wanted and had been refused, perhaps because Mickey, at least in this form, was considered in questionable taste. So one day I found myself in miraculous possession of my heart's desire, snatched from another child's gym locker. I don't remember the act itself or how I was caught out, only the way I felt, sweaty and cold, standing in my mother's bedroom, confronted by both my parents, their gravity worse than anger. "*Why?*" they kept saying. "*Why?*" Why would I, Mary Ellin Berlin, of all children, want to steal something? This particular something? What possibly could be the reason?

There was no punishment meted out, only slow words, unanswerable questions. Punishment the weight of the knowledge that the watch had to be returned to the teacher, who would be asked to return it discreetly to the owner. That I had to go to school in the morning as if nothing happened.

The end of the incident came six weeks later when Linda and I trooped up to the living room on Easter morning. Along with the expected assortment of eggs, gaily dyed egg-hunt eggs, eggs with views, large cardboard eggs, brightly papered, containing a doll or stuffed animal, the Easter bunny had deposited two much smaller papered eggs, small enough to testify to the preciousness of what was within. In mine, on a bed of shredded green cellophane, lay a Mickey Mouse watch, identical to the one returned to the teacher. All Mickey Mouse watches were identical; that was the point. But what did it mean? Slightly tainted goods, that watch, put on with embarrassment as my parents looked at me and then each other. Not revealing their, and no doubt the teacher's, intent. Forgiveness. Acknowledgment, even, of an initial mistake. Certainly not a reward for stealing. Worn a few times but before the spring was out, well before we left for Bedford Village, 1934's summer rental, mislaid.

I had gone into a "difficult stage" and would cause my parents much concern and irritation and myself much woe before it was over. I've blotted out most of it: what I did or said to make my governess cry or, when out with my mother, to prompt the fearful, phony smile that accompanied the frigid glance and the muttered "You are too naughty to take anyplace"; what I did or said on visits to Harbor Hill, the magic kingdom, that caused me to say, "I don't know why Grandpa likes me so much; he has never seen my nicer side." ("He likes you," my mother said, "because when you were four years old you got up on a pony, kicked your heels into him, and cantered off; the groom had to sprint to catch you. Your grandfather is a sucker for spirit.")

A few incidents come back to me: opening the door of my canary cage, having been told not to, watching the poor bird fly out the window, never to be seen again; in bed with a cold having solitary lunch, dropping my silver napkin ring, a heavy, authoritative object engraved with nursery-rhyme figures that for some reason I hated, out the window, not viewing it as a lethal weapon, only glad to be rid of it. Some hours later, on my supper tray, was the napkin ring, only slightly dented, Mademoiselle marveling at the mystery of how it got down to Eighty-sixth Street, where the service elevator man had found it in the gutter; my eighth birthday party, running wild backstage after the matinee of *The Great Waltz*, the life of Johann Strauss set to his music, leading a pack of twenty little girls backward around the revolving stages, up and down ladders, shrieking over the loudspeaker the rudest song I knew: "I smell bacon, I smell ham, I smell Chapin [Brearley's archrival] in the garbage can," the words reverberating throughout the theater. "Never again will I take you backstage, never," said my mother in icy tones, and indeed she did not for a year or two.

Who could blame my father for announcing shortly after this latest episode that he was not, after all, going to do a new revue with Moss Hart but was going to Hollywood to make a movie. If I did not hold myself entirely responsible for his decision to put three thousand miles between himself and me for untold months, I took it exceedingly personally, especially when my mother said he would have to leave before Christmas. It was deemed necessary for him to take me out to a delicious restaurant lunch and to FAO Schwarz to pick out an advance Christmas present and during the hours of the afternoon, in his own brisk but friendly fashion, convey a bit of the excitement he was feeling about this movie, as yet unnamed, with Fred Astaire, which could be wonderful, just wonderful *if*, a lot of ifs always. But in the meantime, I must try to behave myself while he was gone. "It doesn't particularly bother me, but it upsets your mother terribly when you misbehave" (which, of course, was exactly what she said about him).

Then my father was off, telling me to mind Mamma and Mademoiselle and work hard and make him proud.

And in case I needed a reminder, there was the song, the one we had written together earlier that fall when he had come upon me at the piano picking out a tune I said was a song *I* was writing. He said he liked my tune (which much resembled, I'd discover later, the first measures of "Parigi, O Cara" from *La Traviata*) and gave it a lyric.

> *Mary Ellin, Mary Ellin*
> *Is her Daddy's girl.*
> *It must be understood*
> *Only when she is good*
> *Is Mary Ellin, Mary Ellin*
> *Her Daddy's girl.*

As for three-year-old Linda, she might not have been ready for restaurant lunches or friendly sessions at the piano, but she had carved out her own space and was in a particularly cheerful mood, thanks to the departure of mean nurse Hughes. I note a conversation six weeks later, reported by Finny in a letter to my mother, by then also in California keeping my father company. A frequent visitor to the deserted fort, Finny (now Mrs. William Mundy) overheard us chatting while waiting for supper. (We were both in bed with colds.) "I am Mamma's angel and Daddy's sweetheart," said Linda from her bed. "Linda, don't you know that when a man grows up and marries, he cannot have a sweetheart; he just has a wife," I said from my bed. Linda: "A wife, what is that?" Me: "Like Mamma." Linda: "Well, I am Daddy's sweetheart, anyhow, and he can have more than a wife, and I can tell you how." Me: "How?" Linda: "Because, and that is all."

As logical, at least, as stealing a watch and getting another for Easter.

By the time we were a family again, reunited in Santa Monica for the summer of 1935, the movie, now named *Top Hat*, was in its final days of filming. On the soundstages of RKO a famous friendship had been born, that of Irving Berlin and Fred Astaire. A friendship based on more than professional admiration ("Fred Astaire puts over a song better than anyone," my father would say, at home, abroad, to anyone who'd listen, focusing on Astaire the singer as much as Astaire the dancer), or an addiction to gin rummy, or the fact that their wives became inseparable, two Eastern ladies trapped in an uncongenial world who saw eye to eye on bringing up children, being a wife, being a friend. The gentlemen themselves—the cantor's son and the child star from Omaha, Nebraska—were kindred spirits—same mocking humor, same uxoriousness, same personal fastidiousness and sharpness of dress, same perfectionism when it came to work.

Now my father was starting to write the songs for his next Astaire movie, *Follow the Fleet.* The Hollywood years had begun, years unlike the earlier ones, which would not be buried and forgotten, old snapshots pasted in an album without captions, Hollywood years to be proud of, ushered in by what I would always think of as the best summer of my childhood.

PART FOUR

VISITORS
IN BABYLON

The *Top Hat* team: Mark Sandrich, Ginger Rogers, Fred Astaire, Irving Berlin.

17

I T   I S   A   H O U S E   I see first in my memory's eye, cream-colored, with teal-blue shutters and a red tile roof—705 Ocean Front—just a few doors beyond the bottom of the ramp that dropped, as steep as a giant slide, from the Santa Monica palisades to the seacoast road below. Another of my parents' attractive summer rentals, a place people called "full of charm," though "tiny" in Hollywood terms. (Most of the staff it took to maintain us in our usual style lived out, somewhere at the top of the cliff, arriving in the morning, with shufflings and whispers, in time to make and serve our various breakfasts.) A wrought-iron gate guarded a narrow entryway that ran between the house and a row of sweet-smelling bushes and opened onto the brightness of the backyard and the swimming pool.

Beyond was a strip of enclosed sand and a small guest house with a concrete wall from which I liked to jump onto the real beach. "Who do you think you are?" my father asked, "Douglas Fairbanks?" (the owner, it so happened, of the house).

The beach was white and bare in those days—no volleyball nets, no snaking bicycle path—and narrower, about half its present width. The ocean, heard from the house, was loud, and in a storm the waves came right up to the wall. My father worried about the wall (unnecessarily). My mother worried that the surf would keep her awake (it didn't). I worried that a tidal wave would engulf us. (It did, though only in dreams.) But in the real-life waves, big enough, I was fearless as only the innocent and ignorant can be. Jack MacKenzie or my father stood by to pull me out when I got rolled, and urge me back in, taking me beyond the breakers and safely back to shore. Captain Nass, my swimming instructor, was another matter. I trembled before this White Russian who only taught Hollywood's first families, whose mission was to inject   135 a little spine in all those children of the rich and famous. Bronzed and fierce, with bulging muscles like the bodybuilding ads in the movie magazines, Captain Nass came twice a week to teach Linda the basics of swimming and me the refinements—the crawl, the breaststroke, the backstroke, and less successfully, the dives. Why was diving necessary? I asked my mother, who did not dive herself. "So you can dive off a sailboat or a yacht someday," she replied. "You don't want to be left up there on deck."

I remember little of the house's furnishings except for the piano I shared with my father. "Can't you see I'm practicing?" I would say to him when he approached, expecting to use the piano himself. He went away quietly, with no sense of his priority or my temerity. But at other times he got there first. From behind the door came the piano tuner sounds, the mournful thirds and sixths that eventually would order themselves into songs for *Follow the Fleet*. Some pounding and jazzy—"Let Yourself Go," "We Saw the Sea," and "I'd Rather Lead a Band"—others shimmering and melancholy—"But Where Are You?" and "Let's Face the Music and Dance." Gleaming, various, new-sounding songs that, along with those of *Top Hat*, it would be tempting to say, were colored as much by the charms of 705 Ocean Front as by images of Fred Astaire and his partner, Ginger Rogers. Except the *Top Hat* songs—"No Strings," "Isn't This a Lovely Day," "Top Hat, White Tie and Tails," and "The Piccolino"—had been written in the Beverly Wilshire Hotel, and "Cheek to Cheek," before he ever left New York. The landscape that those songs, all the songs, grew out of was portable, in his head.

"By the Adriatic waters, / Venetian sons and daughters / Are strumming a new tune upon their guitars," he sang at the beachhouse piano, as if to make the point. "It was written by a Latin, / A gondolier who sat in / His home out in Brooklyn and gazed at the stars." He looked straight at me, watching to see if I got it. I did. That Latin, I sensed, was my father, and saucy "Piccolino" was my favorite *Top Hat* song.

Indoors or out, my father seemed in his element in Santa Monica, plunging into the pool or surf, eating breakfast in the merciless California sun, late enough that the morning fog had lifted. (In early-rising Hollywood he still kept his own hours.) My mother, too, seemed in her element despite her perpetually ironic manner. "Even the sun is backwards in California," she observed, gazing at the Pacific, where the sun set, flashing fire, instead of rising over the water as it did back East.

"The sun is better in California," I said in response.

"The sun is the sun, for God's sake, and I love it," my father would say.

It became a running joke, my mother taking some little dig at the odd ways of California, my father being reasonable, my planting myself firmly on its side, as if California needed defending, when it was so clear that this was paradise to which we'd returned, with pottery-blue skies, mountains sloping to the sea, orange groves and palm trees, and that whimsy besides: flowers shaped like birds, so bright they hurt your nose, smells you could almost see, a restaurant shaped like a hat, a drink stand like an orange, nothing quite what it seemed and never a house that matched another. But even my mother liked the cool ocean breezes, the easy living and entertaining. There was a message in the salty air as the summer began: We might, just might, move out for good.

To the beach house came guests: Harold Arlen and his future wife, Anya Taranda, the golden-haired Powers model, who recorded the Berlins in a home movie filled with poolside horseplay. (The Arlen-Berlin friendship had begun in Harlem, most likely, at the Cotton Club, where, in the spring of 1933, my father heard Ethel Waters singing "Stormy Weather" and declared he must have her for *As Thousands Cheer*. He and Arlen had also met in the marketplace. On the underside of the "Stormy Weather" record, a runaway best-seller, was the haunting but completely overshadowed Berlin ballad "Maybe It's Because I Love You Too Much.")

Another Santa Monica visitor was Max Winslow, now a producer for Columbia Pictures, one of the men responsible for *One Night of Love*, Grace Moore's most popular movie. Uncle Max played cards with my father and sometimes with me, hearts or casino, till the day I lost badly and threw my cards in his face. (Even in paradise I was still a brat.)

Cousin Alice Duer Miller, in California not just for fun but to confer about a screenplay, arrived and stayed for a while. It was a new view of my proxy grandmother, another one of our family surprises and contradictions. This patrician, Minerva-like lady who in winter gave me lunch at her sunlit apartment by the East River, who listened to my stories and complaints and taught me backgammon, was also the author of best-selling novels (most recently *Gowns by Roberta*), a screenwriter, and a friend of Harpo Marx and the songwriter Harry Ruby (who shared her passion for baseball). She and my mother sat by the pool under sombreros, talking, talking in their upper-class New York accents about everything (including my father, whom Alice, his friend first, called "the sainted Irving"). My mother listened to Cousin Alice as she listened to no one else and heeded her advice even when it was unwelcome. (It was Alice, only Alice, who could say to Ellin in the early days, "My dear, if you don't stop nagging, I don't give this marriage a year.")

I remember pretty ladies coming to lunch, Mrs. Thalberg and Mrs. Goldwyn, look-alikes, with the same brilliant lipsticked smiles, and Mrs. Astaire, blond, perfectly groomed, as small as a twelve-year-old and shy, my mother's new California friend. There was also Miss Crawford, dark, impetuous in manner, who was remembered by the family for kicking off her shoes, flopping on a bed, and all girlish enthusiasm, reading Linda a story; also for basting herself with oil and baking in the sun (ignoring Mrs. Thalberg's best advice). By now I knew that Mrs. Thalberg was Norma Shearer, that she and Joan Crawford were movie stars. How I knew this had to be from those movie magazines I removed from the pantry to my upstairs room, for it was all very played down. They were *friends*. Mrs. Thalberg was simply our next-door neighbor with a new baby girl and a freckled-faced four-year-old, Irving, Jr., who played with Linda and ran to his mother when my sister pushed down his sand castles. As for Mr. Thalberg, the quiet, dark-haired husband with the bad heart she fussed over, who would die, at age thirty-seven, the following summer—his importance was veiled, veiled in a way that went beyond the basic puzzle of what exactly a "producer" did. Sometimes my parents went to the Thalbergs' for dinner. What fun, they said, having old friends next door.

• • •

Played down or not, we were where we were. So I see myself with my friend Sammy Goldwyn, now a gangling eight-year-old who lived a few houses up the beach, my savvy guide to this paradise that was also movieland. We were writing down the names of all the movie stars we knew; the most names won. His list was long, but mine was longer. "You know all those people?" he asked, surprised. "I know their names," I answered. "These are people I *know*," he said. "Oh, well," he added generously, "I live here."

. And the Berlins didn't. We never would. We were transients. At the end of the summer, whatever the talk of staying on, the family returned to New York. And we would continue to return, no matter how often we came, how many months my father stayed or my mother stayed with him. You wouldn't have guessed this, now or later, seeing him go off in his car to the studio or with my mother, as sleek as a movie star herself in an evening dress by Irene or Adrian, to a premiere at Grauman's Chinese or a dinner at the Goldwyns, Selznicks, Goetzes, Fitzmaurices, Astaires, Zanucks, LeRoys, Joe Schenck's or George Cukor's, A-parties at A-houses, or more casually dressed, to Ciro's, the Brown Derby, or some late-night delicatessen to meet Harold Arlen, Jerome Kern, Oscar Levant, the Gershwins, Anita Loos, or Charlie MacArthur. Certainly they were more Hollywood fixtures than the café society wanderers who came for a week or a season—Averell Harriman, Alfred Vanderbilt, Elsa Maxwell, Lady Mendl—or the writers, Kaufman and Hart, Robert Sherwood, Somerset Maugham, who came for a picture or two and then returned to the real world. The Berlins might tarry a while longer but eventually would return as well.

And when it was the whole family, the atmosphere was that of a diplomatic enclave in a foreign land, fenced in, guarded, though we were also eager, as in a foreign land, to see the sights and mingle with the natives.

There were excursions led by my mother, guidebook in hand, to the Japanese gardens in Hollywood and the Mexican section of downtown Los Angeles; to the La Brea tar pits to see the hoofprints of mastodons and the Huntington Museum to see *Pinkie* and *The Blue Boy*. With my father along, there were a couple of evenings, past bedtime, at the Venice and Ocean Park amusement piers and the discovery that my dignified parents liked these raffish places. There were sails to Catalina on Joe Schenck's yacht and an overnight trip to Ensenada with Harpo Marx, Cousin Alice's friend, aboard. Harpo, Mr. Marx to me, had left behind his harp and curly wig and brought along a pretty lady. Uncle Joe, his balding head covered by a yachting cap, also had a pretty lady guest, and there was curiosity on my part about who was engaged to whom. Mr. Marx married his "fiancée" the following year. Uncle Joe continued to have "fiancées," and when I was old enough to catch on, I wondered how a pretty girl could fancy such a homely, potbellied old man "that way." "Power," someone said, "is attractive," an odd concept to a young person. Weren't all adults powerful? (The truth would have seemed even odder: that "attractiveness" in most cases had little to do with it.)

Besides, I never registered Joe Schenck the movie mogul, only the godfather and family friend, fiercely loyal to my father, smoothing things out in Hollywood for everyone, demolishing my reserve with big hugs and just the right balance of teasing and praise, giving me presents—dolls when I was little, jewelry when I grew up—and much sound advice about how to conduct myself out in the world, which I generally ignored. More surprising, my mother loved him, too, I knew. Later I understood that when it came to Joe Schenck, she held back the disapproval other Hollywood lotharios got in full measure. He had never stopped carrying a torch for Norma Talmadge, she said; the girls passed the time, and he was generous with them. And that was that.

A handwritten note from this time gives the bantering, affectionate flavor of their friendship. "Dear Ellin," wrote Joe in answer to a thank-you note of hers, "I am very happy to have had the opportunity to contribute to your pleasure and am grateful to you for having given me the chance. If you want to continue to make me happy, just call on me to be of service to you. The solution to this very complicated . . . mystery is: I love you. Please don't tell Irving anything about it, you know how he is. Can I take Mary Ellin to lunch some day? Love, Joe."

Lunch with Uncle Joe was an event, whether at the Brown Derby, the restaurant in the shape of a hat, or the commissary of 20th Century-Fox (recently taken over by the partnership of

Joseph Schenck and the young, newly powerful Darryl Zanuck). Even more exciting was going on the set. It was what every visitor to Los Angeles wanted to do—European royalty, U.S. congressmen, Nobel Prize winners, Aunt Gwen and Uncle Willie on a Santa Monica holiday—and I was no exception. I remember my father handling with great patience my desire to meet movie stars and have my picture taken with them. Little Miss Berlin, with her black bangs and barely suppressed grin and her black-haired Daddy in tow, and Ginger Rogers, Gary Cooper, Sonja Henie, Tyrone Power, Jane Withers, Shirley Temple, especially Shirley, not even my age but a movie star, the biggest. The next California summer there was even a lunch, in Shirley's private dining room off the 20th Century commissary. Shirley and her mother, me, Linda, and our mother, chummy as could be. What Linda remembers is that Shirley sat in a way we weren't allowed, with one leg up, curled under her on her chair. What I remember is that this friendly child with the dimples and wonderful curls, younger by a year and a half, was gracious to me instead of my being gracious to her. When many weeks later my mother and I ran into Shirley and Mrs. Temple at Bullock's Wilshire and I tried to renew the acquaintance, Mrs. Temple looked blank: Who *are* these people? But little Shirley, who never forgot a face, gracious as ever, said, "Oh, Mother, don't you remember, this is Mrs. *Berlin,* and this is Mr. *Berlin's* daughter."

But even as I was becoming a familiar figure on the soundstages—here comes that little girl with the bangs again—I had yet to see my first grown-up movie. The great day came, finally, one August afternoon in 1935. Eight going on nine, I backed into my generation at last, by way of, what else, a screening of *Top Hat.*

The memory is precise, undiluted by latter-day viewings. I will always see *Top Hat* through the eyes of that eager, dolled-up child, sitting between her nervous parents, in a studio screening room filled with important-looking men. The empty screen, so much bigger to my eyes (though, in fact, smaller) than that of the newsreel theater back home where I sometimes went for an hour of short subjects. The lights dimming, the screen aglow, a big top hat filling the space behind the titles, music surging. *Heaven, I'm in heaven.* Then my first movie began, a black-and-silver world where dimension and color were not missed, deliciously adult (Technicolor would never be so grown-up), yet entirely understandable to an eight-year-old. Not just Mr. Astaire pursuing Miss Rogers, who thinks he's a married man, but Eric Blore and Edward Everett Horton: the room-service steak on the black eye, the turned-around collar. Hilarious. No boredom between the songs, only inner squirming at the way romantic "Cheek to Cheek" went on and on and surprise at what had happened to "The Piccolino," such a big crowd singing and dancing that light, mocking song. Then a lot of happy people afterward, including my parents, relaxed now, center of a buzz of talk.

Of those important-looking men who might have been at that screening—Pandro Berman, the producer, Mark Sandrich, the director, Hermes Pan, the choreographer—only Berman is still alive. At eighty-five, he had no memory, he told me when I visited him a few years ago at his house in Beverly Hills. So he couldn't give me what I wanted, a description of my father at the studio, that place where he went during the week, of which I knew only scattered bits and pieces. Except for the piano. He remembered Irving playing that funny, shifting piano that they moved around wherever he went. "He was tough, sure," Berman said, reminded of his own words that "Irving Berlin was the toughest trader I've ever met in the film business, the hardest-headed businessman I've ever known"; that Irving Berlin had demanded, in exchange for taking less money up front, ten percent of the gross profits, the first such deal in movie history. (Fred Astaire got the second.) A quizzical smile lit up his grizzled, intelligent face. "Music writers can be tough as anyone."

But that wasn't the important thing, said Pan Berman. The important thing, the thing he wanted to tell me, Irving's daughter, was how easy my father had made his life all those years ago. "There wasn't anything I needed to do. We talked, sure. Talked over the script. You could tell him this or that was needed. But you couldn't tell him how to do things. You wouldn't. My job was over when I engaged him." And then, after a pause, "He was a brilliant fellow. Nothing more you had to do than hire him and let him alone."

With the late-August release of *Top Hat*, the Santa Monica summer approached its end. I didn't read the rave reviews (in movie terms the equivalent of the notices for *As Thousands Cheer*), but I remember following the progress of the score on my favorite new radio program, "Your Hit Parade." By the end of September all five *Top Hat* songs were there on the list of America's favorites.

Was that the way it was, then? You sweated blood, put yourself on the line, and the result was a piece of work you were proud of and that the public found sensational? Not necessarily, my father would have said, had I expressed such a thought (unlikely at eight). He would have called the success of *Top Hat* "one of those things," a favorite phrase, and told me, "Don't count on it." (And he was plenty mad when Harry Warren's "Lullaby of Broadway" beat out "Cheek to Cheek" for the 1935 Academy Award.) He would have said the same thing six months later when *Follow the Fleet* opened and similar lines formed around the block at Radio City Music Hall and the critics said that the team of Astaire and Rogers, Irving Berlin, Pan Berman, Mark Sandrich, and Hermes Pan, had done it again.

And I would have nodded gravely, lesson absorbed, and not believed him for a minute, since it was clear he had the golden touch; a touch that, unlike King Midas's, seemed to carry no devastating price.

_____ 18

M Y   M O T H E R saved a lot of mail that first Santa Monica summer, messages from long ago reflecting in part the good time she was having in spite of herself. Thank-you notes from delighted houseguests. A letter from her agent, Otto Liveright, calling her latest story, "The First Mrs. Brooke," "an amazing piece of work . . . the last third is as thrilling as anything else I have ever read." A letter from her friend Consuelo Vanderbilt Smith reporting that rumor had it that Ellin liked the California life so much, she was planning to move West for good (though Phyllis Astaire, East on a midsummer visit, suggested the opposite: "I am really discouraged by your letter because I know that you won't ever be there again and I don't know what I am going to do without you. . . . Don't be too nice to those people!"). A letter from my grandfather approving our tour of the Huntington Gallery, telling of a visit years before to Lord Duveen, the great art dealer, who had helped put together the Mackay collection and who had just sold *Pinkie* and *The Blue Boy* to Mr. Huntington for several hundred thousand dollars apiece. Pointing to the pictures, still on his wall, Duveen said, "Mere decoration, my dear Mr. M, *mere* decoration!"

Yet among all the good cheer were two references to a death, a shadow over the bright summer. One from my grandfather: "We were very sorry to learn of the very sudden passing of Irving's sister which must have been a shock to him. I hope he got our wire. . . ." Another from Finny: "I have been thinking of Irving and you at the oddest moments for the past few days. . . . We were very sorry about Irving's sister. I wrote and tried to tell him so but there is so little one can offer or say in a letter."

The sister was Sarah. The death, a tragedy I learned about years after the fact. But even when my parents told me, they did not place it in time, only said that long ago, when I was a little girl, something terrible had happened: my father's older sister Sarah, who struggled with depression, had killed herself.

The facts are bald and cruel. One Friday afternoon in early August 1935, Aunt Sarah went up to the roof of her apartment building in Brooklyn, and while her husband was downstairs, fetching a chair, she fell or jumped. "Fell" was what the family said to the newspapers, "as the result of an attack of vertigo." "Jumped" was what they said among themselves. My father flew East for the funeral. The shocked relatives gathered: Aunt Gussie, Uncle Ben, the Kahns, the Robinsons. The reporters gathered, too, at the entrance of Washington Cemetery, for the story was headline news across the country . . . "Famed Songwriter's Sister Dies in Plunge."

I have no memory of being told at the time. "Daddy's gone to New York for a few days, he'll be back soon"—that would have been it. Given my age and the circumstances, they might well not have told me at all, kept the tabloids hidden, or told me in a way that allowed me quickly to forget.

For Sarah was not in the cast of known characters. She had been to see me when I was little, then faded from view. In my father's family the female relative I knew best was Aunt Gussie, forceful, smartly turned out, married in those days to jaunty Ed Rice, in the paint trade (and father of two sons from a previous marriage, said to be one reason why, seven years after their 1931 wedding, the Rices were divorced). "A Jewish Aunt K," I liked to say (and was thanked by neither side) of buxom, vivacious, temperamental Aunt Gussie, who gave wonderful presents—homemade jams and jellies, hand-crocheted afghans, even little diamonds one Christmas to me and Linda—who worked tirelessly as a Braille translator but who also fought with everyone, except her sister Ruth, from whom she was inseparable. Gussie and Ruth, I'd hear later, were a problem for Sarah, third oldest of the five Baline daughters. Sarah's special friend was Ethel, the oldest daughter, mother of the Robinsons; but Ethel died in 1915, and Sophie, Sarah's other close sibling, also died young. And the sisters who remained sometimes shut her out.

What you would also hear later about Sarah was that she took an interest in her motherless Robinson nieces—but did not have the vitality of her brothers and sisters and was sad, always sad. For she had no children, and her marriage, to Abraham Henkin, nicknamed "Sender," was a disappointment. A single surviving photograph of Sarah confirms my mother's description—that she was small, dark-haired, probably charming looking as a girl. There is another brief characterization in a letter the spring I was three from my mother to my father: "Sarah and I had another long conversation. . . . I described to her in what seemed to me a plaintive voice my summer plans. Bernardsville two weeks, Great Neck four days, California two weeks, Bar Harbor two weeks, and she said, 'Well, traveling is very interesting isn't it?' She was sweet, understood she hadn't seen Mary Ellin because the child had been ill. *Really* understood . . . with no chip on her shoulder."

"Poor Sarah," my father would say gruffly in later years, the comment prompted by some lesser family misfortune or some narrowly escaped peril. "When I think about poor Sarah . . ." That was all. And I never wondered if he questioned whether he had done all he could. Did she need more than the money he gave her, a kind of regular contact that he seemed unable to offer a moody older sister?

In a news photograph of Uncle Ben, my father, and Mildred Kahn arriving at Sarah's funeral, the brothers look wiped out under their straw hats; Mildred looks incongruously pretty for such a grim occasion. "There was not much talk in that car," recalls Mildred, who also remembers that Sarah was "nervous, but always very nice to me"; that Henkin was said to come from a once prosperous family in Russia, to be well educated but an idler.

Whatever the brothers' memories and feelings—grief, guilt, dismay—they would have been controlled, pushed under. Thoughts of Sarah as a young woman, taking a job in a sweatshop, bringing in her share of money. Sarah as a bride. Was my father at her wedding? Was she at my father's to Dorothy Goetz, in Buffalo, the bride's hometown? At Ben and Nettie's 1914 wedding in Brooklyn? Did she visit her mother on Friday evening? Was she at Leah's burial? Sarah was fifty-three in 1935. A bitter time for a childless, not so happily married woman, in poor health and reduced circumstances, prone to melancholy, embedded in a family of close relationships, none of which seemed to include her.

So there it was, another tragedy concealed, another block in the dark side of my father's life, building itself, stone by stone, death by death, in some other dimension; though who knows how big a space Sarah occupied; how often she came back, unexpectedly, to haunt him in the night. "I know how you feel," he would say years later to a close relative over another tragic suicide. "Just how you feel."

Not long ago, a friend of mine, a fellow writer, asked if I was uncovering any surprises as I worked on this history. "You mean skeletons?" I asked. "Not necessarily," he said. "Just surprises." None so far of fact, I said, but quite a few of juxtaposition. Sarah's death, coming midway into the *Top Hat* summer, was one of them. There would be others. There had been others. My father's "don't count on it" had deeper roots than I could possibly have imagined; though as Hollywood friends said of him in those years, he seemed a happy sort of person, and he certainly seemed so to me.

19

CENTRAL TO THOSE Hollywood years, pulling my father East for large chunks of 1936, postponing any final decision about moving "out there," was the birth, the following June, of my sister Elizabeth, an occasion of great joy. It was months into my mother's pregnancy, however, before I learned what was up—and not from her but from my pregnant science teacher, who, after being pestered by me about her interesting condition, suggested I address some of my questions to my own pregnant mother. "Well," said my mother, annoyed at the other woman's spilling the beans, "I'd been waiting for you to notice. I wasn't dying to be stared at sooner than necessary." "Well," I responded, "my science teacher said I should put a hand on your stomach and feel the baby kick." "Why don't you put your hand on your teacher's stomach," retorted my mother, embarrassed as well as annoyed.

Until this exchange (which for some reason my mother enjoyed recalling), I only knew that she was vaguely unwell and that my father was pitching in. This time it was he, on my birthday, who escorted twenty young ladies, nine-year-olds now, to the Hippodrome Theater, where this year's matinee favorite, Rodgers and Hart's *Jumbo,* was playing. Jimmy Durante, the great "schnozzola" himself, a bespangled leading lady, Gloria Grafton, Rodgers and Hart's "The Most Beautiful Girl in the World," and big Rosie the elephant—these were mere background to the carryings on in our two boxes. My father bought us all the things mother forbade— whips, cotton candy, lemonade, which we blew at each other through straws, from one box to the next, howling with mirth. "Enough now," he said, "that's enough, I tell you." Nobody listened, least of all me.

It was a grand success. My stock rose in school. My classmates said I had the nicest father, and wouldn't I ask him to join the father's chorus at the annual Brearley Christmas assembly. "Oh, God," he said, turning me down, though he dutifully appeared, supporting my mysteriously ill mother, at 9:00 A.M. to watch me play Joseph in the lower school's nativity play.

Then, on Christmas morning, he handed me an envelope.

And there was the announcement, all in verse ("pack your pyjamas, we're off to the Bahamas"), that he and I were catching the
Florida train that very night, leaving for a ten-day holiday in Nassau. Was he out of his mind? Not quite. Mademoiselle was going
along to take care of evenings and early mornings. (As for abandoning my unwell mother: not up to traveling herself, she wanted
him to have a holiday with me.)

It was quite a package, put together for my enjoyment by my
father, himself in pursuit, as always, of "a little sun." My first trip
outside the continental United States; my first airplane ride, from
Miami to Nassau in a seaplane; my first resort hotel, the British
Colonial, set in tropical gardens; my first experience of traveling
without my mother, with a man.

There was no daytime dumping me with Mademoiselle, who
stayed in the background after one fishing trip when Monsieur
served up from the rolling ship's galley his special scrambled eggs.
"Ah, non, pas des oeufs brouillés avec de l'oignon sur un bateau,"
cried Mademoiselle, and promptly threw up. Every day my father
took me fishing or to the Emerald Beach Club or another beach,
reached by glass-bottomed boat. In the late afternoon there were
carriage rides to see the sights of the town. Wherever we went
there seemed to be music playing, island music. "Mama don't
want no peas, and rice, and coconut oil," I sang, "All she wants is
brandy, handy all the time," till my father told me to stop.

The calypso music went with the flat turquoise-and-cobalt
sea, the boys on the pier diving for coins, the black faces and costumes like the dancers in "Heat Wave," the Gilbert and Sullivan
policemen, the English voices. We were in the red, I said: a tiny
dot of red on the map that matched the huge patches of red representing The British Empire on which the sun never set. In the hotel I met Empire-style grown-ups, men dressed for the tropics,
women in garden-party hats, a man with a flushed face, introduced
as the lord of Nassau, Harold Christie, who tried to sell my father
a house. Preferred company were two friends from New York, Hassard Short, known as Bobbie, the person responsible for the elephant in *Face the Music*, the rotogravure children in *As Thousands
Cheer*, and his companion, Billy Ladd; friendly, amusing men, one
dark haired, plump, and balding, one slim with bleached blond

hair, who chatted in the sun and took movies of our holiday. (Of Mr. Short and Mr. Ladd my mother would say later, "I disapproved, but as time went by, I couldn't help noticing that theirs was the happiest marriage of the group, my own excepted, of course.")

Winter after winter I'd received postcards from my parents in some balmy place. Now I was in the balmy place, writing: "Dear Mamma, I think Nassau is wonderful. The water is the color of the sky. . . . We are going fishing today. Then we are going to have a picnic lunch on Rose Island. Daddy and I are having a lovely time. I miss you and send you lots and lots of love. . . ."

No, he was not out of his mind. He was a smart father who understood that what every child needs, at some point, is a little special attention. If it comes in the form of a trip, a child does not forget. The parent earns a lot of points for a future rainy day. Or, put another way, my father was a great traveler—so my mother always said, and now I'd discovered it for myself—adaptable, charming company, endlessly curious. But I was too, he let me know by word, look, and gesture. And something shifted, moved a little, in the way I felt about myself.

And though I would not put too much emphasis on a single holiday, it is a fact that 1936, launched in Nassau, known in the family as the year Elizabeth was born, was also the year when I emerged from bratdom and became, give or take a few lapses, a generally satisfactory and satisfied child. I made a school friend at last, and then another. I stayed out of trouble days at a time. Coincidentally, strictures were easing up. I grew my hair and got a permanent wave, curls like Shirley Temple, and Linda; hideous, but I loved it. I began seeing an occasional movie (what else, now that my father made them?) and having an occasional grown-up supper with my mother, when we talked about grown-up things like books and ideas, small breaks in the routine that fostered the illusion I was taking tiny steps toward that distant, so desired, goal of being grown-up myself, an illusion enhanced by the change in my reading—Oz books replaced by Louisa May Alcott and all the Scribner classics.

And where the bad dreams came from I did not understand, why at nine I still had screaming nightmares, terrifying not only to myself but to everyone else in the household. Sometime that year my pregnant mother, who had been so mean about my putting a hand on her stomach, who had to be a mother in her own way, gave me a locket, pink enamel, shaped like a Gothic window, within, engraved on gold in minuscule letters, the Lord's Prayer. When I was scared at night, she said, I could hold it. Maybe the charm didn't stop the nightmares entirely, but it reassured me, and it was very pretty besides.

Elizabeth made her entrance into the world on June 16, 1936, more than two weeks late. "Took her own good time," my mother would say, "an independent spirit from the start." Her middle name was Irving: "Elizabeth Irving Berlin—it scans," said my father the lyricist, my mother the writer. If they were disappointed about having another girl, they never said so. Later, my mother would tell June Levant, wife of Oscar L, who also had three girls, "It's really better for men like Oscar and Irving, who don't do all those boy things, play catch and baseball, to have daughters." She would also say to her daughters that in terms of a famous parent, ours was the only good combination. Famous father and son was difficult, famous mother and son worse, famous mother and daughter not so great; but famous father and daughter, that was "pure velvet."

My mother had almost as many theories as she had rules. My father did not have theories, and his rules, of which there were plenty, conveniently hid behind hers. He just had a few sayings, like: "Your mother is in charge of raising you girls, I just bring home the bacon" (an oversimplification at best). Or, "Famous, forget about famous, just marry a guy with a nice little business." Or, "It's important to be smart in school, but it's even more important to be smart about yourself." Or, later, "You may not like to hear this, but there are good girls and bad girls, and in the end it's easier to be a good girl." Which had nothing to do with childhood naughtiness and everything to do with an old-fashioned father watching with some concern his darlings growing up.

So now there were three of us, photographed for the 1936 Christmas card on the dunes of Westhampton Beach (this summer's rental), in Hungarian costumes my parents had brought back from a midsummer visit to Budapest. Three daughters widely spaced, five years between me and Linda, four between Linda and

Elizabeth, but tagged and lumped together from then on in people's minds: the three little Berlin girls, with their Mademoiselle
and their new Scottish nanny, Janet Tennant, brisk, kindly, and
droll, who had been hired to care for Linda, shifted to infant Elizabeth, and eventually would ride herd on all three of us and the entire household as well.

And was this the moment to move us "out there"? Now that
my father was embarked on his next movie, *On the Avenue,* this one
for 20th Century-Fox, with plans for yet another; had an office in
the 20th Century Music Building, a California secretary? It was
not. My parents had decided: We children would be raised in New
York, with its top private schools, its traditions, its old-fashioned
ways. During the school year my mother would continue to divide
her time between Beverly Hills and Manhattan, taking the baby
with her sometimes, and we would all be together for summers and
holidays. And someday things would return to normal—my father
would return to Broadway.

It was, no question, an eccentric way of life. But I was kept so
busy, so surrounded by the household and various proxy parents—
Finny, Cousin Alice, Aunt Gwen and Uncle Willie—that I have no
memory of feeling deprived. I missed them terribly. But life was
calmer when they were away. And there was a certain cachet in
saying, "My father is in Hollywood making a movie," or, "My
mother is in Hollywood with my father."

Besides, they were never far out of mind, thanks to my
mother's long and frequent letters with pictures that, however much
they had to do with her or me, inevitably focused on my father. "I
can't draw," she would say, but managed to catch the essence of her
favorite subject—in bathing trunks, in bed with a cold, in a dressing gown at the piano, off to the studio on a raw day in his hat and
overcoat—the blackness of the hair and eyebrows, the jut of his
nose, the trim body. He himself sent postcards, brief scrawls in a
sharp black hand. And then, the caretakers back in New York were
sure to keep the absent ones in mind with a story here, a story there
(not to mention the constant orders from afar, the long arm of the
law reaching from the Beverly Wilshire Hotel to 130 East End Avenue: "Your mother says . . ." "Your father wants to know . . .").

As for those weeks when my mother was in New York, writing my father long letters: he only said he hated the separation, the hotel living, the pseudo-bachelor life. My mother said she hated the separation, too, except for the first week, when she could catch up on things left undone when he was all engrossingly present. But, she would add, maybe a bit of separation wasn't bad for a marriage, kept a marriage interesting long after it might otherwise have settled into habit.

A final note for 1936, election year. Politics had now entered the family. In Los Angeles that fall my mother organized a Roosevelt-Garner ball at which my father entertained. Back in New York I remember being proud that I was one of only two Democrats in Brearley fifth grade. I knew we were not only right but *good*, on the side of good. And I saw no more incongruity in my well-heeled parents being Democrats than in the aristocratic Roosevelt himself being a Democrat.

By the time I was nine I was being drawn into conversations about current events, urged, uselessly, to read the papers. (Books were what I read, stories of bloodshed and derring-do in brightly colored, olden times.) Grown-up talk mostly was my newspaper— talk about FDR, who had closed the banks, created jobs, given people hope, prevented a revolution, FDR the savior, upholder of the American way. In one sense my parents were simply getting on a bandwagon. (All but two states went for Roosevelt in the 1936 election.) In another, they liked his being "a traitor to his class," the independence of it. Weren't they in their own way traitors to theirs? "That man in the White House" was *their* man in the White House. And once they adopted a cause, they threw themselves into it, my mother naturally more noisily than my father, speaking on street corners, on the back of trucks, on the radio. (Aunt Gwen remembers Irving sitting next to her in the theater during a campaign year, saying, "Do you remember when we could just talk about the children and Ellin was *calm?*")

Roosevelt was my president, too, if not my very first president, the only one I remembered. Later, when my parents switched and Ike became their man in the White House but not mine, they would say they only had themselves to blame. They had brought me up a New Dealer, and as sometimes happened with childhood religions, this one did not lose its grip.

_____ 20

F O R   A   F A M I L Y   constantly on the move, it was significant that 1937 was always remembered as "the year we went to Alaska." For the head of the family, of course, this spectacular trip was only one month out of a busy twelve that began with the release of *On the Avenue,* starring Dick Powell, Madeleine Carroll, and Alice Faye, like a dozen other movies of the day, a musical about a musical. But the score was almost as original, and remarkable, as *Top Hat*'s: "I've Got My Love to Keep Me Warm," "This Year's Kisses," "The Girl on the Police Gazette," "Slumming on Park Avenue," "He Ain't Got Rhythm," and "You're Laughing at Me," this last, one of those orphan songs from the dry period, pulled out of the trunk for Mr. Powell to sing in his smiley, upbeat voice.

In the works all that year was *Alexander's Ragtime Band,* a movie designed to span three decades of American show business and Berlin songs, something exciting and different, so the word drifted down to the children's level during spring vacation in Phoenix; but there were "headaches," not unconnected to a name that also drifted down, "Zanuck," a name to inspire respect and wariness. Never before had my father been in quite such a feudal relationship, its flavor caught in an interoffice memo from I.B. to D.Z. protesting the plan to drop "I've Got My Love to Keep Me Warm" from *On the Avenue:* "To take it out would be just the same as if they'd decided to take 'Let's Face The Music and Dance' out of *Follow the Fleet* . . . I know your sense of story values is much better than mine but I think my judgement on the value of the songs for this picture is pretty good." The story was the number-one problem of *Alexander's Ragtime Band;* scriptwriters were fired, replacements brought in. But there were also cast headaches, money headaches, scheduling headaches, and so many postponements that at year's end my father took time off to write the songs for RKO's new Astaire-Rogers film, *Carefree*.

But however fruitful or fretful the rest of the year had been, he would hark back to that August trip as something unique. And it was something he'd personally arranged, thanks to a tip from that same Darryl Zanuck (a hunter of Alaska bear): to whip us off on an adventure, in the middle of another Santa Monica summer, leaving Hollywood behind for a while.

For it had been a strange summer so far. On one level, it was everything I had remembered from two years ago, only more so. Another delightful beach house, this one a bit of old Normandy with leaded-glass windows and a huge wrought-iron chandelier, the property of another old-time movie star, Uncle Joe's ex-wife, Norma Talmadge. More afternoons with my California buddy, Sammy Goldwyn, no longer up or down the beach but in a rambling white Beverly Hills mansion with a swimming pool twice the size of ours, a pool pavilion, a tennis court, two croquet courts, and a glorious rose garden—my home away from home then and later. More studio visits, Linda along; meeting our father in his small, cluttered office in the 20th Century Music Building, known as the "Hall of Fame" for the busts that lined the inner court, Mozart, Beethoven, Grieg, Tchaikovsky, Debussy, and Arthur Sullivan (and working in their shadow, Irving Berlin, Harry Warren, Harry Revel, Richard Whiting); lunching with him in the commissary, with its murky, Radio City–style murals of the world's great cities; being introduced to some of his colleagues, paying little attention (they weren't movie stars); wandering about the bright white soundstage village that was his new habitat; and dropping in on the *Heidi* set to see Shirley Temple, the *Thin Ice* set to meet Sonja Henie (though not I.B.'s set, for his movie wasn't shooting yet).

Piano lessons this summer were from Edward Steuermann, friend of Stravinsky, Schoenberg, Gershwin, and Oscar Levant, one of the foremost interpreters of twelve-tone music on the concert stage. Courtly, gentle, with a very long face and pale, reflective eyes, Steuermann shared a house in Santa Monica canyon with his sister Salka Viertel, the screenwriter, friend of Thomas Mann, Charlie Chaplin, Ernst Lubitsch, and Greta Garbo (who, alas, never dropped in on my music-lesson day). What business had I studying with Steuermann? None, but we both seemed to enjoy the encounter. Like my grandfather, he respected my gall: He liked my wish to play pieces out of my class. I liked his kindness, his passion for music. "Listen, child," he would say, "listen to how it gets from there to here, the most beautiful bridge in Schubert, in Beethoven." Sometimes he would play Schoenberg and Webern, make the odd (to my ear trained to melody) music sound as seductive as Schubert or Beethoven—or the George Gershwin of *Rhapsody in Blue* and *Concerto in F.*

And to the beach house, one night in June, part of the summer's first heady weeks, came Gershwin himself, a friend of my father's since 1919, when he refused to hire twenty-year-old George as an arranger, saying, "Stick to your own songs, kid, you're too good to be arranging some other songwriter's music." My father introduced "the kid," by then the great George Gershwin, to my mother in Paris, in the spring of 1926. She was newly pregnant and sick; Gershwin, never without a cigar, filled the Crillon suite whenever he dropped by with vile blue smoke, an inauspicious beginning to an eventual warm friendship. Since Gershwin's arrival in Hollywood to write songs for *Shall We Dance?* and *A Damsel in Distress,* he and my father had seen each other a lot, dined with Harold Arlen and Oscar Levant, sat up nights playing poker with Jerome Kern. One day, Gershwin, a camera bug, took a time exposure, brooding and arty, of the two of them, old friends from Broadway in a new land.

So there he was, at our house, asking me during the cocktail hour how I liked Steuermann, did I think he was a good teacher, and my father invited me to sit down at the piano and demonstrate. I played, as I remember, a Mozart sonatina. Next Gershwin played some of the songs he'd written for Fred Astaire: "They All Laughed," "They Can't Take That Away from Me," and "A Foggy Day," and the song he'd just finished for *The Goldwyn Follies,* "Love Walked In." His hands were big on the keys; his playing was precise, with a strong beat and many flourishes. He bent over the piano, looking up now and then with a quick, sweet smile. Dark-haired with a high forehead, he looked a little like Moss Hart without a widow's peak. Then the grown-ups went into dinner and I went to bed.

Not for years did I hear about the rest of the evening from another guest, June Levant, then the actress June Gale, just beginning to date Oscar, at the Berlins' for the first time. How, after dinner, she and Oscar found George sitting on the running board of his car, his head in his hands, groaning. "He's doing it again," said Lee Gershwin, standing there with Ira, helpless, looking frightened.

The summer's other level.

A few weeks later, Gershwin was dead of a brain tumor. Sunday, July 11, 1937: I remember the sense of shock and sorrow in our house. Thirty-eight years old. A life, and God knows how many great songs, how much great music, ahead of him. Later, my father said to me, "You could have been the last person he played for."

Some of his respect and love for George Gershwin is conveyed in the lines written the following year for Gershwin's memorial:

> *I could speak of a Whiteman rehearsal*
> *At the old Palais Royal when Paul*
> *Played the "Rhapsody" that lifted Gershwin*
> *From the "Alley" to Carnegie Hall.*
> *I could dwell on the talent that placed him*
> *In the class where he justly belongs.*
> *But this verse is a song-writer's tribute*
> *To a man who wrote wonderful songs . . .*

My father would talk to me about the wonderful songs of many composers, the ones who were friends, like Gershwin, Porter, Kern, Arlen, Rodgers, Harry Ruby, Johnny Green; the Tin Pan Alley and Broadway cronies like Milton Ager, Richard Whiting, Burton Lane; and the ones he admired from afar like W. C. Handy. "If I had to pick one song I wished I'd written," he once said, "it would be 'St. Louis Blues.'" (Concerning the ones he didn't admire, silence was the rule.) Later, after the war, he would talk with enthusiasm of the newer generation—Frank Loesser, Lerner and Loewe, Jule Styne, Leonard Bernstein. But about Gershwin there was a special feeling always, a mixture of nostalgia, affection, musical kinship, I'll-be-damned admiration, and disbelief that fate could be so cruel.

• • •

He had another reason, then, that summer of 1937, for wanting to give himself and his family a breather from Hollywood, to suddenly announce, in mid-July, that he had chartered a boat and we would be spending the month of August in Alaska.

From Seattle to Juneau and back it was the fishing trip to end all fishing trips: rainbow trout and big cutthroat trout and salmon running up to thirty pounds; lake fishing, stream fishing, and bay fishing for halibut and bass. All of us—my father, my mother, Linda and I, our guest, Sammy Goldwyn—in hip boots and slickers. We caught fifty or sixty fish a day, three times as many thrown back as kept and eaten. There were salmon eggs for the trout if you were lazy, flies for the skilled adults, great shiny spinners for the salmon. Sometimes we fished at the mouth of a stream rushing into a bay; at other times, to reach hidden lakes veiled in mist, we walked for miles in pine forests so thick that neither rain nor sun got to the forest floor. From the trails we saw bears playing, fishing themselves for the salmon that swam upstream to spawn. As we cruised farther north, there were schools of porpoise and whales. The water turned milky green, and we began to see small icebergs and then glaciers, three-hundred-foot stony walls, not glistening white, dirty and gray, but still: the Ice Age.

It was the Berlins discovering the wilderness, though, one had to admit, in Berlin style. The "boat" was a luxurious, diesel-powered 107-foot yacht with a crew of six. Except for one rough day crossing Queen Charlotte Sound, we cruised in calm inland waters. Accompanying us were Hermine, nominally in charge of "the girls" (she never took off her city hat and coat, hated the whole experience) and Jack MacKenzie, who loved every minute and was in charge of Sammy (regularly spanked for disobedience). And in the salon was a piano. From time to time my father interrupted our games, chased us away, and worked. "What are you doing?" asked Sammy. "I'm working on a new song," he answered. It was the first time, Sammy said later, he realized that Mr. Berlin did something other than play cards.

My father was my father even in Alaska. He chewed gum while fishing. He rarely sat still. When we went to a restaurant in Sitka, he caused me familiar embarrassment by insisting on going into the kitchen to discuss the specialties of the day. He emerged triumphant. The cook had once worked at Dinty Moore's.

But there was no long-distance telephone (only a wireless sparingly used). He was away from it all, as he had perhaps never been. He *looks* away from it all, in the movies Jack took, casting into a foaming stream, letting Linda hold his rod, showing me how to land a salmon; helping us scramble up the sides of Muir glacier, none too steady himself; talking on deck to Sammy, shaking a finger to make a point, giving my mother some delicacy he has cooked over an open campfire; even she, who hates to be photographed, gives the camera a big smile.

Jack MacKenzie's movie ended as all good travelogues do, with a sunset, though in actuality the trip ended in total confusion a half week before it should have: Linda, three days out of Seattle, down with a raging fever; she and my parents taken off the boat in the middle of the night by a small private seaplane (the coast guard plane refused to land in such bad weather) and flown to Seattle. In the hospital, polio, spinal meningitis, a burst appendix, were ruled out. The nasty bug withdrew. And it was back to reality. New York, after a few more weeks, for us; Hollywood for Daddy.

But something had happened on that trip to my city-boy father. He had found a secret self, one foreshadowed the summer on Loon Lake, now fully exposed. Something really quite major going on with him in that northern region of rushing streams, waterfalls, pines, something that puzzled me later, when I thought about it. Where had it come from, my sun-loving, beach-loving father's affinity for nature, for what he called "real country," the mountains, the woods? An affinity, as I grew older, I did not share. Was it the green dreams of a poor boy imprisoned year round in city cement? Or something even further back, from Russia? But then who can ever say what triggers infatuation, whether for a person, a landscape, a dwelling place, a time of day or night.

For years we ran Jack's movie and said someday we'd go back with Elizabeth, the baby who wasn't along. But we never did, never really thought we would, especially not after my father found his own bit of wilderness closer to home. And eventually my mother put away the movie, refused to look at it. It made her too sad, she said, to see herself and Daddy young.

My father was, in fact, in his fiftieth year.

21

THERE WAS NO fiftieth birthday party. Bringing us out for spring vacation at the Inn in La Quinta, a small ranch hotel in the desert beyond Palm Springs, was the closest we came to a celebration. Suddenly, we were all there again, our instant family under a hot sun and palm trees, lodged in blue shuttered *casitas,* ringed by red mountains that turned purple in the afternoon. In spirit, as distant from Hollywood as New York. Four of us on horseback in western clothes, the fifth (who'd been in California with Tenny and my parents all winter) toddling about in her baby cowboy outfit, my father, by the pool, asking his older children, "What gives?," wanting to hear the news from Manhattan. How's so-and-so? What's going on in kindergarten, in Brearley sixth grade? In a great mood. Why not?

After all, he had given himself, or been given by Darryl Zanuck, in *Alexander's Ragtime Band,* as fine a fiftieth birthday present as a songwriter could ask for. Two great singers, Alice Faye and Ethel Merman, the best of the screen, the best of the stage, delivering the best of Berlin, nearly thirty years of hits, wrapped up in a big, slick 20th Century-Fox package, with Tyrone Power, Don Ameche, and a cast of hundreds.

And somehow Irving Berlin had managed to get what he wanted, a showcase for his songs, without allowing what Darryl Zanuck had originally wanted, a hoked-up version of his own life story. Studios would do it to Kern, Gershwin, Victor Herbert, Sigmund Romberg, W. C. Handy, Kalmar and Ruby, Rodgers and Hart, and to his pal Cole Porter at *his* suggestion—an oft-repeated tale. How in 1943, during the filming of *This Is the Army* at Warner Brothers, Jack Warner had told Irving Berlin that he must let the studio do his own life story next. "You don't want to do me," said I.B. "The person you should do is Cole Porter. There's a really *won*derful story." And he proceeded to outline it: the café society darling, married to a famous beauty, who becomes a great songwriter; the terrible riding accident, the thirty operations and the comeback, better songs than ever—a story that could be an inspiration, in wartime, for thousands of disabled servicemen.

Afterward my father fretted and fussed: What the hell had he let his friend in for? But Porter was flattered by Warner's invitation, delighted with the money and the eventual result—being played by Cary Grant—whatever others might say about *Night and Day*, and sent his dear Irving a gold cigarette case in appreciation.

So, over the next decades, Hollywood would do it to all those fine fellows. (Only George M. Cohan would get a movie biography to be proud of.) But they hadn't done it to him. They had hung the Berlin songs on a fiction, mostly of his own invention, about a band leader named Alexander. To get what he wanted and also satisfy Zanuck had been a two-year ordeal. Now it was done and being talked of as the Movie of the Year.

"Dear Mary Ellin," he wired the week after his birthday, when we were back home, "the preview was a big success and I only wish you and Linda could have been here to see it. I am very happy about the picture and think you will like it too."

There was a slight pause before I was permitted to see the great movie, and into that pause came Camp Treetops, the great outdoors in a slightly less pleasant version than Alaska.

Eventually, camp became a story I would tell my parents and anyone else who would listen. I hated Treetops, and it hated me. I hated the cabin with three roommates, bad reading lights, and un-comfortable beds that had to be made, every morning, with sharp hospital corners. I hated the whistles and gongs. I might have en-joyed canoeing, but I couldn't master backpaddling. Mountain hikes were agony going up (I had no wind), though I scrambled down faster than anyone, which earned me no points. My solace was reading old novels by Fannie Hurst and E. Phillips Oppen-heim in the clubhouse (supposedly for the counselors) while others played games. It was back to third grade; I was counting the days till my return to Ventnor, New Jersey, this summer's seaside rental, just ten minutes away from Atlantic City, the great playground. Then the blow fell: Linda was exposed to measles, and I would be staying on for the two-week extra session.

Actually, with just a dozen children left, other abandoned boys and girls like myself, things loosened up. To entertain us, and themselves, the counselors suggested we organize a revue. My act was a marionette show. I wrote the script (cribbed from an old fairy tale about a princess who turned unwanted suitors into pearls for her necklace), made the costumes, coached a helper. The playlet had everything: humor, suspense, special effects. At the end, there were cheers. Later I played the piano, something I'd not done before at camp. I picked out "I've Been Working on the Railroad," "Clementine," and "If you Roll a Silver Dollar," and people gathered around. "You're okay," the other children said, if not in words, in gestures and looks. "Not such a spoiled rich brat, after all." A last-minute save. Applause at the final curtain. Mary Ellin a hit. Not quite.

Later, my mother told me in high indignation that at summer's end she had received a letter from the camp director suggesting she (1) fire my governess and (2) send me to a psychiatrist. I, too, was indignant (what had my governess ever done but be nice?) and also hurt. Hadn't I made it come out at the end? "Apparently not," said my mother.

So I missed the opening of *Alexander's Ragtime Band,* a big hit with the public and many, but not all, of the critics. But the biggest excitement, as far as I was concerned, was the spread in *Life.*

My favorite magazine and I did not agree about the movie. I bought the whole thing, honky-tonk Alice Faye introducing stuffy Tyrone Power to ragtime, his rise as a bandleader, hers as a singer, their quarrels, their rebound romances with Don Ameche and Ethel Merman, their eventual reunion on the stage of Carnegie Hall, she come down in the world, he in his hour of glory, and all those songs along the way. It seemed to me desperately romantic, right up there with *Lost Horizon* and *The Prisoner of Zenda. Life,* however, said the story was "insipid" and the movie corny except for that musical cavalcade confirming what everybody already knew, that Irving Berlin was "the world's greatest writer of songs."

What *should* have been up there, and then it would have been a great American movie indeed, was Irving Berlin's own story, said *Life*—and proceeded to illustrate the point in thirty-four pictures and captions. Not just the stepping-stones of an amazing career but the personal stuff, too. Poor dead Dorothy the first wife, my grandfather ("who objected to Berlin"), my parents on their honeymoon, hounded by photographers, Grandpa and Aunt Anna. ("Before Mackay married Anna Case, opera star, he became reconciled to daughter's husband.") And, wonder of wonders, a large half-page photograph, taken by Uncle Willie, of my camera-shy mother and my reticent father walking on the Atlantic City beach, holding hands. There was even a snapshot of us children. For *Alexander's Ragtime Band,* every house rule concerning personal publicity seemed to have been broken.

I was riveted, understandably. What eleven-year-old wouldn't have been? I must have known by then about Grandpa's "objecting," but to see it in print! I must have known by then, however hard my parents might try to play it down, that my cozy, quirky, affectionate father, who made his living writing and publishing songs, was a famous man, as famous as Charlie Chaplin, as Babe Ruth, as Charles Lindbergh, though perhaps not quite so famous as Albert Einstein or the president. Still, to see it there in print! From my parents came no comment other than my mother saying, with a tight little smile, that it was nice for Uncle Willie to have a photograph in *Life.*

One issue later, *Carefree* was *Life*'s movie of the week, with Astaire and Rogers on the cover. A doubleheader. The golden touch in fine working order. Before long, "Change Partners," from *Carefree,* and "Now It Can Be Told," the new ballad from *Alexander's Ragtime Band,* were on "Your Hit Parade."

And yet all of a sudden that September there was a sense of things coming apart, new movies and hit songs not quite that central. Our beloved Scottie, Charlie, was run over on a Ventnor street. The new chef, replacement for Mary Hauck, chased a maid around the kitchen with a butcher knife and had to be removed by the police. I remember storm warnings, windows boarded up, though in the end the killer hurricane of 1938 bypassed Atlantic City. And on the wireless, the staticky voice of Adolf Hitler, screaming hysterically in German, being interrupted by the roars of the equally hysterical crowd. And then Munich. My father returning from a business trip to London with the first real talk of war. Public events, along with small private misfortunes, bearing down, darkening a time already dark because of my grandfather—the real reason I had been sent to camp that summer.

My jolly grandfather, whose "objecting" was such an old story, so irrelevant now, was dying.

I had known for months that Grandpa was sick, though not how sick; not that the old cancer, cured by Dr. Blake, had returned two summers ago, had been there hanging over the rest of 1936, 1937, and 1938. Certainly he had seemed well enough during the previous school year; had presided over Thanksgiving dinner at Aunt Gwen and Uncle Willie's; had entertained us in the eighteenth-century farmhouse that was his new country home, still my buddy who had liked me when I was a brat and liked me now in transition, no longer a little girl nor quite yet a young lady; still pulling five-dollar bills out of the curtains (I was never too old for a five-dollar bill), challenging me to a conversation in French, arguing with me about Napoleon, my hero but not his.

That Grandpa could no longer afford to live at Harbor Hill and had moved into the original manor house of the property; that he had lost a fortune in the crash and had been through a good part of the money left; that the paintings, the sculptures, the majolica vases, and Italian wedding chests and armor were being sold off, piece by piece, to the Metropolitan Museum and the dime-store millionaire Samuel Kress—I knew nothing of these facts till after his death, no more than I knew about his cancer. I accepted my mother's explanation that the move was "sensible" and Grandpa's own joking comment that he and Aunt Anna were tired of rattling around in that huge place on the hill. This was much cozier, this prerevolutionary homestead, with its beams and fireplaces and wide polished floorboards. And in New York there was still Seventy-fifth Street, the great town house where we had Easter lunch. (The story that my father bailed out my grandfather after the crash with a gift of $2 million was just a story—denied always by my parents. Nothing has turned up since their death to contradict this denial. My father's contribution to my grandfather's declining years was to be nice: an affectionate, respectful son-in-law who, whatever his true inner feelings, appeared to hold no grudge.)

So I also accepted that Grandpa's being in and out of Roosevelt Hospital for this and that was nothing to worry about; an operation called a "tonsillectomy"; a treatment for a "throat abscess"; more treatment; an actual appendectomy. (Terrible to have to put him through that, too, my mother said later, when the doctor knew there was no hope.) "No, of course he's not going to die; you don't die of an appendix," she said. All the while, as the last of his money ran out, he kept up a cheerful front, going to his office as long as he was able, dealing with a personal matter that was causing him grief and displeasure: the divorce of Aunt K and Uncle Ken and Aunt K's remarriage to Robert Hawkins, her Reno lawyer.

But now, as the summer ended, I knew my mother was visiting his sickbed in the hospital or at home. "Could I see him?" I asked after we moved back to town. "When he feels better," my mother said. Afterward she explained, "He didn't want you to remember him sick; he wanted you to remember him the way he was." But I was angry. "I should have been able to say good-bye," I said. *"Now I'll never see him again."* The finality hitting me.

He died on November 12, the day after Armistice Day. I remember being called upstairs to the library where my parents waited, grave, horribly calm. When they told me, I bawled. However, the next day, when they came into my room to discuss the funeral, I was myself again. I asked if I would wear black. When they replied no, I said, "You are spoiling the whole day for me." The spoiled brat was back, and on a bleak day, they said later, I had actually made them laugh.

It was my first funeral. We gathered at Seventy-fifth Street, I remember, in the marble foyer with the fountain: my mother, Aunt Anna, and Aunt Gwen in black and veiled (Aunt K could not get back in time from Hawaii, where she was on her wedding trip with Uncle Bob); the men with black arm bands and black ties, I in muted blue. When we reached St. Patrick's, Fifth Avenue was lined with people, policemen on horseback holding back the crowds. There were photographers, newsreel cameramen, for however diminished his life, my grandfather's death was front-page news. In the *Times* the day before there had been an editorial extolling Clarence Mackay, chairman of the board of Postal Telegraph, as a businessman, a patron of the arts, a "leading Catholic layman." We as a family were conspicuous in a way I had never known before.

It was my first time in St. Patrick's (in any Catholic church other than St. Mary's, once or twice in Roslyn). The size of the cathedral, the grandeur of the ceremony, and the very full house overwhelmed me. The theatricality. The sadness. The coffin before us covered with a blanket of red roses. The minor-keyed music played by members of the New York Philharmonic in honor of the man who had once headed the orchestra's board. The sense of an event in the life of the city. At the end there was the sight of the Postal Telegraph boys in their blue-gray uniforms lined up on the church porch and all the way down the steps, on either side, saluting. All that for Grandpa. Until that moment I had not known what an important New Yorker he was, or once had been.

22

CHRISTMAS, 1938, a sad holiday. My father still wearing his black arm band in memory of the man who took so long to become his friend. My mother in mourning, trying to be cheerful, but Linda and I knew it was a pose, that she felt terrible, and what on earth was going to make her feel better? And so my father's surprise on Christmas morning. An envelope somewhat larger than the one a few years earlier announcing our trip to Nassau. "Oh, Irving, what have you done?" my mother said, already guessing as she tore open the envelope. "I bought it for you," he said. "It's yours."

"It" was a house and fifty-two acres in the Catskills, in a town with a funny name for the mountains, Lew Beach ("Not a beach," he kept saying, "Lew Beach, the man who founded the town"), and a funny split personality. A half hour north of Grossinger's, still in the heart of the borscht circuit, with its own Jewish hotel, the Edgewood Inn, and an orthodox camp run by a rabbi, Lew Beach was also an outpost for non-Jewish "old New Yorkers" who liked to fish or live the rustic life. My parents had been introduced to the community by my mother's friend Consuelo Vanderbilt, whose second husband, Henry Davis, as stuffy as they came, had a farm there. She had taken my parents to see this old, ramshackle house set between a stream ("Irving loves to fish") and a steep evergreen hillside, which could be had for a song, she said, enjoying the pun. Now the fantasy was a reality. If my mother thought, What *has* he done?, she didn't miss a beat. The eyes teared up; the "You are something," came fast. And then, to us children: "Think of it, our very own country house at last."

A few days later, we went to have a look. My father was nervous—what had he done indeed?—my mother loud in her expressions of delight as we drove through the tumbledown town of Lew Beach, past a white-steepled church, a green-shuttered farmhouse, then to the right onto a wooden bridge over a partly frozen stream. And there, across a snowy field, it stood, "our very own country house": no pillars, no broad terrace and tall French windows, just an old, low-slung dwelling with peeling white paint and a dingy roof. "It needs a little work," my father said as we looked about the icy inside. A lot of work. There were two poky parlors, a dark dining room, a kitchen that looked as if it hadn't been used in years; upstairs three low-ceilinged bedrooms and an attic; a house with possibilities, couldn't we see the possibilities?

And then he took us out the back door and across to the brook, which was running fresh between icy banks; and upstream was a shining cascade and above that a real waterfall breaking through sculptures of ice and above that a really big fall, dropping between gray-green rocks into a deep black green pool, big enough to swim in. On the rocks high above was a "tea house" where in the summer you could watch the fall. Beyond, stretching into the thick pine woods was more stream and one would guess a lot of fish, since this was Shin Creek, a tributary of the Beaverkill, one of the finest trout streams in America.

"Are you excited?" my father asked, and before I could answer, he said, "*I* am." We were all excited, including two-year-old Elizabeth, but he was the most. I had not seen him that excited since the day he took me to meet infant Linda in the hospital.

So we had fifty-two magnificent acres and a house of sorts, the Berlin homestead. My father putting down roots at last. Anchoring us forever in the East with a wonderful family project.

Well, not exactly. He was still a songwriter and still these days, whether he thought of himself that way or not, a movie song-writer. The project that would have kept him in New York, a new *Music Box Revue,* had fallen through. Now he was finishing up *Second Fiddle,* starring Tyrone Power, Sonja Henie, and Rudy Vallee, and working on the treatment for yet another 20th Century-Fox movie, one like *Alexander's Ragtime Band,* that would mix old songs and new. Many of his pals had moved West for good—Jerome Kern, Harold Arlen, Ira Gershwin, Harry Ruby. It had to happen. The separation wasn't right.

And so the news was broken, the entire plan unfolded. The Catskills was to be not only our new summer home but our East Coast headquarters. For the rest of the year home would be a hill-top hacienda high above Los Angeles, a house I'd adore, in that place I adored, though, of course, I wouldn't be there that much. Because that was the other part of the arrangement. Not only was I leaving Brearley, now beloved Brearley, I was going to boarding school. There was no Brearley in Los Angeles. The nearest equivalent was the Katharine Branson school for girls, outside of San Francisco. Out came the brochure, the account of my mother's visit and a second visit with my father so he, too, could make sure it was right for me. Boarding school was fun! She had loved her convent, her St. Timothy's. The more she talked, the lower my spirits sank. I was saying good-bye to New York, to my school chums, to 130 East End Avenue—I could barely remember before it. And to Mademoiselle—I could barely remember before her—who was being abandoned as well. How could they do this to me?

I never imagined an Irving Berlin song being written for me, beyond "Blue Skies," that is. But "I'm Sorry for Myself," the snappiest number in *Second Fiddle,* did make me wonder if my father wasn't more observant of his sulky twelve-year-old than I gave him credit for.

And then it was June and we were moved into our Catskills estate, which had undergone quite a few changes since last seen. The house, though still a bit poky, had now, thanks to my mother and her clever decorator Anne Urquhart, acquired charm. It had white-painted woodwork, cozy, girl-sized, wallpapered bedrooms carved out of the attic, Linda's rose-strewn, Elizabeth's ivory beige, mine blue, with shelves filled with our East End Avenue books; in the new upstairs playroom my little gray desk and doll's house, now Elizabeth's. Downstairs, in the new, long living room made from the two parlors, were more bookcases, an Adirondacks-style stone fireplace, and East End Avenue stuffed furniture, covered in appropriately homespun material but way too big for the room; in the dining room, wallpaper with grazing sheep and my father's dark, English-style bachelor dining set, too big as well but lending character. (My parents' idea of interior decoration, handed down to their offspring, was to utilize your past; everywhere were reminders of West Forty-sixth Street, Harbor Hill, East End Avenue.)

And this "main house" was now only part of a complex. An old barn-garage had been transformed into servants' quarters. The "tea house" had been made sleepable. Most important, beside the lower fall where, in the nineteenth century, there had been a mill, now stood a brand new cottage—"Mamma and Daddy's cottage"— white clapboard with black shutters and a big picture window looking out on the fall.

"If you share that house with the children," Consuelo had said, surveying what her suggestion had wrought, "you'll sell the place after one summer and never come back." A year or two later, Consuelo herself would divorce Henry Davis and never come back except to visit my parents. But the Berlins would never leave.

Now, in the summer weather, it was even more apparent that my father had fallen in love with this piece of land. In his Alaska clothes, with his Alaska gaze, he went about with tree men, ordering the moving of mature pines, hemlocks, and maples as if they were saplings; with masons, carpenters, and woodsmen, arranging for the building of a dam, the blazing of trails, a lower trail crisscrossing the stream, an upper trail high above through the woods. "For the first time in my life I'm interested in something besides my work," he said. "I hope it lasts."

In those early days he didn't yet stock the stream with golden trout my mother became too fond of to eat. We fished for what there was and spent hours upstream, by a deep, narrow pool we called "the coffin," watching for an enormous old trout that refused to be caught. We swam in the icy pool under the big fall; we had picnics on the flat gray rocks, a procession from the house bringing food and drink, a uniformed butler with the silver cocktail shaker, maids in pink bringing the salads, the homemade potato chips, the herring from Grossinger's, the steaks from Dinty Moore's that my father grilled on an open fire.

When guests came—Moss Hart, the Mackays with Michael and little Mary Rose, Gilbert Seldes and family, Cousin Alice with her son Denning and daughter-in-law Alison—there were treasure hunts, croquet matches, and a lot of smart, fast talk. But mostly it was plain old-fashioned country living, supported admittedly by a staff more suitable to a house in Southampton. We had our own spring; we made our own electricity; we took our own ice from the icehouse; we picked apples from our own apple trees; we bought milk, cream, butter, and eggs from the farmer next door; we hiked up our hill, and up a bigger hill we called a mountain, with a ranger's lookout and a spectacular view. Buying this place was the best thing he'd ever done, said my father, who was more than a little hurt when I returned in mid-August from a stay in Maine with my classmate Buffy Rappleye and said I'd had such fun I never wanted to come home.

For Buffy's country place had the one thing, besides a beach, Lew Beach lacked: boys. A gang of youngsters, twelve to fifteen years old, whose families summered on a lake called Mountainy Pond, in log cabin camps with wood-burning stoves and gas lamps. At Mountainy I smoked my first cigarette and got my first crushes, on Buffy's dark, handsome cousin and her blond, handsome older brother. From Buffy I learned crucial information about what people did in bed (slightly wrong) and two kinds of kissing, regular and French, information unconnected with reality: the giggling night swims in the nude, the threat of the boys watching us. (They didn't; they couldn't have cared less.) I was teased about my well-developed figure and acquired a nickname, "Cricket," after the family cocker spaniel for my long floppy brown hair and generally eager behavior.

Why wouldn't I be eager? I'd never had such a time or been in a summer house like the Rappleyes' where the mother cooked and did the housework and the distinguished father, dean of the Columbia University Medical School, did the outdoor chores and the kids washed up. I dropped dishes and was called "butterfingers"; on the tennis court at the Mountainy "clubhouse" I was told my backhand resembled spaghetti. But they took me on. I wasn't a bad rower or swimmer; I had conversation; and when we played records in the clubhouse parlor—Tommy Dorsey, Jimmy Dorsey, Glenn Miller, Artie Shaw, Benny Goodman, Duke Ellington, the Andrews Sisters—I could hear a song once and sing it back, carry a tune. But I'd almost forgotten that part, the connection between me and popular music.

So I came home with stories of *real* outdoor living, *real* wilderness, and a bunch of songs that I sang continually, *my* songs, "Deep Purple," "Beer Barrel Polka," "And the Angels Sing," "I Let a Song Go Out of My Heart," "Moonglow," "Sunrise Serenade," "Three Little Fishes," and last but not least "Marie." Not Irving Berlin's original "Marie" in three-quarter time but Dorsey's swinging version of the song with interpolations.

"Livin' in a great big way, yourself," said my father who had an adjustment to make, a line of his own to cross. For he was about to become the parent of an adolescent.

What is strange, given my apprehension about the summer's end, is that I now can't remember when the countermand was given and everything was revoked; and suddenly, after all, at the last possible moment, literally two, at the most three, weeks before we were to leave for California, we weren't moving, after all. And though it was too late to get back into our apartment, though Mademoiselle would not be reinstated, it might not be too late to get back into Brearley. I remember being ecstatic; that was all. Except it was September 1939. I couldn't really be ecstatic because of the grim news from abroad, which obviously had something to do with the reprieve. The war's effect on business, on Hollywood, on everything. The change of plan was all mixed up with the newscasts on the portable radio that my mother kept at her side all day and allowed my father to bring into dinner though that was something she ordinarily frowned on.

Now, reading the correspondence between my father and Darryl Zanuck, it appears there was indeed a business reason for the change of plan that had nothing to do with the war. The indefinite postponing of *Say It with Music,* the new Irving Berlin movie that was to surpass *Alexander's Ragtime Band* and was having similar script problems. Only times were different. The studio, the stars, the director, couldn't wait. An unpleasant developing situation to do with competing properties, a changed mind on the part of Zanuck, or in any case, lousy timing. 20th Century-Fox was suddenly out of the picture and Irving Berlin, the "movie composer," was faced with peddling himself, his stories, his songs, not that there weren't plenty of studios eager for his services. Still. He had his excuse to do what he'd wanted all along, stay in New York and do a show.

Which was the part my mother related long after the war was over. "It wasn't the war," she said. "It wasn't even certain business things. . . ." A wave of the hand, dismissing 20th Century-Fox matters as too boring to talk about. "When it came down to it, your father couldn't bear to move, to make it permanent."

"You look so depressed," she'd said to him one night. (I wasn't the only one feeling sorry for myself.) And then he'd confessed. "There's no Lindy's in Los Angeles," he said. "No paper at two in the morning. No Broadway. No *city*." "We don't have to move," my mother said. He looked at her. Was she crazy? The house on Angelo Drive. The New York apartment let go. The schools.

"Of course I can arrange it," said my mother, delighted with the change in plan, though not perhaps with the timing. "Haven't I always?"

Impossible, some might say. An impossible man, however full of charm. But never my mother. Whatever he did, however notional or unpredictable, it was okay with her, or made to seem that way.

"Did you and Daddy never fight?" I'd ask her one day, for you could hardly count as serious fighting those periodic explosions at the family dinner table. Fight? Of course they fought, she would say, plenty of fights before, almost always, she gave in. "I remember in the early days, I'd get so mad sometimes when your father said no I'd go into my room and pack my suitcase. Then I'd think, but where will I go? Not home to Mother. Certainly not home to Father. To a hotel, that's it! Only how would I register? My own name? A false name? It would be all over town the next day. And so, sadly, I would unpack my suitcase." But thirteen years into the marriage, the suitcase was no doubt more in the mind than in actuality; they agreed on politics, agreed on friends, on how to raise their children and how to live; with their long-standing pact on religion, there wasn't all that much to quarrel about other than money, my mother's chronic extravagance, and the engagement book, my father's well-known distaste for most forms of planned or formal social life. Whatever the battles, they were, as always, behind closed doors.

If the Hollywood years had petered out in a so-so movie, *Second Fiddle,* and a disagreeable studio hassle, this was nothing I took in at the time, for life seemed to race along—off with the old, on with the new. The new show, *Louisiana Purchase,* was beginning to take shape (producer, B. G. De Sylva; book by Morrie Ryskind, the coauthor of *Of Thee I Sing;* stars, Victor Moore and William Gaxton)—and in the meantime something quite extraordinary was going on with a new song.

Kate Smith introduced "God Bless America" on the radio on Armistice Day, 1938, the weekend of my grandfather's death. She sang it again on Thanksgiving; and after that, every week for many months to come, she signed off with it. I'm not sure when I first heard it. I just remember this presence among us, all of a sudden that rich, round, carrying voice singing this new and quite peculiar Irving Berlin song. And a story that quickly became public property: how Kate asked Irving if he would write something for her Armistice Day broadcast; and he said as a matter of fact he had been tinkering with an old song out of the trunk, one that had seemed too solemn for *Yip, Yip, Yaphank,* a soldier show, but that seemed just right for the ominous, uncertain autumn of 1938. He'd added a verse about storm clouds gathering across the sea, made a couple of lyric and melody changes in the chorus, and there it was: "God bless America, land that I love . . ."

Big Kate, with her double chin, cheerful demeanor, and hearty voice, wasn't my favorite singer. My idea of a singer was Alice Faye: a throaty voice with a catch to it. But there was something so simple, yet thrilling, in the way Smith sang this particular song that I had to respond, in spite of an initial disappointment that it *was* so simple, simple enough for a small child to sing, for my sister Linda to sing while I accompanied her on the piano. It got no less simple when you heard it again and again and again. But no more simple, either. It didn't wear thin. Weekly the satisfaction repeated itself: the way the verse led into the refrain; the way the phrase "white with foam" led to the end.

By the late summer of 1939, "God Bless America" was already earning a tidy amount, for the future God Bless America Fund (and the Boy and Girl Scouts of America); across the country it was being sung in schools and churches, at political rallies and national holidays. Though dance bands were forbidden to play it and swing arrangements were ruled out, a Bing Crosby record had become a best-seller. Now the song was being pushed as the new national anthem despite protests from Kate Smith and the composer, who said, "There's only one national anthem, which can never be replaced." He also said, "I think that 'God Bless America' is the most important song I've ever written. I'll tell you more about it in five years." (Just a year later it had sold 500,000 copies and made $40,000 for the Scouts—a hefty sum in 1940.)

After a while I became aware of negative talk. Not just the crazies who asked what right an immigrant Jew had to call on God to bless America or a protest artist like Woody Guthrie, who would write "This Land Is Your Land" as an ironic comment, but middle-of-the-road columnists and broadcasters who called the song flag-waving, sentimental, jingoistic, simplistic. I didn't understand what they were saying. The song was what it was. But I was troubled. Then, one day at a Boy Scouts rally in the Catskills, I heard my father sing "God Bless America." No other singer, not Crosby, not Judy Garland, not Kate Smith herself, or a long procession of opera stars performing it on state occasions, could give it quite that conviction. He meant every word.

He meant it then. He meant it thirty years later when he sang it as an old man, on the *Ed Sullivan Show* that celebrated his eightieth birthday. How nervous he was, my oldest daughter would remember (all four of my children were there, snapped with him afterward in a classic 1960s photo); more and more nervous sitting beside her, pulling at his handkerchief, stretching his legs into the aisle, as he waited to go on; and then he sang it beautifully, a whole lifetime going into that frail but still true delivery.

It *was* the land he loved. It *was* his home sweet home. He, the immigrant who had made good, was saying thank you. And even if in later years he and I disagreed sometimes about the way that land did things, when he sang that song, I could not fail to be profoundly moved.

Though not to get too "heavy in the hand," as my father called taking things too seriously, I should note that a year or so after the song was written, the composer came upon his youngest daughter one day at the piano, picking out the tune and singing in her childish soprano, "God bless Elizabeth, girl that I love . . ." He thought it hilarious.

"God Bless America," you might say, was the real fiftieth-birthday present Irving Berlin had given himself, the one that looked forward rather than back, even if it came out of the trunk. For it was the beginning, whether you liked it or not, for better or worse, of a new image, though it would be a while before we in the family caught on.

PART FIVE

SEVENTY-EIGHTH STREET INTERLUDE

Portrait of a happy marriage, 1942.

23

IN THE BROAD SWEEP of Irving Berlin's life, it is easy
to leap from "God Bless America" to *This Is the Army*, to skip
right over 1940 and 1941. One might give a brief nod to *Louisiana
Purchase*, the hit show with the smart, spirited score that marked
his entrance into the 1940s and return to Broadway after six
years away. There would also be a note that the songs for *Holiday
Inn*, the 1942 hit movie that launched "White Christmas," were
written in this curious interim period—the period when Europe
was at war but not yet the United States and people like my parents, however busy leading their literary, theatrical New York
lives, were also deeply involved in politics, emotionally already
at war. And that could be it.

But then I would leap over the father of my early teens, a
character dear to me, and to a lot of others still around, who were
the girls I went to school with, the boys who were our first dates.

We were in a house now, a five-story double brownstone on
East Seventy-eighth Street, just off Lexington Avenue, that my
mother had somehow found, on no notice, available for rent. After
years of apartment and hotel living, my father enjoyed having his
own front door, coming and going as he pleased. If our new city
home had a somewhat formal aspect, it was shaken up by his casual ways—the midnight excursions to the newsstand or Lindy's,
the icebox raids, his habit of wandering about the third floor fresh
from his bath, a towel wrapped around his waist and his hat on, to
keep his slicked-down hair in place. (*"Daddy,"* I shrieked, if I
came upon him thus in the company of a friend, and he would duck
back into his bedroom or bath.)

As always, from behind the study door came the nocturnal
tinkling of the piano; the study in this new house was no longer the

out-of-bounds room at the top of the stairs as on East End Avenue. It was now at the heart of the house, but the sounds were mysterious nonetheless. In this new world of Seventy-eighth Street, my father sometimes aired his songs along the way to completion, mostly to my mother but occasionally to a child who happened to be nearby. I once asked my mother if she ever offered suggestions—I certainly didn't. "Of course not," she replied. "I say, 'That's wonderful, dear.' Then he'll come back in an hour and say, 'Listen to this,' and it will be better, and later even better. Maybe he can tell something from the way I say 'wonderful.' But what do I know?" (My mother would occasionally point out an error in a lyric, e.g., that in the "White Christmas" verse, "Beverly Hills, L.A." was incorrect, that in "Sun in the Morning," "moonshine" couldn't "give you the Milky Way"; my father said he didn't care, that was the way he wanted it.)

"Like a house in an English children's book," Linda remembers Seventy-eighth Street. At seven, she liked the front and back stairs, the dumbwaiter that went from bottom to top, the children's bedrooms on the fourth floor, with Dutch tiles around the fireplaces, the breakfast table in the dining-room bay window that looked out on tall trees. Enhancing the illusion was the nursery presence of Miss Tennant, with her brown bun, turned-up nose, and her brisk, humorous manner. "There's a bear in my room," cries small Elizabeth, curly-headed mistress of Tenny's heart. "I don't see it," says Tenny, a faint Scotch burr coloring her speech. "It's gone under the bed," says Elizabeth. "If it's small enough to fit under the bed, it's nothing much to worry about," says Tenny, displaying that reasonable attitude toward problems that would enable her to survive forty years of working for the Berlins.

For me Seventy-eighth Street was simply a satisfactory launch pad for my new life as a teenager. I liked the privacy of my bedroom, at the back, away from Tenny and "the children," with a piece of roof adjacent to one window where I smoked forbidden cigarettes till caught and caught again. I liked our new living room which was the width of the house, and blended the old East End Avenue living room and library into one opulent package. At the far end, opposite the fireplace, was a wall of floor-to-ceiling books, the ceilings high enough for our library steps (from which one afternoon, on the top shelf, I discovered the complete works of Havelock Ellis).

The best part of living on Seventy-eighth Street was the Allen-Stevenson School for boys across the street; boys arriving every morning as I left; boys who looked over from their classes into Linda and Elizabeth's bedrooms. Living opposite Allen-Stevenson became something to talk about, a feature of my adolescent "line," prepackaged chatter suitable for every occasion. I patiently explained to my father about lines, good lines, bad lines, lines that fooled you, lines you could see right through. He understood, he said; grown-ups had them, too. You had to watch it, though, for a line could get awfully old, awfully fast.

The teenage years had begun, a time when some fathers of daughters bowed out, but mine was eager to stay friends. He took me to my first Toscanini concert and to dinner before at the Roosevelt Grill. It was my first nightspot. While we were there, Guy Lombardo played only Berlin songs. I was embarrassed and proud at the same time and careful not to let my father know that I considered Lombardo and his Royal Canadians ("the sweetest sound this side of heaven") corny, if not worse. But later I had to admit I, a restless teenager, found Beethoven's Ninth a bore, though Toscanini, hair flying, eyes burning, baton lashing the air, might have been the most exciting performer I'd ever seen. My father, though surely he, too, had found the Ninth *long*, was disappointed. Was I not the family concert- and opera-goer, his musically trained child of whom he boasted? I was, I was. "I won't tell on you," he said.

And then there was the night, in the winter of 1940, we wandered into *Du Barry Was a Lady*. My mother was in the country, my father taking me to Dinty Moore's for a steak. After dinner he suggested a newsreel. "That's so dull," I said. "Tell you what," he said, "there's a show that's just opened, Cole Porter, Ethel Merman, Bert Lahr. I hear it's great."

Because *Du Barry* was such a hit we had to settle for the second row of the balcony; nonetheless, one could hear and see clearly. The raffish plot (a nightclub washroom attendant who dreams he's Louis XV), the bathroom-bedroom humor, was just right for a thirteen-year-old. Merman, with that wicked, savvy lilt, was just right, too, as were the songs—"It Ain't Etiquette," "Do I Love You, Do I?," and the naughty "But in the Morning, No!" I did notice that my father was coughing a lot and peering at me in a concerned fashion. At the first act's end he gave a big fake yawn and said, "I think this is sort of boring. I've got a *wonderful* idea, let's go to the Newsreel Theater." "But Daddy, I love it." "Don't argue with me. I say it's boring"—a little perturbed, perhaps, that I didn't find it boring at all. We left.

Each new phase seemed to interest him. When my friend Buffy and I decided to give a dance for our Brearley classmates, he found us a band for a suspiciously small sum. At the dinner I gave before the dance he got thirteen-year-old boys at the same end of the living room as thirteen-year-old girls by playing and singing some of our favorites—"Alexander's Ragtime Band," "Easter Parade," "Blue Skies." When it came to the dance itself, to help things get started, he cut in on all my friends and remembered the next day who was who, who looked snappy, who could stand to lose a little weight, who could follow. He also remembered one of the boys, Tim Seldes, son of his pal Gilbert Seldes, sitting gloomily on the sidelines, staring at people's feet. "What's wrong?" asked my father. "I'm trying to figure out how they do it," replied Tim, whose progressive parents had never forced him to attend dancing class.

Not that my elusive, work-preoccupied father had suddenly turned into a social butterfly. That same Tim Seldes liked to recall his escorting us to some party, sitting back in the family Lincoln, saying, "You know, Tim, if it weren't for you children, I wouldn't be riding around in a car like this. I'd just as soon be sitting on some desert island in the sun."

Still, there he was, chaperoning, talking, joking, and apparently doing it, not out of duty but because he enjoyed it. More of a chore were those hotel ballrooms I introduced my parents to: the Lincoln, where Harry James played; the Pennsylvania (Glenn Miller), the New Yorker (Benny Goodman), The Astor (where my father said, a bit ungraciously, to Tommy Dorsey, "You realize I'm only here because my daughter dragged me"). Having decreed, never mind what my friends were "allowed" to do, that at fourteen and fifteen I was too young to go dancing unchaperoned, the compromise was to take us themselves. Being with Mr. and Mrs. Berlin meant the best table and more often than not finding the band-leader sitting with you between sets—a reasonable exchange for being on your own, my friends assured me. (I did not agree.)

Besides, they liked my genial father, who happened to be Irving Berlin, and my pretty, chatty mother, who could "bring out" the shyest youth. And my parents liked them, treated them, girls and boys alike, as individuals. My father made dangerous pronouncements. After the Brearley production of Shaw's *Saint Joan,* he told Buffy, the lead, she might have a future; it set her on a theatrical path, she said (till marriage intervened). After the ninth-grade variety show, the Brearley Hilaria, he said to Monique James, the class comedienne, "I'll give you a part in my next show." (To me, who had blown the playing of "Limehouse Blues," he only commented, "Maybe you should have practiced a little more.") He had them all sorted out, Buffy, Nancy, and Marian the actresses, Sylvia the poet, Ginny and Patty the class leaders, funny Monique, smart Jessy, Timothy the philosopher, Bill, God's gift. When they came to Lew Beach, he walked them about, in casual country fashion, quizzed them, and let them talk, not too long but long enough that they felt his main concern was their problems. And then, quick change, he was back, in town, in a glossy dinner jacket, breaking the ice at a Junior Miss dinner before a Junior Miss dance.

Now, these dances I went to, it should be noted, were not all school parties. A lot of them were subscription dances—dances that New York girls of a "social" background belonged to—a form of club.

With adolescence came acknowledgment of "the problem," a problem so successfully handled that until the spring I was thirteen, I had no direct knowledge of what might politely be called "social" anti-Semitism. Not way back in the dark ages of my mother's youth. Current. "What are these things called 'the dances' that my friends are going to next year?" I asked my mother. And finally she had to level, explain not in abstract or airily waved-away terms, a word here and there about some silly club or resort that didn't take Jews but quite directly about the world "out there," not in Nazi Germany but in the good old U.S.A., that was not like our private world, so mixed I hadn't a notion of who was

Jewish or not. How the skating club at Madison Square Garden wouldn't take me so I learned at Radio City. How the Robinson dancing class wouldn't take me so I went to open-minded Mrs. Hubbell's (and made there lifelong friends, Fifi Little and Lucille Harris, who later, with their husbands, would become my outposts in high society, as I and my family would be theirs in a more bohemian world). And now there were these subscription dances that might not welcome me. But she would find out, and presently announced, after lunching with some ladies who counted, that though no Jewish girls seemed to belong to the Junior Holiday Dances or the Junior Get-Togethers, not to mention the older Holidays, senior "Gets," the "Mets" and "the Colonys," all those parties she had gone to as a girl, there were no "rules on the books."

She went to work, and in the winter of 1941, there I was, a little pioneer at my first Holiday dance, with my two escorts (in New York, girls invited boys, preferably two, to ensure a stag line and plenty of cutting in); leading the way (a few others would be let in, in my wake), a "half" abroad in a ballroom of Gentiles, or at least Gentile girls. Things weren't so rigid when it came to those sought-after boys. And I had a dandy time and appeared to pay no price, feeling only a vague uneasiness when two Brearley pals who happened to be Jewish said they couldn't go and how come I could?

And my father? He was leaving that side of things to my mother. If my fiercely loyal mother, member of the Woman's Congregation of Temple Emanu-El, who took us to Friday music services, who arranged for Passover in Baltimore with his friend Rabbi Morris Lazaron, if Ellin said it was okay, then it was okay by him. His world, the freewheeling world of show business, she would point out when challenged, did not organize for young people like her world did, whatever its faults.

So an illusion was fostered: that Irving Berlin's daughter, who was also Ellin Mackay's daughter, belonged in that old, exclusive enclave; that it only enhanced my belonging to have this out-of-the-ordinary father who was such a hit with my friends—friends who were as innocent, most of them, as I was of the nuances of prejudice inherited from an earlier generation. They would soon fade, these nuances, to nothing alongside the horrors that we and the world at large would have to acknowledge overseas. But not really to nothing. Snobbery and prejudice were not so easily erased. My father's "difference" had nothing to do with his being a Jew.

"For a lot of us your father was our first exposure to a really famous man, and he bore the responsibility well," one of those friends, the magazine editor Bill Rappleye, would recall years later. "He always had time, or made time, to talk to us; above all, he was committed, when with us, to that particular moment. At a party he would watch us without trying to participate (he wasn't one of those *embarrassing* fathers), but still he wanted to know: What's that song? What's that dance? What's that rhythm? What's that expression? As if he were taking notes for his own next song." And then, jumping ahead a couple of years: "When I was heeling [i.e., trying out for] the *Yale Daily News*, I interviewed your father in his office. He could have turned me down so easily, but he didn't. I remember him dark, wiry, and compact behind a big desk. It was the fall of 1942. *This Is the Army* had opened, and we talked about war songs. He said that so far no great war song had come out of World War II and he didn't think one would. For himself there was 'God Bless America,' but that wasn't a war song. There was 'This Is the Army, Mr. Jones,' but that didn't compare to George M. Cohan's 'Over There.' I was amazed at his candor, at the things he had to say about the song business. I also remember that having once decided to see this brash young fellow, he made me feel I was a professional."

But it is not yet *This Is the Army* time. It is the spring of 1940, late May, and *Louisiana Purchase;* the Seventy-eighth Street show has just opened and is the town's new "number one musical." Solid, if not brilliant, reviews. Sold-out house. A lighthearted tale of corrupt politicians trying to frame the U.S. senator who is investigating them, just racy enough to seem the height of sophistication to thirteen-year-olds. It could have been written for me and my friends, I thought, with its fresh, bouncy tunes, its clever, topical lyrics, though that was scarcely the intent of the composer, who said simply, "Without seeming immodest I think I have the best collection of songs I've had in a long time." And looking back, they were quite remarkable.

It's the forties now, and the sound is changing. Two ballads,

"You're Lonely and I'm Lonely" and "Fools Fall in Love," are in the old thirties style. "It's a Lovely Day Tomorrow," one of my father's great songs, can't be pinned to any musical time. But most of the numbers—"Louisiana Purchase," "You Can't Brush Me Off," "Outside of That I Love You," "Latins Know How," "Sex Marches On," "What Chance Have I with Love?"—have a new beat. Big-band swing influenced this score, along with the current rage for things South American. And an unknown big-band singer, Carol Bruce, my father's discovery, was the show's surprise hit, almost, but not quite, stealing the evening from its stars, Victor Moore, William Gaxton, Vera Zorina, and Irene Bordoni, the twenties favorite making a delightful comeback.

The new score set the tone for our second Lew Beach summer, which included many weekend guests to break up the mountain solitude and stifle my complaints that there was nothing to do but *read* (though, in fact, reading was my greatest pleasure). Moss Hart came, and Bobby Dolan, musical director of *Louisiana Purchase,* and were led, whether they felt like it or not, on long hikes up the stream and into the woods; Cousin Alice came, played her uniquely vicious and expert game of croquet and between times talked with me and my mother about Time, the fourth dimension. (We were all three reading Dunne's *Experiment with Time,* I from my vantage point, they from theirs, which made interesting, non-condescending conversation.) The Seldes family arrived; Timothy announced to anyone who would listen that there was no God; Marian danced on the lawn in diaphanous scarves; Gilbert read *Junket Is Nice* aloud to Elizabeth, while Mrs. Seldes, smiling serenely at all the show-offs, won the treasure hunt. Leonard Lyons, the columnist, decided to teach Linda how to skip stones at the big pool, then jumped in and interrupted one with his nose—scarred for life. Harry Ruby, composer of "Three Little Words" and "Who's Sorry Now," loose-limbed as a ball player, engaged in horseplay with me and my sisters and reminisced with my father. (They'd been friends since 1918, Camp Upton days, when Harry had taken down the songs for *Yip, Yip, Yaphank,* my father's soldier show of the First World War, and comforted his nervous buddy, who, along the way to a hit, kept moaning, "I'm not *there. . . .* I can't face the disgrace of this thing.") Afterward Harry wrote Irving, "My best to Ellin and those three little girls from the Catskills. I never enjoyed the company of children as I did theirs." An exaggeration, perhaps, but still it was one of those early Lew Beach summers when everyone had a wonderful time and said so.

And yet. And yet.

Every evening that summer on the stage of the Imperial Theatre was a still moment at the heart of all the escapist foolery when Irene Bordoni sang "It's a Lovely Day Tomorrow," with its crystal-clear verse

> *The front page of your paper is bound to make you sad,*
> *Especially if you're the worrying sort.*
> *So turn the front page over where news is not so bad,*
> *There's consolation in the weather report . . .*

and its chorus holding out a hand, "Come and feast your tear dimmed eyes / On tomorrow's clear blue skies . . . ," a songwriter's modest reminder of where the world really was in the summer of 1940, the summer of the fall of France, of Nazi tanks rolling up the Champs Elysées and Nazi planes pounding Britain and Nazi trains carrying prisoners of war, and many others, to destinations unknown.

And in the privacy of their rooms at night, in the cottage by the waterfall, or, when the summer ended, on the Seventy-eighth Street third floor, my apprehensive parents listened to those increasingly ominous reports and talked about what they would do with themselves and their family if the unthinkable happened.

_____ 24

LOOKING BACK, I'm always surprised at how untroubled my own memories are of this period, given my parents' concern, not all of it invisible.

"The news is bad tonight," my father would say. The radio would come into dinner over my mother's halfhearted protests. I would try to share the fear, the distress. But it was too far away, too horrible, too enormous to grasp, like the pictures in *Life* of the Frenchman in tears, of St. Paul's rising above the smoking ruins of London. I was grateful when my mother turned to me to discuss plans or tell an amusing story.

For my parents, though, the war in Europe remained frighteningly close. Later, my mother would say they genuinely believed, in the summer and fall of 1940 and well into the next year, that the Germans would win. With Europe gone, with Rommel in North Africa, Hitler seemed unstoppable, even if commentators called the Battle of Britain a draw. Eventually, so went their worst imaginings, he would conquer England, then Canada, then "make an arrangement" with the United States that would amount to conquest. And if that happened, how would they protect their half-Jewish children? Flee to South America?

Politics became the stuff of their lives. As there were Democrats and Republicans, so now there were "interventionists" and "isolationists" (though not all Democrats were the former or all Republicans the latter). Isolationists in our interventionist family became the enemy, or at best, if close friends, the misguided ones. Early joiners of William Allen White's Committee to Defend America by Aiding the Allies, supporters of all of Roosevelt's pro-British moves, my parents campaigned for the president even more vigorously in 1940 than they had in 1936. My father gave money and performed at a rally and on the air. My mother spoke from the back of campaign trucks on street corners and on the radio up and down the East Coast.

In school, doing my own modest bit, I wore my Roosevelt button, quoted my mother's barbs, and collected clothing for "Bundles for Britain," while Republicans parodied the president—"I hate *war* (pronounced *wah*), Eleanor hates *wah*, even my little dog Fala hates *wah*"—or, if the joke didn't take, hinted darkly of secrets in FDR's past. Things got so nasty in the halls of Brearley that Sarah Roosevelt, the president's granddaughter, a classmate of Linda's, was kept home the final week of the campaign.

I can still see my parents that fall setting out from Seventy-eighth Street, part of exciting events, a couple with a mission. My mother was so deceptively ladylike in appearance, honey blond hair under a velvet skull cap, breaking in soft curls around her face, ivory skin set off by a smart dove-gray suit, a creamy ruffled blouse, three strands of pearls, or a dusty-blue silk dress under a mink coat; my black-haired, black-browed father handsome in broadish pinstripes, thin, shorter than my mother when she wore heels, which she did going into battle or out on the town, but never smaller in her mind or anyone else's. Even when she was the principal performer, she was a wife first, fiercely so, who walked out on one radio show—forget FDR, forget the campaign—because the host asked if Mrs. Berlin didn't find "God Bless America" a little corny and sentimental.

If they had once seemed frail to me, in need of protection, they did no longer. Though sometimes volatile, they were basically solid, reliable, surefooted, and annoyingly strict figures. Their appearances in the sporadic diary I kept are confined mostly to such dry observations as "Storm broke at home because Mamma found out about my smoking, i.e. breaking my promise . . . Had a serious talk with Mamma and Daddy and everybody is very gloomy," or, "had a long argument about going to the movies alone," or, "we are having a lot of trouble with cooks as Mamma and Daddy are quite hard to please," or (in Lew Beach), "Worried about my report. Mamma must have gotten it and she hasn't phoned in two days . . . she and Daddy are probably meditating on what steps to take," and, zeroing in on the problem, "It's more peaceful here when Mamma is away but also a lot more boring."

They were certainly not boring, and it was clear even to me, as I came around the bend, into my teens, that not all parents behaved with, and concerning each other, as mine did. Though they seemed most definitely of the older generation—my mother, not yet forty, just as ancient as my father in his fifties—there was a spark to them that was not old at all. Later, my mother would recall the two of them, after some "gloomy" exchange, laughing at the picture of themselves, the great romance, become scolders, watchdogs, caretakers, moral arbiters.

I wouldn't have said my parents resembled those sparkling, sparring married couples of the silver screen—Myrna Loy and William Powell, Cary Grant and Irene Dunne, Hepburn and Tracy—but there was a flavor of matched wits, banked fires. Their little oddities aroused my adolescent curiosity. The business, for instance, of my pretty, sociable mother not dancing, not even with my father, who sometimes, in a restaurant when an orchestra played or in one of those big-band ballrooms I "dragged" them to, would hold out a hand and say, "Come on, Ellin," and she, widening her eyes, would say, oh, so sweetly, "You know I don't dance." "Oh, I did when I was young," she would say when one of my dates, doing the polite thing, or some gentleman of her acquaintance asked her. "But I was never very good at it. Now I don't have to, so I don't." It was like her tin ear, only not quite. Not for years did I tell my mother my theory: that my father, who was not lacking in jealousy in their younger days, had made a fuss one night about someone, said he didn't want her out on the floor again with that particular man, and she said, "All right, I won't dance with him anymore, I won't dance with *anyone* ever again, including you." Afterward he was sorry, really very sorry, but it was too late. She did not comment, only gave me a smile that she sometimes gave when I had guessed correctly about something that she considered none of my business. The smile was confirmation enough.

The not dancing went along with the story of being so mad she packed her suitcase, part of the early years of a marriage that had not, in its second decade, in its days of new, high purpose, remotely given way to indifference or habit. (If my mother had an equivalent possessiveness, it was just a sense of general vigilance concerning a husband constantly exposed, in his business, to beautiful, seductive women. If he had had a wandering eye she would have been a tigress, but he didn't. I remember his talking a bit too much about Carol Bruce, his wonderful discovery, and my mother giving quite a few *humphs* and the talk ceasing, rather abruptly. That was about it.)

When the 1940 election was over, my parents remained politically engaged. My father, waiting for his next project to come through, the movie *Holiday Inn*, seemed to be spending all his time singing "God Bless America" at civic events and writing war-related songs: a sad song about ruined London, "A Little Old Church in England"; another about England's enemy and the world's, "When That Man Is Dead and Gone" ("Some fine day the news will flash / Satan with a small moustache / Is asleep beneath the lawn"), a clever ditty some people found lacking in taste; and, at the request of the U.S. government, "Arms for the Love of America" and "Any Bonds Today," my favorite of these patriotic efforts, given a swinging rendition on a Decca record by the Andrews Sisters.

My mother, beginning work on her first novel, a romance with an anti-Nazi theme, launched an attack on the America First Committee, William Allen White's opposite number, in a series of network radio speeches. I remember those broadcasts, written by herself, the edge to her voice, the sharpness of her reasoning as she lit into the foes of Franklin Roosevelt and aid to Great Britain. A formidable opponent of tycoon and senator alike, she saved her most bitter words for Col. Charles Lindbergh, the fallen hero ("[who] says 'I prefer to see neither side win' "), and was little gentler to Anne Morrow Lindbergh, targeting her scary little book *The Wave of the Future*, "which speaks of democracy tenderly but speaks of it as though it were dead—drowned in that wave of tyranny against whose inevitability Mrs. Lindbergh is not willing to fight."

I also remember that before she made a speech my mother was so nervous she couldn't keep anything on her stomach and afterward took to her bed. But my father, who fussed over her, did not order her to stop for he was too proud of her.

At Seventy-eighth Street in the winter of 1941, the "right" and "wrong" sides of the political scene were symbolized by two slim volumes. The first was that chilling blueprint of a totalitarian world by Mrs. Lindbergh. The other was *The White Cliffs*, Cousin Alice Miller's fiction in verse about an Anglo-American marriage, with its much-quoted final words about the heroine's adopted country: "I am an American bred, / I have seen much to hate here—much to forgive / But in a world where England is finished and dead, I do not wish to live."

In the family, Cousin Alice, my father's old friend, my mother's proxy mother, my sister Elizabeth's godmother, everyone's favorite, was, all of a sudden, center stage. I can see her now, a handsome, gray-haired older woman with a sloping bosom, a diamond-chained lorgnette, more for decoration than snapping and peering, a long, bony face, who liked to tell of turning down, a year or so earlier (she knew her limitations), an offer to play

Franklin Roosevelt's mother in *I'd Rather Be Right*. Our senior wise woman was so old-fashioned, a near contemporary (though not a friend) of Edith Wharton's, yet so with it and so delighted with herself and us, for being delighted with her. Called in the late thirties a has-been, her novels of love and society passé, Alice Duer Miller was once again on top of the best-seller lists. A poet in her youth, before she began writing fiction to make money, author of one previously admired tale in verse, *Forsaking All Others*, she had watched with horror and pride the British retreat from Dunkirk and in less than a month had written *The White Cliffs*. Her publisher, Coward-McCann, had been enthusiastic but cautious. Only a few thousand copies were printed. Then Lynn Fontanne gave the poem an impassioned reading on NBC, and the orders poured in. The book returned to the printers twenty times. "Success is always sweet," said Cousin Alice, "but never sweeter than when it comes after sixty."

My father got a big kick out of Cousin Alice and let you know it. She and my mother took his mind for a minute or two off his worries, of which there were more, in the winter and spring of 1941, than the war in Europe. "Headaches" over his brainchild *Holiday Inn*, originally planned as a revue, now a movie, hung up in negotiations. "Headaches" at the office, and the first intimation, when the name Saul Bornstein came up, a hitherto neutral name, of darkening coloration, of major trouble brewing between my father and his partner of twenty years, temporarily on hold because of the biggest headache of the lot, "the ASCAP mess."

On January 1, 1941, the notorious boycott had begun. No songs by members of the American Society of Composers, Authors and Publishers on the air because the broadcasters had turned down a new ASCAP contract. This meant nothing by any songwriter you had ever heard of, including my father, nothing, that is, that wasn't in the public domain. As a fourteen-year-old I had plenty to say about this, more than my father wanted to hear. Did he know that "Jeanie with the Light Brown Hair," written fifty years before "Alexander's Ragtime Band" by his idol Stephen Foster, was number one on "Your Hit Parade"? (He did.) Had he heard those insipid numbers by the songwriters of BMI, the broadcasters' answer to ASCAP? "Jim," "I Hear a Rhapsody," "I Understand"—these were supposed to replace Jerome Kern, Irving Berlin, Cole Porter, Richard Rodgers, George Gershwin, Duke Ellington, Harold Arlen, etc. etc. "I'd be careful what you say about that, kid," he cautioned, though he himself had been heard to say, "The public has been getting the cream of the bottle, after the first of the year they will be getting skimmed milk."

And then, as a kind of wild footnote to this time of real and necessary concerns, there was the affair of Mary Blake, my mother's youngest half sister, a "headache," riveting to the younger generation, and impossible to conceal, what with all the comings and goings, the phone calls, the conferences behind closed doors, that second year at Seventy-eighth Street.

A tall, fat eighteen-year-old with a gorgeous face and sullen manner, spitting in the eye of the family, Mary was carrying on with a German diplomat, one Ruprecht von Boeklin, more than twice her age, an acknowledged Nazi, and married besides. Ordered by my parents, her sisters, and her guardian Uncle Willie to end the romance, Mary said she and Woolie were planning to marry as soon as he divorced his wife, waving in my father's face as proof the diamond swastika on her charm bracelet. Told she couldn't, as a minor, marry without permission, she threatened to move into von Boeklin's suite at the Carlyle. She did just that, too. Eventually, when she turned twenty-one, she would marry her Nazi lover, who shortly thereafter appeared, thinly disguised, as the villain of that novel my mother was writing, *Land I Have Chosen*. (Swastikas notwithstanding, von Boeklin did not return to Germany, but settled down with Mary in New Jersey, pursuing, somewhat reclusively , the life of a gentleman farmer.)

After all this, how pleasant to report that in this winter of irritation, my father had someone else to be proud of besides my mother, Cousin Alice, and those charming younger daughters straining at the confines of the nursery floor. His A student, now in ninth grade, who, despite some adolescent capering, was surely, in these serious times, hitting the books harder than ever. Alas, in these serious times, his A student was heading, like Pinocchio in the Disney movie, straight for Pleasure Island, was already there.

This was the year I was allowed to go to the movies, too many of them, unchaperoned, at "nice" theaters, the Translux, the Plaza, the Normandie (the ones patronized by my mother's friends, who might tell if they caught me smoking or laughing too raucously with my buddies), the year I hung out for hours at the Liberty Music Shop listening to records—Frank Sinatra, Helen O'Connell, Benny Goodman (buying something, maybe). It was the year I became unbearably superior, in my mind, to "the little ones," that is, Linda and Elizabeth, reestablishing relations only at supper, entertaining them with the stories I loved to make up (though all they remember is my looking in on them, on my way out, and saying, "What are the *children* having for supper?"); the year I joined Womrath's lending library to read such inappropriate items as *For Whom the Bell Tolls* and *The Sun Is My Undoing;* the year I neglected my practicing of Mozart sonatas in favor of boogie-woogie. Above all, it was the year I spent hours on the phone comforting my lovesick friends and being comforted by them. What time was there to study?

The predictable result was a ghastly midterm report: C+ in history, C in math, D (the first ever) in Latin. My parents were on a holiday in Florida, but my father had come to New York on business. He did not get the report till the morning he was heading back south. I had already left for school.

For two weeks I received my mother's usual cheerful letters, with only a brief but ominous mention of the reality at hand. "Daddy will be in New York soon and will discuss your report with you then."

Now I see myself arriving at Dinty Moore's for dinner. No outing *à deux* would ever stay more clearly in my mind. I have dressed carefully, Marie Antoinette preparing for the guillotine. I am wearing navy blue pumps, a navy blue skirt and coat, a pink silk blouse, a navy blue hat with a rolled-up brim and too much veiling, and just a suggestion of lipstick; my father was not thrilled with the purple smear we fourteen-year-olds favored.

The hostess escorts me to the table: "Here she is, Mr. Berlin, what a lovely, grown-up young lady; you must be proud." There is the polite exchange of news, the nervous munching of oyster crackers, the arrival of steak and baked potatoes. Then: "You know your mother and I were both disappointed with your marks," he begins. "Your mother was *very* upset. Of course, you know I don't get as upset about these things as she does. . . ." Even in my anxiety I know that had my mother been there instead, she would have said, "Of course, I take this with a grain of salt, but your father . . ." And she, in fact, would have been telling the truth.

"You have a very good brain, Mary Ellin," he continues, "but it doesn't do you a bit of good if you don't use it. You kids don't know how lucky you are. You take a lot of things for granted. I want you to have a good time, go to your parties. But the most important thing you're doing right now is learning, and never forget it. When you do well, you have no idea, you couldn't, how proud it makes me." Pause. The heavy eyebrows come together. The look is earnest. "Well, anyhow, your mother and I have decided that if your marks don't improve, if New York is too distracting, we will have to send you to boarding school, where you can concentrate."

"Oh, no." My first words since he began. The lower lip trembles.

"Now, none of that. You know your mother and I love you. It would hurt us more . . ." (Oh, no, not that one, I think, lower lip firming up.) "Enough, now. You know how I feel about you. Just think about what I've said." Period. Discussion closed. With my father in a "serious" talk, points were made briefly, firmly; then it was finished. There was plenty left unsaid that I could fit in for myself: the bit about the Lower East Side kid with minimal schooling, the newsboy, the singing waiter helping to support a widowed mother who had no advantages, while we had everything. He could have gone on for quite a while, but he didn't.

And instead of taking me home in brooding silence, he took me to Loew's State, where he said he should catch someone's act. (George Jessel? Jimmy Durante? I can't remember.) The manager ushered us down to the front row. The famous comic came on. Midway in his routine (not funny, according to my tastes) he paused, announced that his dear friend Irving Berlin was in the audience: "Come on up and say a few words to the folks, Irving." To a big hand and the strains of "Alexander's Ragtime Band," my father climbed up on the stage and said simply that his friend had his toughest audience in years, his fourteen-year-old daughter, who loved every minute (as if he hadn't felt me squirming by his side).

"Let his daughter take a bow," someone shouted in the balcony. The spotlight found me. I stood up, nodded, and smiled a discreet smile that didn't reveal my braces. There was polite applause—not only saved from the guillotine but acclaimed by the populace.

That spring I made a notable academic recovery, or at least enough of one to stay in Brearley. A year later, Womrath best-sellers and Hemingway were being supplemented by *War and Peace* ("a wonderful book, though golly it's long"). By the summer of 1943, a Bryn Mawr applicant, history my proposed major, I was up there with the class brains. "I'm not only glad about the marks for myself but for you and Daddy," I wrote my mother, the butter unmelted in my mouth. "I guess you get rather discouraged when my work isn't up to standard, especially Daddy, who must be made sick to see the opportunity of the best education going to waste."

Lesson digested and not forgotten. Though what the good marks, the brain, the education, the hard work, those things my father cared about so desperately, were leading up to—that was something else to be addressed later. If someone had asked me at this point what I wanted to be when I grew up, I would have answered, not too originally, an actress, though with my loud voice and dark looks, boys' parts were all I seemed to land: Bloody Tybalt, Pluto, Judas Iscariot, Napoleon Bonaparte. In fact, I liked a lot of things—music, history, writing. In fact, I hadn't a clue. And if someone had asked my father what *he* wanted me to be when I grew up? I'm not sure. To be good at whatever I did, to stick with it, whatever I did, to make something of myself. But what? Well, that was up to me, he would have said at this point, and later too.

In September 1941, my father went to Hollywood to work on *Holiday Inn,* in production at last. All spring and summer he had been writing the songs, on keyboard and typewriter, a whole new batch to accompany the one written a year or more earlier called "White Christmas," a secret song he felt from the start so strongly about he'd made it part of the contract with Paramount. More songs, for this tale of a country inn open only on holidays, than for any previous movie, some of them throwaways, some future standards like "Happy Holiday," "You're Easy to Dance With," and most notably, "Be Careful, It's My Heart," a light, elegant ballad delivering a message: that even in serious times, Irving Berlin, the troubadour of moonlight and romance, was still around.

There was still plenty to fuss about. ASCAP politics even as the boycott ended; a hassle over "Angels of Mercy," written for the Red Cross, a nice gesture entangled in red tape; continuing problems with Saul Bornstein. But things were back to normal, or at least as normal as you could get in the fall of 1941, with the country heading into war. From California in October "the boss" sent Dave Dreyer, the man he now relied on in the office, a cheerful bulletin: "With the exception of the opening chorus the score for *Holiday Inn* is complete & . . . the reaction to the songs here is really great." Once again he was making plans, the minute he got back to New York, to do that show of his heart, a new *Music Box Revue*.

A great show *was* around the corner. But it would not be a *Music Box Revue*.

On December 7 my parents were in Beverly Hills. I have no idea how they reacted that Sunday when the news came, what their feelings were now that our involvement in the war, which they thought inevitable for so long, was finally a shocking fact. As for myself, I was at a friend's house studying when my friend's mother came in to tell us that the Japanese had bombed Pearl Harbor and I'd better go home.

And then, in the spring, my father joined up.

From the war department came the formal invitation—result of weeks of behind-the-scenes discussions—to mount "a revival of your own World War I musical show Yip, Yip, Yaphank . . . in behalf of Army Emergency Relief." Not losing a beat, my father sent a reply that seems oddly formal coming from him: "I am delighted to accede to your request."

_____ 25

ONE FINAL NOTE on the Seventy-eighth Street years, which were about to end in a burst of glory. Though we lived in remarkable closeness in our large, upstairs-downstairs house, adult

concerns, especially painful ones, were kept separate. Thus, I
have only the most fragmentary recollections of a central event of
this period, pushing aside even war jitters, something my father
carried around with him for the better part of three years—the
matter of Joseph Schenck.

It seemed to have little connection with "Uncle Joe," my father's friend from the old days on the Lower East Side, for decades
one of the most important men in Hollywood, board chairman of
20th Century-Fox; or with Uncle Joe, my own dear godfather, who
came to the house for dinner, took me to the theater and the Colony
restaurant, the grown-ups' territory, and asked if, for a lark, we
could go to El Morocco, the nightclub where café society rhum-
baed and loitered on zebra-striped banquettes (and was told certainly not). But there it was, no more than a subsurface murmur at
first, a sense of something going on that wasn't disclosed, and finally, at some point in the winter of 1941, disclosed to me in a few
words and as quickly put aside: the nasty fact that Uncle Joe had
been indicted on a charge of income tax evasion and was to stand
trial in New York.

I have a dim memory of my father, who testified on his behalf,
muttering, "It will be fine, the government doesn't have a case,
they're just trying to make an example," of my mother saying,
"Don't bring it up with your father, with anyone." Maybe his ac-
countant made mistakes, she said, but Joe had done nothing others
hadn't done, and he'd paid up all the government said he owed.

Certainly there was no mention then of the complications:
that behind the tax case was union business, the paying off of
racketeers to grease the wheels of Hollywood productions, something all the big studios, including 20th Century-Fox, were suspected of doing. "Joe took the rap for a lot of guys," my father
would say later, and try to explain how it was that Uncle Joe,
though engaged in questionable dealings, had been a form of Hollywood hero; that the other studio chiefs, also dealing in illegal
payoffs, had families; Joe, the only one without children, had volunteered to stand for the rest.

But at the time it was just this "tax case" that my mother kept
saying would be "fine" and then unhappily was not fine at all. Joe
Schenck was convicted and sentenced to a year in jail. I remember

asking if I could visit him—visions, no doubt, of myself bearing baskets of food to my poor old godfather behind bars. No one was permitted to visit, I was told, except his brother, not even my father.

So it falls into place, a difficult undercurrent to difficult times, a painful interlude but no interruption to an ancient friendship: my fifty-five-year-old father, in late April 1942, back at Camp Upton, in Yaphank, Long Island, to write *This Is the Army;* and a week later, sixty-four-year-old Uncle Joe, the Hollywood leader, locked up in Danbury prison. A further irony was that a quarter of a century earlier, that same Joseph Schenck, already a power in Hollywood, had told General Bell, commanding officer of that same Camp Upton, that Irving Berlin was much too old and too delicate for army life and should be discharged immediately. He wasn't, and *Yip, Yip, Yaphank* was the result.

Uncle Joe was paroled after serving four months and back within the year at 20th Century-Fox, back in my life when he came to New York, nothing changed, apparently no worse for the experience, though later my father would say, "Joe never got over it"; those months behind bars, brief as they were, had left an indelible mark.

My father, meantime, for more than thirty years the country's favorite songwriter, had embarked on the biggest undertaking of his life.

PART SIX

THIS IS
THE ARMY

Opening night, London, 1943—the first stop overseas.

26

THE OPENING NIGHT of *This Is the Army* was Saturday, July 4, 1942.

This particular memory of my father is intensely private and yet not private at all. It is one that I, a dazzled fifteen-year-old, attending my first opening, and my mother, veteran of many such nights, but never one like this, shared with an audience of two thousand people packed into the Broadway Theatre. In spirit you might say it was shared with a whole nation, since it was the first Fourth of July after we entered the war. But that is what gave the night its potency: that it was so public and yet so personal. I have nothing that I can possibly compare it to.

I remember the crowds gathered outside the theater, people who had been hearing six months of bad news, who had sons, brothers, fathers, husbands in uniform, who needed something to cheer for and participate in even if they didn't stand a chance of a seat. Inside was another special wartime audience, the uniforms, gold stars and ribbons, the big brass, red-faced, gray-haired men and their well-coiffed wives; and the dressy civilians who had to be the regular first nighters, some of whom I knew because they were family friends, others whom I simply recognized; but also the crush of more plainly dressed citizens and servicemen making their way to the balconies. I remember the special vibration at the fourth row center where we sat—my mother, myself, and Tim Seldes, my date for the evening—embedded in generals to the front, generals to the back, generals to the right and left, with a few familiar faces salted among them—Aunt Gwen and Uncle Willie, Consuelo Vanderbilt (now Mrs. Jack Warburton), Moss Hart, Robert Sherwood, the Kaufmans, the George Backers, Herbert and Maggie Swope. Excitement in the pre-curtain talk that this benefit opening alone had raised thousands and thousands for Army

Emergency Relief; that already the movie rights had been sold to Warner Brothers for many more thousands that would also go not to Irving Berlin but to military charities. The word from people who had seen a dress rehearsal was that something wonderful was about to unfold.

Then the orchestra struck up the overture, a half-dozen tunes heard for the first time ever, plus a couple of old favorites; the curtain went up on a stage filled with soldiers, bleachers filled with them, three hundred young men in khaki delivering the opening chorus. "You thought that many, many years ago / You saw the last of ev'ry soldier show / But here we are yes, / Here we are again." Then they sang the title song, and the entertainment took off and built, the way a good show will, number by number: a raucous song, "The Army's Made a Man Out of Me" sung by Sgt. Ezra Stone, radio's Henry Aldrich, also the show's director; a comedy routine by Pvt. Julie Oshins, late of the nightclub circuit; jugglers, tumblers, a magician; a handsome corporal with a high, melodious tenor singing "I'm Getting Tired So I Can Sleep"; a second sweet-voiced boy singing "I Left My Heart at the Stage Door Canteen," the ballad that would climb to the top of "Your Hit Parade"; soldiers getting their laughs dressed up in crinolines for "Mandy," carried over from *Yip, Yip, Yaphank*, tapping out a hot swing tune, "What the Well Dressed Man in Harlem Will Wear," saluting the navy in a rousing first-act finale. Soldiers in greasepaint, mostly amateurs, putting on one of the best revues, so went the intermission talk, that anyone had ever seen. Irving Berlin, the man people called in 1942, without thinking twice about it, America's top songwriter, had delivered again.

I can remember in the intermission feeling so proud. Though I was used to hearing about my father's success, I had never experienced it live and head-on. Openings, movie premieres, the great celebrations, my parents had always decreed, were no place for children. Fifteen was just over the wire. (My sisters would attend a matinee. But at the matinee they, too, would see what I had seen and would not forget.) I can still picture the way we all looked. Myself, bright-eyed, dark-haired with my signature bangs, in a Lanz evening dress, red dotted Swiss skirt, white lace blouse, red suspenders, the height of teenage fashion. Tim Seldes, tall, gangling, an Exeter lower-middler, looking suave in his dinner jacket, though the sleeves are slightly too short.

My mother, is svelte in a black-and-white print sheath and green jacket that matches the emeralds she has taken out of the vault for the occasion—the Mackay family jewels, "left over from the good old days," she says, as if there had ever been a day or night to equal this.

She is every inch the excited, happy wife, but being a little artificial, the way she is when nervous. The show isn't over, and her husband still has to get out on that stage himself and sing his song. After yesterday's dress rehearsal, which she and I attended, she joked approvingly, "He is a ham at heart, up there again at last." But dress rehearsal is not opening night.

The second-act curtain goes up. There is a tuneful salute to the air corps; a dream sequence; the evening's funniest skit featuring impersonations by the GIs of the stars of the Stage Door Canteen: Jane Cowl, Alfred Lunt and Lynn Fontanne, Gypsy Rose Lee, Vera Zorina.

And then, there he is at last, sitting up sleepily, swinging his legs over the side of a cot and standing up, alone, stage center. A small, black-haired man in an old doughboy's uniform with a high-necked jacket and puttees. It is the first perfectly still moment since the evening began. He looks down, then up, and out at the audience, mouth open, ready to sing. Then the silence is broken by a roar, as sudden as thunder, and the pounding of applause. Everyone around us is rising, cheering now; and we are on our feet, too, applauding furiously—there is no question of family modesty. The demonstration continues for a full ten minutes as my father stands there looking down, looking up, opening his mouth, closing it again.

Finally, he is allowed to begin his song, the one I've grown up with, not as every soldier's favorite lament in the First World War but as both my parents' everyday theme song: "Oh! How I hate to get up in the morning, Oh! How I'd love to remain in bed." The voice is high, with a slight rasp, familiar, sweet; not the world's greatest, but who cares; he knows how to put over a song. After the wobbly first few bars, he seems at home up there, dropping twenty-five years, impish, with his rumpled forehead and raised brows, beating time with the hat against his knee, building up to the punch line, his words, his music, his frail, exactly appropriate voice: "And then I'll get that other pup / The guy who wakes the bugler up / And spend the rest of my life in bed."

When he finished, the cheering began all over again. I felt my mother's hand take mine and saw a suspicious glitter in her eyes. "He was *good*," I said. My mother nodded, not trusting herself to speak.

Then the moment passed. We were back with the marvelous soldiers, lined up one last time for the finale, back in the hurrahs for everyone, for the whole evening that had even the critics on their feet applauding. This was something that never happened, so someone remarked, the gentlemen and ladies of the press putting themselves publicly on the line, as they would put themselves on the line in the Monday papers. Richard Watts of the *Herald Tribune* spoke for one and all when he wrote, "*This Is the Army* is at once delightful entertainment and a song of American democracy. . . . Because [it] does not try to capitalize on patriotism it is one of the most truly patriotic works I have ever encountered. Because it always keeps its sense of humor and never tries to be emotional it is one of the most moving events in theatrical history."

And finally, in a huge crush backstage, we found my father, the man the company called "Mr. B," still in his costume and orange greasepaint. I remember the look on his face, a mixture of wonder, satisfaction, and exhaustion. Under his eyes black circles showed through the greasepaint. But the eyes danced.

A bit later we returned to normal. After a hot and crowded hour's celebration at the opening-night party at the Biltmore Hotel, my parents announced they were going to the Stork Club. Would they take me? What did I think? Tim and I could go to Hamburger Heaven. I was cross and did not entirely conceal my displeasure. Back to normal, indeed. Except not quite.

Life in our family had always been in compartments. The private and public carefully separated, the symbol those sounds from behind a closed door that became the songs the world sang. They were very private, those sounds, as our family life was private, as the man who was our father, although the world's Irving Berlin, was private. Even when I went to the shows and the movies, and up there on stage or on the screen were his songs, even if my father and I were dancing to a band playing a Berlin medley, and I felt proud and embarrassed at the same time, still it didn't quite connect. Though clearly I knew that the man I called "Daddy" was a world-famous songwriter, his celebrity was somehow a distant thing.

But that night I saw fame—and something more. I saw and felt love—love for this man, my father, for what he had done, bringing into being *This Is the Army*, for what he had given people his whole life, as a songwriter and as an American.

On that night, halfway through my sixteenth year, everything came together. The public and private Irving Berlin converged. Witnessing in that theater the affection and pride that echoed even deeper feelings of my own, I knew something about my father, and who he was, that I had not known before, that I'd never be allowed to forget.

Again and again in the days and weeks that followed he answered friends who had sent wires and letters, telling them how happy he was. He wrote to Alexander Woollcott, Moss Hart, Robert Sherwood, Hassard Short; and to the ailing George M. Cohan, his mentor, who had welcomed him into the Friars Club in 1912. He wrote to China Harris, widow of Sam Harris, his Music Box partner, who had died a year earlier; to Grace Moore and Belle Baker, Berlin stars from way back; to Frank Tours, the conductor of *As Thousands Cheer;* to his brother Ben and sisters Gussie and Ruth; to Mark Sandrich, Damon Runyon, Gilbert Seldes, Howard Lindsay, Russel Crouse, Ira Gershwin, Cole Porter, Jerome Kern, Harry Ruby, Harold Arlen, Sam and Frances Goldwyn, Fred and Phyllis Astaire, and on and on. "So happy about the whole thing," he'd write, about the show itself, a smash hit—he had never had such a hit—about the money it would be making for Army Emergency Relief, about the way it seemed to be lifting civilian morale and the attendant excitement in Washington. "The best thing I've ever been connected with," he'd write. Or to put it another way, "It was a tough job but as is always the case, there's nothing wrong with the stomach that a big hit can't cure."

Reading that correspondence now, I'm reminded of how excited he was, how he bounded in and out of rooms, how he gleamed, how different it was, somehow, meeting him at Moore's when I was in from the country, going on to the Broadway Theatre and witnessing that same outpouring from an ordinary, any-night audience. But there is one letter, surely the most touching of all he received, that makes me very sad, as it must have made him very sad, the letter Cousin Alice Miller, dying of cancer, sent from her room at Roosevelt Hospital. "Dear Irving," she wrote, "I cried when I read the *Tribune* review, and that was not illness or senile decay, but delight at seeing in print such an estimate of you as those who love you have always held. You have stepped into your rightful position in public esteem, and you have done it by going quietly about your own business doing what you felt was right. . . . I am getting well in order to see the show." "Dear Alice, I can't tell you how deeply touched I was by that sweet note," my father replied. "I would rather get that from you than anybody I know. Just as soon as you are well enough I want you to see the show."

She never made it to the theater. She left the hospital in late July and died at home a few weeks later. "I saw [Alice] about a week before she died," my father wrote their mutual friend Harry Ruby, "and all she would talk about was the Army Show. She knew, of course, that she was going to die and I had the feeling she was trying to keep my mind off that. It was so like Alice. Ellin has taken it quite hard and last night when I tried to comfort her, she said, 'I feel very peculiar and the only one I can talk it over with is Alice.' "

The death of Cousin Alice, like the death of my grandfather, stayed in my mind always. I remember my heartbroken mother afterward, in Lew Beach, going off for long walks alone, closing herself into her cottage, sobbing behind the shut door, so Tenny would report, howling like a child, but in company incapable of sharing her grief, translating grief into unnecessary nagging that for once I understood and forgave.

Then cousin Alice's death was pushed aside, into the place where my mother kept her sorrows. At summer's end she was in Washington, D.C., where *This Is the Army,* now launched on a national tour, had had another roof-raising opening. There had been a cast party at the White House; on another night my parents dined alone with just the president and Harry and Louise Hopkins. My father had lunched at the Senate, where Sen. Alben Barkley made a speech about him. "Irving is having a wonderful time," my mother wrote Woollcott from the Willard Hotel. "He is getting through this show the rewards of all the shows and all the years."

She was getting them, too, of course, though she would say to anyone who cared to listen, including her daughters, that her real reward was simpler: It was being married to him—for nearly seventeen years now it had lasted, the marriage the world said couldn't last a year—still enjoying herself with the man she had fallen for, if not at first, then at second or third sight, shamelessly chased and finally caught.

As for me, my parents' oldest child, I saw that he had done it again, this amazing Mr. Berlin who most of the time was simply a parent, less annoying, more charming and straightforward than most, the father I loved.

Four months later, in January 1943, Alexander Woollcott, Cousin Alice's best friend, my father's biographer and good comrade since his bachelor days, died of a stroke: another loss in a year of losses. (Max Winslow had died in June, George M. Cohan in November.) I realize I have come far without a memory of this famous Woollcott, so dear to both my parents. But he was never around that much. He didn't come to Lew Beach or, that I remember, to family dinner in town. It is my guess, though he was named my sister Elizabeth's godfather, that he didn't much like children. Certainly I was never invited to accompany my parents on their visits to "the Island," his Vermont retreat. My clearest memory of Woollcott (aside from his books, which I enjoyed) was of a plump, double-chinned, rather haughty man in a dressing gown who wandered into Cousin Alice's library when I was there for lunch (he lived in the adjacent apartment); he'd address a few words to me, say what he'd come to say to Cousin Alice, who adored him, and depart.

So it was revealing and poignant, all these years later, to come upon my father's words on the subject in a letter to Irving Hoffman, the Broadway columnist: "I was really depressed by Alec's death, though I have been prepared for it for many months," he wrote. "Dr. Gus Eckstein . . . one of Alec's oldest friends . . . told me that it was only a question of time because Woollcott wouldn't stop being himself and Eckstein thought it was just as it should be. I thought some of the obituaries were a little mean, though it was all made up for by Frank Sullivan's kindly and sympathetic piece. I never really thought that Alec was as cold-blooded a person as his reputation made him out to be. . . . He did brush aside many things he didn't want to do that most of us let ourselves in for because it's the easiest way, but I know of so many times when he put himself out to be kind and gentle and considerate that it seems unfair to me to see the emphasis put on the mean side of his character. . . ."

27 _____

NOW, FOR LONG STRETCHES of time, he is going out of sight, my wartime father, out of reach. Direct memory gives way to stories and latter-day discoveries; to a search long after the fact for the reality of those years that he would indicate later were the most exciting, the most valuable, the most extraordinary of his life, that were the great divide . . . before . . . after.

I experience little or nothing firsthand of what happened once the show left New York. There was a flurry of excitement, Christmas of 1942, when my mother, sisters, and I, our wartime priorities clutched in our hands, boarded the train, crowded with "cute" servicemen ("Keep moving, dear, no talking to strangers, dear . . . *dear*"), to meet our touring father in Detroit. A few more days of being in the thick of things. A photographer snapping us in our suite at the Book-Cadillac, with our hotel Christmas tree, for next year's card, my mother said, but also for the Detroit papers, permissible publicity considering the cause. Backstage meeting some of the "boys" my father was close to: Sgt. Alan Anderson, his stage manager; Cpl. Milton Rosenstock, the conductor; Pvt. Robert Sidney, the choreographer; Sgt. Carl Fisher, the business manager; Pvt. Julie Oshins, the comedian; and the company member, Sgt. Ezra Stone, with whom he had been close and was no longer, for reasons never discussed. ("We had a falling out," my father said later, and changed the subject. Whatever his fights, my father was tight-lipped about them, which is perhaps why, in many cases, though not Ezra Stone's, they were later made up.)

Everywhere now at the side of "Mr. B" was Cpl. (later Warrant Officer) Ben Washer, publicist of *This Is the Army*, the new Benny Bloom in his life, pleasant in manner and looks, savvy, keeping my father organized, handling travel plans, tickets, schedules, communiqués from the War Department. New names, hard to keep straight, punctuated their conversation: Major General Phillipson, head of Army Emergency Relief; Major General Surles, public relations director of the War Department; Col. Frank McCarthy, aide to General Marshall. There were constant reminders that those soldier-actors performing nightly were a "division"—the only fully integrated division in the U.S. Army. They marched in formation to and from railroad stations; they stood reveille every morning and drilled in their spare time. And despite this holiday hotel suite, my civilian father took orders like the rest.

Then we were boarding the train back to New York, and on my mind were parties where I would dance with my beau, a Yale freshman, so baby-faced and wholesome my mother actually allowed me (properly chaperoned, of course) to attend football weekends in his company. And everywhere I went they'd be playing—as if *This Is the Army* weren't enough—the country's number one tune, "White Christmas," not only the instant property of homesick servicemen across the seas, but a song boys and girls on the home front danced to, fell in love to, adopted as "their" song. However seasonal the words, we didn't hear it as a Christmas carol, we heard it as a ballad that Bing Crosby had sung to a blonde in a movie. The song sneaked up on your feelings, with a special meaning for me. Hearing it, I smiled to myself, thinking I had a secret, as if everyone, everywhere, by this time didn't know exactly whose daughter I was. As if I didn't know they knew—which was another side to this shiny coin. With "White Christmas," reinforced by my sixteenth birthday, came the realization, dim at first, gradually strengthening, that as gratifying as it was to see that flash of interest in others' eyes when they were told who I "was," there was a price for a teenager, a question for the child of a celebrity. Would I ever be liked, respected, and found interesting on my own?

To my mother's "pure velvet" was being added, little by little, another, somewhat more realistic truism: "There are no free lunches." My father, long accustomed to fame, if never quite at ease with it, always minimized it, pushing it aside. Somehow he got out of its way. He was disturbed by the thought that his children could not always do the same. And so, as best I could, I kept those conflicts—celebrity's daughter *vs.* normal teenager—to myself, unlike others of a more domestic nature that were part of anyone's growing up: the desire of parents to protect and control, the desire of children to try their wings.

After a few more weeks on the road, my father went to Hollywood, to turn *This Is the Army* into a movie. No mere transcription of the stage revue but a sentimental story of father (George Murphy, the future senator) and son (Ronald Reagan, the future president) and two world wars, with chunks of the show scattered throughout. However disappointing to the fans of the original, the picture was a major hit at the box office in the summer of 1943, part of the snowballing *This Is the Army* excitement. Later, even my father would call it "one more big musical movie," important mainly for the whopping $8 million it made for Army Emergency Relief but nothing to compare to the live show, which at summer's end he took overseas.

And so Irving Berlin, at fifty-six, joined that adventurous band of entertainers circling a world at war, thousands of them, from the smallest pickup USO troupe to the great stars—Al Jolson, Bob Hope, Jascha Heifetz, Martha Raye, Frances Langford, Marlene Dietrich, and Katharine Cornell touring the battlefronts with *The Barretts of Wimpole Street.* But nobody yet had taken a complete Broadway musical on that rough, heroic road.

During this period, I remember my father returned less and less frequently to Lew Beach or our new city apartment on Gracie Square. Our wartime home was a third the size of the old one, suitable to the new circumstances of the head of the house earning no money whatsoever from his all-consuming enterprise, not even taking expenses. He was the one who briefly livened the atmosphere in the all-female household, though he exasperated my mother by using up a week's butter ration in a single midnight feast and upset me, who also spent a lot of time at the icebox, by saying if I didn't watch out I'd look like a *tanta* (puffing out his cheeks in case I didn't know what a *tanta* was—in Yiddish, a big fat woman). He annoyed me further by agreeing with my mother (when did he ever not?) that no, I couldn't take a summer job in New York working for the USO or on a farm picking fruit for the boys overseas—co-ed, adventurous jobs to make me a worthy daughter of the creator of *This Is the Army*. But he'd be delighted if I took that just-as-worthy job at a convalescent home for underprivileged boys (no one in the ward over eleven) in Chappaqua, New York—which was what I did, earning so much parental praise via the mails for my ingenuity in handling my unruly charges that I had to forgive them both for not letting me do as I pleased. Besides, I was enjoying myself.

And then my father, one October afternoon in the fall of 1943, said goodbye to all of us—big hugs, no fuss now. And was off on an army plane to London, where bombs fell nightly, to open *This Is the Army* at the Palladium, then tour the British Isles. (The mission now was the improvement of Anglo-American relations and British morale; every cent earned at the box office, and from a new song, "My British Buddy," would go to British war charities.) The apartment felt empty without him. My mother put on a show for me and my sisters, a big smile to hide the anxiety that would be there till the day, after Europe, after the Southwest Pacific, when he came home for good. Only occasionally, in apology for being cranky once too often, would she admit it wasn't just being overtired from war work, running parties for Ship's Service, working as a Gray Lady at Halloran Hospital; it was fear. He needn't have gone. He was too old to have gone, she said, and too curious. That curiosity would get him in trouble, she knew her husband. Her mood was not improved by calls from Aunt Gussie saying she had had another dream that Irving was dead. Had Ellin heard from him? How did she *know* he was all right?

Then the stories began, the reassuring, amusing ones my mother told out of my father's or Ben Washer's letters or that my father related when he came home between tours of duty. Stories I listened to sometimes with half an ear, for I was involved in my own life. But when I did listen, the stories told me that even on his great odyssey he remained the character we had always known, whether having tea backstage with the king and queen of England and the little princesses (who, according to the tabloids, wanted to meet their favorite songwriter) or lunching with Winston Churchill (who did or did not mistake him for Isaiah Berlin, depending on who told the story); whether greeting in bombed-out Bristol the queen mother—Queen Mary—who pleased him by asking for an autographed copy of the score, or visiting Tenny's mother outside of Glasgow, bearing gifts from New York, or in Dublin spending the day with his old friend John McCormack, the Irish Caruso whose records of "Always" and "Remember" had been all-time best-sellers for Victor records when phonographs were still Victrolas. A favorite story concerned an Irish rabbi. Everywhere my father went, he met with a representative of the local Jewish community and listened to complaints—till he got to Belfast, where a rabbi, asked by Mr. Berlin if there was a Jewish problem, answered in a thick brogue, "Ah, no, there are only three hundred Jewish souls here, but we have a big job patchin' things up between the Catholics and the Protestants."

And then, back in London, Eisenhower came to the show, breaking his rule of no theater in wartime, went backstage, and told the company he was recommending that they be sent to the front to play for their fellow soldiers.

So next there were the stories of my father in Italy, still jolly but with a subtext furnished by the headlines that gave my mother increasing concern. He opened the show at the San Carlo, one of the few structures standing whole in ruined Naples—imagine, he wrote my mother, *This Is the Army* on the stage of the second greatest opera house in the world where Caruso made his debut* and out front, in that magnificent gold-and-crimson hall, were more soldiers, nothing but soldiers trucked in from the front just north of Caserta. And then they moved up front themselves, to the little town nobody had ever heard of, Santa Maria, where the show played for the men of the Fifth Army most of the spring of 1944. My father made it seem like an oasis. He mentioned nothing about the sounds of war coming up the valley, the land mines, the nightly air raids and strafings. Instead, he wrote about the great apartment

*In fact, Caruso made his debut at the *other* Naples opera house.

he shared with Ben Washer, with its sunny balcony, its fine piano; the doting landlady Signora Polito, who cooked delicious spaghetti, the landlady's eccentric relatives, a home away from home. "If you and the children were here it wouldn't be hard to take at all," my father wrote. "Of course [that's] only one side of it," he added. But of the other side, what those men trucked in to see the show were returning to, who exactly those men were in the front-line hospitals where he entertained every other morning, he wrote only sparely and talked about, when he came home, almost not at all.

Then on to Rome, a week after the city fell to the Allies: the Rome opera house, the royal suite at the Excelsior Hotel, recently vacated by the Germans. And I'll never forget the audience-with-the-pope story: how my father, by a half hour early for his morning appointment, sat with others in a Vatican waiting room, not even noticing that His Holiness had walked through the room, giving a blessing. When a monsignor asked him to leave now with the rest, my father said, "But I have an audience with the pope." "You've had your audience," said the monsignor. "I believe I have a private audience," said my father. "Nobody gets to see the pope twice in one day," said the monsignor, as the little man in khaki was motioned into the pope's private chambers. And so Pope Pius XII told Irving Berlin of his visit to Harbor Hill in the 1930s as Cardinal Pacelli and blessed the rosaries my father had brought for Finny and my mother. But the real reason my father had requested an audience was as a Jew, to thank the pope for all he had done on behalf of "my people" in Italy. "Some of the stories of his help are amazing," my father wrote my mother at the time, and never listened when later a different kind of story about Pope Pius was told, that his Holiness had sympathized with the Germans and closed his eyes to the Holocaust.

But nothing from those months, I have to admit, made such an impression on my teenage mind as a news photograph of my father sitting on a rock with Marlene Dietrich "somewhere in Italy," which made it to the pages of *Time*, got him in some trouble with his wife, and subjected me to much teasing by my friends, especially the junior Henry Luce, who asked what my father was doing in his father's magazine sitting on an Italian hillside side by side with Marlene, gorgeous even in her trouper's fatigues.

Such colorful encounters, so fixed in my youthful memory, are obviously not the whole picture. Now, reading the diary Ben Washer kept in Italy and the notes of Maj. Jock Lawrence, on special "Irving Berlin" detail in London, not to mention my father's own letters, I have a clearer view. The nonstop days and nights, the shows, two a day, six days a week, the hospital appearances, the officers' club and Red Cross shows, the broadcasts, the social demands, as many in the field as in the cities of Great Britain; the command lunches and dinners with Field Marshal Alexander, Gen. Mark Clark, Field Marshal Wilson, Lieutenant General Eaker; the evenings with the middle brass, the officers in Special Services, and the morale-boosting meals with members of the company. And all the day-to-day business, the meetings of the "committee," the eight-man *This Is the Army* inner circle that ran things, the arrangements for the men's housing, food, transportation, and general well-being, the rehearsals to make sure the show kept fresh and alive, the new songs being written and added to suit the occasion, some fifteen in all, the flights in noncombatant crates, the jeep rides to frontline hospitals, the air raids, the constant movement that had my mother frantic back home, although it was always framed in reassuring terms. "Please don't worry about my safety," he wrote. "I couldn't be further away from harm." And then she'd hear from Ben about his wandering off in Algiers, en route to Naples, lost in the souks, just looking for a cup of coffee; or about his joyride in a P-38, taking off with a wild-man pilot from a mountain road nearly straight up, the loop-the-loops, barrel rolls, a power dive: Irving Berlin as Gary Cooper, as Harold Lloyd.

Nor were the honors along the way dwelt on—the praise heaped upon my father and the men of the company, the letters and official commendations from the British, from the American generals at home and in the field—Marshall, Phillipson, Eisenhower, Bradley, Devers, Mark Clark; and later, in the final part of the tour, from every base commander encountered in the Southwest Pacific, stacked up now in my father's files. Though the "test for the long pull" he would say later, was what the GIs were writing home, the things he'd hear from the officers who censored the mail.

And then there was the letter my mother received about the single civilian performance of the Italian tour, a benefit for Rome's orphaned children, that ended with songs requested by the crowd—"Always," "Cheek to Cheek," "Alexander's Ragtime Band." "It was a difficult audience and a critical one," wrote Lydia di San Faustino, daughter-in-law of the late Princess Jane di San Faustino, my parents' friend from Venice in the old days. "It had been and still was *deeply* suffering under the knowledge of the futility and shape of the struggle it had made, and the bitter tears and losses. . . . Then Irving came on, a simple doughboy such as the Italians had fought side by side with in the last war. He *didn't* preach and he didn't promise, he simply stood and sang the old songs he was asked for. He didn't talk down to the Italians, he simply made them feel the heart of America. . . . Then he did the one *perfect* gesture. He told [them] he wanted to sing them the song he'd learned from Italian children when he was a boy, 'Oi Marie.' The audience *roared!* . . . I knew that America could send no more perfect ambassador."

(The story behind the story, as my father would report privately afterward, was that he had planned from the start to sing "Oi Marie" to that particular audience—that the real meaning of the "perfect gesture" was to hear all those well-dressed, upper-class people, Fascists among them, singing this song of the streets as if it were the Italian national anthem.)

The day after the benefit was the final Rome performance, the final show for the men of the Fifth Army before the company headed over to Foggia and Bari to play for the air corps. One last time Mr. B sang "The Fifth Army's Where My Heart Is," the rough-toned, affectionate comedy song he had written in Naples, and the Fifth Army returned the compliment without jest, presenting the *This Is the Army* detachment with the official Fifth Army Plaque and Clasp "for exceptionally meritorious service during April, May, and June 1944," the months of Anzio and Cassino.

Many years later, in the winter of 1990, a few months after my father died, I went with my husband to Italy, to the places the army show had played. It was not my first trip to that part of the world, but my first on such a pilgrimage, looking for my wartime father.

If I found him, caught for an instant a ghostly presence, it was not in Naples or Rome, in the flashy, famous, familiar towns, but in Santa Maria (once the ancient Roman town of Capua) and even more unexpectedly, in backwater Foggia, places I had never been before.

There, at the heart of Santa Maria di Capua Vetere's *cèntro stòrico*, stood the provincial opera house where the show had played, the Teatro Garibaldi, instantly recognizable from a 1944 news photograph in one of my father's scrapbooks, with its balconied facade, its busts of composers—Rossini, Bellini, Pergolesi—and the GIs lined up in front of this same theater, waiting to get tickets for *This Is the Army*.

When I looked out from the opera house balcony, the old geography was clear: within the sprawl of modern buildings, a charming dusty rose and yellow town, its narrow streets cobbled, its houses balconied and shuttered like the house (address unknown) in the photograph of my father and Signora Polito. It is a soft, worn, painted view of a place an artist or writer might have settled into long ago, off the main drag, with a café life. There was also a park with a bandstand and beyond, a line of beckoning blue mountains. I could picture my father somewhere in the view, on his balcony in bathing trunks, writing my mother in his black scrawl: "My Italian neighbors are singing—each a different tune from some opera and I feel like Grace Moore in her movie 'One Night of Love' when they all become part of her singing lesson only my boss is 'Mama' who is struggling in the very clean kitchen trying to toast some bread over an improvised contraption placed on the stove while Grace's boss was Harry Cohn reading her contract in his office." And again: "If it weren't for the swell job that is being done here, I would feel a little ashamed to have such comfort and food."

And I remember that those blue mountains are the Apennines, where, in May 1944, the Germans held the line and the Allies pushed toward Rome and where the bloodiest fighting of the Italian campaign began. Just eight miles from the front, an hour's jeep ride from Santa Maria, were those field hospitals where my father went every other morning, the part of the job "most satisfying for me," he wrote my mother. "The shows are mostly outdoors on an improvised platform . . . the stunt lasts about a half hour and is very informal and different every time. It's all ad lib and sometimes when the mike is good I play for myself." The grimmer aspects are only in Ben Washer's notes: singing in the midst of stretchers, visiting the amputation wards, taking down the name and address, faintly whispered, of a dying soldier's wife, to be written as promised.

That's one side of my father that is suddenly real to me. A man with other men, doing what was called back then "a man's job," a man his wife and three daughters would never truly know.

But over in out-of-the-way Apulia, in circumstances quirky yet typical, a more familiar character appeared.

I was following up my father's reference, in a V-mail note to my mother, to "a visit to one of your cousins, John something. . . . He lives close to a famous monastery. . . . I spent some time with the priest there. It was very interesting. You will know who he is when I tell you about it." Ben Washer's notes elaborated. The priest was Father Pio, the Franciscan peasant world-famous for having received the stigmata, an object of veneration and pilgrimage for years. The monastery, some twenty miles out of Foggia, was in the small town of San Giovanni Rotondo, and the cousin, a devotee of Father Pio's, was an eccentric Italian nobleman who had married "out of his social strata."

At the monastery, tripled in size, it seems, since 1944, heart of a large settlement devoted to Father Pio's memory, a burly, genial English-speaking monk, one Father Joseph from Brooklyn, was excited to learn that Irving Berlin had once paid a visit. Making me feel less on a fool's errand, he said he knew all about my mother's cousin John "something" who had to be Count Gianni Telfner, a founder and administrator of the Padre Pio hospital, the region's finest. Of course: one of our Italian relatives, a grandson of Marie Louise Mackay's sister Ada. Gianni's widow, the contessa, the monk added, lived right down that street in a charming yellow villa.

She remembered Irving well, said Contessa Caterina, who once long ago had been a beautiful young milkmaid on the Telfner Tuscany estate and was still, at seventy, in black and pearls, an exceptionally pretty, gracious woman. "Intelligent" was her first impression of this family connection dropped down into their wartime lives; then "handsome . . . sympathetic." "Irving talked with Gianni about the family and about music," she said. "Gianni loved the opera and afterwards Irving sent him records." She remembered the visitor making the point that he was not a Catholic—he wanted to be clear on that—but would of course be interested to meet Gianni's friend the famous monk. And Gianni saying of Ellin's Jewish husband, though not in his hearing, "He may not be a Catholic, but he is a good Christian."

But what on earth did they talk about, in a whitewashed monastery parlor, with a chaplain interpreting, my agnostic Jewish father and the bearded peasant in his cassock, with the burning eyes and big hands, gloved to hide his wounds? It was something friendly, certainly, for at the visit's end Father Pio kissed Irving Berlin on both cheeks and blessed his journey home.

The answer would come back in New York, where mysterious snapshots in the file marked "Italy" suddenly made sense. That unidentified bearded man was Father Pio. And what my father, grinning broadly, showing him a copy of *Time* magazine, was talking about was my mother's book.

The whole time he was overseas, my father had been writing my mother about *Land I Have Chosen*. Published in June 1944, it became an event back home, something to celebrate. It was a tale one sat up half the night finishing, about two women who change places, a German actress who chooses America, a Southampton girl who chooses Nazi Germany. From Santa Maria my father had written and fussed about a front-page story in *Variety* on her $150,000 movie sale (a deal he personally negotiated on a flying trip between England and Italy). From Rome he commiserated over a bad notice in the *New York Times*. "You hit hard in what you have to say and many people won't like it. . . . The subject is dynamite and you always knew that, but that is what makes your novel important." A fortnight later, "I saw the *Time* review . . . and it certainly should make up for any disappointment you had in the N.Y. Times review. It's a wonderful notice as *Time* does not go in for log rolling or being soft."

Thus, he is showing the saintly monk (whatever serious talk may have preceded) the *Time* review and the photograph of his wife, Gianni Telfner's cousin. That is my mother's devoted and ever curious husband, on a day off, in a far-flung Mackay outpost in the middle of a war.

And then from Bari in late July came his last letter from

Italy: "Playing for the Air Corps is thrilling and they can't do enough for us . . . the characters for your [next] book sound swell but I would take my time if I were you. It's blistering hot here but I brave it every day so I can come home with a healthy tan."

I have never budged from my generation's conviction that World War II was necessary, "the last good war" (a curious phrase). But one has to put on the old blinders, step back into the time of the clear enemy, the clear end, however brutal, however wasteful of lives, the means—into the skin of that civilian Mr. Berlin, consumed with patriotism, who, though scarcely warlike himself, could nonetheless be observed by Ben Washer, at dinner with General Alexander, having a "fine time in conversation analyzing game of war as analogous to song-writing game."

Afterward my father made no pretense: He loved the U.S. Army, the "boys," the officers, the esprit de corps, the determination to "get a tough job done." And he would continue to love the army right up to the night when, at age eighty-five, in the spring of Watergate, he sang "God Bless America" for the returning Vietnam POWs, at Nixon's White House with the beleaguered president chiming in. It was the last public appearance of his life.

_____ 28

I C A N   S E E   H I M still at the Lew Beach dinner table, just back from Italy, his deep tan camouflaging the weariness. He is animated with his stories, his souvenirs. But I knew, watching him walk up the path to the cottage with my mother, that this was a man badly in need of a break. And that's about all I knew, because no more than a few days later he left the country for town to tend to "business," very complicated business that he did not want to discuss, concerning Saul Bornstein and the office. Then, after some weeks in New York, he left for Hollywood, and after a few more weeks for Milne Bay, to rejoin the company.

For those of us back home, the time in New Guinea, the

Admiralty Islands, and the Philippines was the hardest to grasp, out of reach even in the imagination: the jungle, the equatorial heat, the proximity of the fighting, the ruggedness of one-night stands in remote outposts on makeshift outdoor stages; the shows played in tropical downpours in front of the huge audiences. As the skeptical commander of one remote base in the Admiralties wrote in his letter of commendation, "The idea, the effort, the expense, in short everything connected with sending a show of [this] size to the South West Pacific was not alone to me preposterous—that it had been done was stupid—till I saw the show. . . . May I take this opportunity to thank those who had the courage to send *This Is the Army* to this theater. . . ."

The stories were of a different order: my slugabed father up at 6:00 A.M. for breakfast in the mess after a bad night under inadequate mosquito netting; en route to Milne Bay singing "White Christmas" with a group of soldiers on Christmas Eve in a Red Cross canteen in Hollandia, the songwriter not in Beverly Hills, L.A. but in that South Seas scene he had heard about so often; improvising a new staging for "God Bless America," now the show's finale, dousing the stage lights, asking the men out front to light their lighters or matches ("to see an audience of 17,000 light up like so many flickering stars would even impress Hassard Short," he wrote my mother. "Every new place we played I told you was the most thrilling . . . well this is really it"); writing still another finale for the Leyte opening, "Heaven Watch the Philippines" because he had heard the Filipinos singing "God Bless the Philippines" to the tune of "God Bless America"; a hundred schoolchildren joining the soldiers onstage—"I can't tell you how thrilling [it] was."

"Thrilling" was a word we'd hear a lot after my father came home, about this performance or that; he would speak with emotion of "the boys," the ones in the show, the ones in the audience. As for himself, he had done a job, the most exciting of his life, at an age when most men stayed home. He was the one who should be doing the thanking: thanking the U.S. government for making it possible for him to be part of it all. Only to my mother did he express his real feelings. "I feel . . . I will have done a harder and better job here than anywhere else," he wrote her during the Pacific tour. And again, "The show continues to tremendous audiences—at different bases and of course different theatres. This is tough on the boys but the result is terrific. . . . I have come in for much personal praise and attention. I wouldn't say this to anyone but you, but I am greatly pleased with the dividends here." And finally, at the end: "I'm not tired any longer, I'm simply numb. . . . The past three years, between T.I.T.A. and Bornstein has taken a lot out of me. Just being three years older is something [but] all of it has been worthwhile and I really believe that apart from any personal glory or satisfaction—it's good for the children. That may be conceit on my part—so I would never say it to anyone else—certainly not to the children. . . . Of course I'm not fooled. Things are only important to the one most interested. And outside of you and a few others, my doings are mostly mine—to crow over or be stuck with."

So there was another subtext to the story of those triumphant years . . . *Bornstein* . . . the brushed aside, darkly colored name, the weight my father carried around with him the whole time of *This Is the Army*, there in my memory always, the Bornstein affair, but never before precisely dated.

The situation is set out starkly in a letter my father wrote Maj. Jock Lawrence, his number-one army contact since London, explaining why, after Italy, he must take time off from the show. "As you probably know I have tried to split with my music publishing partner for the past two years and hoped to do so when I went home [between England and Italy]. I not alone wasn't able to get anywhere with him, but I left my affairs in serious condition. The copyrights of all my songs are involved."

The copyright question—did Irving Berlin personally own his songs, or did the firm—was the core of a many-layered fight between two partners, one of whom had run the business (basically very successfully), while the other devoted himself to the creative end and didn't keep his eye on the shop. The relationship (as described by my father in a lengthy memo to his lawyer George Cohen), troubled since the mid-1930s, had become a "dog fight" over "God Bless America" ("he didn't mind my giving my royalties away but objected to the lost publisher's revenue") and a full-scale battle over *This Is the Army* for the same reason. The immediate battles brought to the surface the underlying battle: Was Irving

Berlin free to split with Irving Berlin Inc. and take his incalculably valuable songs with him?

In September 1944, after a final month of threats and counterthreats, an agreement was signed. My father kept his songs, free and clear, his publisher's name and the privilege to give away royalties and publisher's revenues as he saw fit. Bornstein got the rest of the company catalog, all those great standards and the Disney scores, plus $400,000, and became Bourne Inc. In December, Irving Berlin Inc., now Irving Berlin Music Company, moved a few blocks north into new Broadway offices; the style, the confusion, unchanged; nothing really changed. My father would continue to publish other people's songs, I was told (though this would stop after the war), and if he didn't, he had enough songs of his own, well over eight hundred, to keep a publishing company busy overtime.

I remember a moment's pang when the announcement was made, losing all those old sheet-music friends, a pang I knew was childish and not to be expressed, for my father got a bad look on his face when anything to do with Bornstein came up. He dismissed it. It was a battle finished, a divorce he had wanted. That was that. But, like any divorce, the process was traumatic, causing my father to say, in the period before he went back overseas, for no apparent reason that I could see, that he felt very old all of a sudden.

And then, one spring weekend, my father came back from the Pacific, a family milestone I remember too sharply for reasons having nothing to do with this joyful homecoming. We are down from the heights now, back to ordinary life, and I am facing, with his return, a reckoning.

A reckoning because not once, since a long letter to England and a short note to Italy enclosing my final Brearley report, however proud I may have been of him, have I written my absent father. My mother wrote almost daily. Linda and Elizabeth were sat down once a week and made to write, and how those letters cheered him up, my father would write in return. But I was too old to be "made" to write. I was asked, no doubt, if I had, and I am afraid I answered yes even if I hadn't. Because I would, of course, though I was frightfully busy in the spring, with senior year and graduation, earning that final report that prompted a wire of congratulations from Rome. And even busier the following winter as a Bryn Mawr freshman who, though not a "Debutante"—my mother made that clear to everyone—still went to the wartime deb parties, the Allied Flag Ball and the superstuffy Junior Assemblies, just like my mother before me. Procrastinating, procrastinating, and then, having waited so long, embarrassed to put pen to paper.

So I relive the scene at 1 Gracie Square: my mother and my just-returned father in the library, which doubles as his bedroom, deep in conversation. He greets me warmly; my heart gives a joyful bound at the sight of him. We hug each other, I ducking my head a little. Then I present him with two letters, "found," I say, in my desk drawer, never mailed. A quizzical look as he takes those proffered envelopes. "Fine, fine, it's all right," he says. "Your sisters wrote. I'm glad to see you, Mary Ellin." A hand on my arm, hard. "Now tell me about yourself."

I felt very small all of a sudden, and then it was finished. It wasn't important. Even from my mother there was only modified irony, as if, for once, thoughtlessness, really quite callous behavior, from a supposedly devoted daughter didn't matter. It didn't matter even that she probably guessed that those two letters had been written by a trapped rat within the past twenty-four hours (the beginning of my own career: writing fiction). What mattered, and all that mattered, was that her husband was home safe at last. And to me, I had to admit, as well.

Less than a week later, back at college, taking the sun on a Bryn Mawr lawn, I heard the news shouted from a window: *The president is dead . . . President Roosevelt is dead.* When I talked on the phone to my parents, there was shock in their voices. A few months earlier, my mother had stayed overnight in the White House, had written my father a note on White House stationery: "Look where I am! This is really exciting—but not fun because I haven't you." My father responded, "Who has a better right? No one has worked harder for the President nor longer." Now "their" president was gone. "Our" president was gone, the only one I'd ever known. Never again in the family, between the generations, would there be such political unity, such perfect clarity. But then clear days in general were coming to an end. The postwar was about to begin.

PART SEVEN

BRIGHT DAYS
BEFORE
A FALL

In the sun in Palm Springs, after the war.

29

AFTERWARD I WOULD always think of the summer of 1945 as the first great postwar summer, though the war didn't end till August, though the young men passing through our house in Beverly Hills were still in uniform, waiting to be shipped out to the Pacific, where the Japanese were fighting suicidally on.

But my father was home, working on an old-fashioned, before-the-war-style Bing Crosby musical, *Blue Skies.* In appearance at least, he was none the worse for wear, though too thin, his face under the jet-black hair deeply creased. He wore glasses a lot of the time now, but if anything, the glasses made him look younger, covering the circles under his eyes.

We were sprung from the quiet of Lew Beach; I was sprung from my job at the convalescent home to go to California. For the first time in eight years we were back there, a paradise still: the landscape, the air, the rainbow colors by day, the purple night skies over the Hollywood Bowl. There were more lessons with Mr. Steuermann, my favorite piano teacher, and a surge of music, classical and popular, everything enhanced by the return of my father, Mr. Music himself; having him hear how good I had become on the piano, hearing him play his new song for the movie. "From out of the past, / Where forgotten things belong, / You keep coming back like a song," he sang in his true, wispy voice, and I knew my own father was really home with this twilight, thirties-style ballad—one of those songs about songs that were his signature.

Part of him, of course, was still overseas. All summer he would be writing the "boys" he left behind in the Pacific—Carl Fisher, Milton Rosenstock, Alan Anderson, and people in Washington—about getting his "boys" promotions, home leave, discharges, or reassignments, about winding up the show and the possibility of his rejoining the company for a final performance in 227

Honolulu. That he was having a hard time winding down was not apparent, however, except in conversations I'd hear between him and other men, the exchange of war stories that I found boring, not having been there, not knowing, not really understanding. As far as I could tell, he was back with the family, making up for lost time, catching up with my sisters, not such little girls anymore, and figuring out how to deal with an eighteen-year-old (myself) loose in Hollywood. Unfortunately, he had not just one but two eighteen-year-olds; my cousin Katherine O'Brien, something of a lost child since Aunt K's remarriage, was spending the summer with us. It was easy enough to find a few approved playmates for Elizabeth, nine; still possible with Linda, thirteen. But how on earth were my parents to keep us grown-up girls, with our new privileges (nightclubs, later curfews, permission to drink "non-hard" liquor), from going Hollywood, losing our silly brunet and blond heads over the wrong boys, the wrong set.

Things got off to a shaky start, with my father taking us to dinner at Romanoff's, where we were joined by Pat di Cicco, the agent, former husband of Gloria Vanderbilt, and his current girl-friend, Gussie Moran, the tennis player, instantly recognizable in a skintight red sweater. Moving on to Mocambo's, Katherine and I danced not only with my father but with Pat, who, though old, forty at least, and not much to look at, was quite a dancer. On the way home I pronounced him "very nice and so attractive"; my father shuddered but thought it a joke; the next day, my mother shuddered and did not think it a joke, nor did she laugh when Pat di Cicco telephoned, suggesting another "family" evening.

Next, my parents' friend George Cukor volunteered to find "the girls" more suitable action, providing a navy ensign and army lieutenant, both sleek as juvenile leads, to take us dancing. We were disappointed not to hear from them again, and my mother refrained from sharing her suspicion that these particular young men in uniform would not be interested in us or any other young ladies, beyond doing George a favor.

No matter. George had more to offer including his houseguest Somerset Maugham, who became a regular at our house for dinner. He took his place alongside Uncle Joe, the Astaires, the Levants, the Goldwyns, the Capras, Robert Riskin, the screenwriter, and his wife, Fay Wray (that rarity, my mother said, a movie actress who "seemed real"), Madeline and Bob Sherwood (in town writing *The Best Years of Our Lives*). The great Maugham, instantly recognizable from book jackets with his look of a wise turtle, at the height of his fame, was not above talking to a young person. He let me discuss my favorite Maugham novels, *Cakes and Ale* and *The Moon and Sixpence,* and he answered good-humoredly questions about the meaning of *The Razor's Edge,* being filmed that summer. One evening after dinner, though already in his seventies, he lay flat on the floor, balanced a glass of water on his forehead, and rose to his feet without spilling a drop. "An old Indian trick," he explained when no one else, my father included, could do the same. At summer's end he presented me with a photograph of himself, inscribed "from a very old party to a very young party"—an endearing gesture from a wonderful storyteller who has gone undeservedly out of fashion.

So yes, my cousin and I were kept well occupied for a while, rubbing elbows with celebrities, tagging along with the grownups. Some of the celebrities, of course, were such familiars, you couldn't remember when they hadn't been around, that you hardly registered their presence, like "Mr. Astaire," who at least three nights a week, if not already at the house for dinner, would knock on our door afterward, an impish, smiling, balding man arrived to play gin rummy with my father. From an alcove off the living room, behind a fringed curtain, you would hear the slap of cards, the murmuring and occasional chuckle, the sudden shouts of "gin" or "you so-and-so." At other times we went to the Astaires' house and, before the men retreated to the card table, showed each other home movies; Elizabeth played with Fred, Jr., and little Ava, Linda and I struggled to "bring out" Phyllis Astaire's painfully shy sixteen-year-old son by her first marriage, Peter Potter; and the two pretty, prissy mothers exchanged cryptic humorous *tut-tut*s concerning the latest Hollywood foible or scandal.

Some encounters were less predictable, like the night Charlie Chaplin and his girl-bride Oona O'Neill turned up at the Goldwyns'.

I had never met the great Chaplin, though my father's acquaintance with him dated back to the mid-1920s, an occasion I heard about years later from that keeper of ancient lore, Helen

Hayes. How Alice Duer Miller had given a dinner to introduce Chaplin and Irving Berlin but Chaplin never showed up. As the guests were leaving Alice's apartment—Helen, Charlie MacArthur, Irving, and a furious Alexander Woollcott, sponsor of the evening— a taxi rolled up; out tumbled Chaplin begging everyone to forgive him and get in the cab. "We went to Irving's place," recalled Miss Hayes, "and those two geniuses set out to honor and impress each other. Charlie gave his interpretation of an actor doing the soliloquy from Hamlet, an actor in deep trouble, for he had picked his nose and had something on his finger he was trying to shake off, a lesson in pantomime. Then Irving went to the piano and sang a song in that high, gentle little voice. Then Charlie did another routine, then Irving a song, on and on till light began coming through the window. It was a night never to forget." The two geniuses had seen each other in Hollywood, throughout the thirties, at this gathering or that, though during the war (my memory now) my father's friendliness had cooled when Chaplin stayed put in California instead of going home to England. "What would I do there?" Chaplin had been heard to ask. "All he'd have to do," my father said, "was stand in the middle of Piccadilly Circus and say, 'I'm here.'"

On this night, though, in the summer of 1945, there seemed to be no stiffness. My father and Chaplin shook hands warmly. Chaplin gave me a smile, saying, "I remember this child when she was in her cradle." Meanwhile, I was being embraced by Oona, only two years ahead of me at Brearley, last seen in the school elevator, a blasé senior in a baggy green sweater, already a celebrity: not only Eugene O'Neill's daughter but the Stork Club's Glamour Girl of the Year. With his wavy gray hair, Chaplin seemed even older than my black-haired father (they were both fifty-seven); an old man married to a girl more or less my age. I did not see that he was a sexy, dangerous fellow. I was shocked, and even more so when, during the after-dinner movie, the two of them held hands and snuggled.

There was also tea with Katharine Hepburn and the disappointment when Spencer Tracy (somehow I knew about that) did not arrive and join us. Miss Hepburn, Bryn Mawr '28, asked me how I liked her alma mater. Instead of telling her the truth, "Not much," and why, which might have interested her, or at least stirred things up, I said it was wonderful. No Tracy, no fireworks, just another Hollywood tea party.

But meeting celebrities, and there were many around that summer, was not exactly the "action" my cousin and I craved. Living on the grounds of the Beverly Hills Hotel, we imagined adventure at every turn, on the palm-bordered tennis court, at the cabana-bordered pool, in the Polo Lounge, center even then of Hollywood deal making. And so, when the first of the suitable young men from the East appeared, he was greeted by Mr. and Mrs. Berlin with open arms. (My old buddy, Sammy Goldwyn, a tall, remarkably handsome army lieutenant, got a similar welcome from my parents, who did not realize he was driving me up Topanga Canyon and across the top of the Mulholland Drive at eighty miles per hour.)

"That famous California summer," one of those suitable young men, the writer Warren Leslie, would recall years later, "when your mother and father took us in, all the young men from New York on their way to the Pacific, navy ensigns, marine privates. I remember their marvelous easy hospitality, the way they fed us, housed us, introduced us quite casually to people we had never dreamed of meeting, and sent us off to the Strip with Jack MacKenzie behind the wheel to make sure we got home safely. I remember the bitter night when, a month's pay saved up, I took you to Ciro's. A month's pay barely took care of the cover charge, let alone dinner, and Jack had to be summoned from the parking lot to bail us out. I also remember our poor friend Mary Jo [my former Brearley classmate] with her bare-midriff dress and your father, concerned (we were going into dinner), saying, 'I wonder what is keeping Mary Jo,' and your mother saying, 'She is busy powdering her stomach.' It amazed me that such a sweet fragile-looking woman could have such a lethal tongue. And I remember your father as the master of the kindly put-down. One afternoon I told him about this obscure song of his I liked called 'When I Leave the World Behind.' I was excessive in my praise, the eighteen-year-old bypassing the obvious hits for something elusive. Your father told me very pleasantly the story of the song, then added, 'But I'll tell you, Warren, it really wasn't a very good song.' "

So Pat di Cicco and any number of unsuitable men-about-

Hollywood were held at bay by my parents, who kept young visitors on their toes without apparently losing any points.

Not everything that summer was so lighthearted—and certainly not *Blue Skies,* the reason for our being in Beverly Hills in the first place. The project seemed jinxed from the March day my father, still in the Pacific, received the shocking news that the movie's director, his longtime colleague Mark Sandrich, had died at forty-four of a heart attack. Then there was the matter of Mark's protégé, the glorious young blonde Joan Caulfield. The new director, Stuart Heisler, wanted her replaced; meanwhile, she and the married Bing Crosby had begun an affair. "We'll see about *that,*" said Bing, and she stayed. Then Paul Draper, the dancer, the third star, in his first bit of dialogue, could not get out the heroine's name—"M-M-M-M-Mary"—because of a disastrous stutter. Over a weekend, Draper was out and Fred Astaire (who had turned them down earlier) in: a brilliant save but "headaches," my father would say, an old word from before the war, "you can't imagine the headaches."

And behind the scenes: "My doctors tell me when I finish this picture I should take six months off, a complete rest," my father wrote George Cohen, his Hollywood lawyer. "But you know me, I'm better off keeping going." And he went on to describe his next project—a Broadway revue.

But that was not something I knew or thought about. Even my father's worsening insomnia was pushed aside. "How did you sleep, Uncle Irving?" my cousin Katherine would ask when he appeared midmorning. "Not a wink, Katie, not a wink," he would say in a manner calculated to make you laugh.

And then the war really was over. It was V-J Day: everyone stood by the radio, and the sounds began, all over Los Angeles, horns honking, bells ringing, and someone was shouting, "Come on, everybody's jumping into the swimming pool," and we ran down to watch the fun, though we were too timid or too well brought up to jump in ourselves. And there they were—starlets, businessmen, a waiter or two—splashing fully dressed about the spotlit pool, an image more appropriate to an Ernst Lubitsch comedy than the curtain raiser to Armageddon.

In our household, the full meaning of the events and images preceding V-J Day—the bomb, the second bomb, the fireball, the mushroom cloud, the dead and dying below—didn't quite sink in at first, horror lost in awe, in the sheer, crude excitement of having brought, with a dreadful world of the future weapon, the war to an end.

When it did sink in, when back in New York the subject suddenly escaped constraint and exploded at the family dinner table, it was the first crack in the old solidarity: My parents, however appalled by the death and destruction, lined up solidly behind Truman's decision, talking about the lives saved, the months, the years, of fighting avoided; I questioning, talking of the evil genie let out of the bottle; everyone getting disagreeable and then retreating, pushing discord back down.

At summer's end, General Marshall invited my father to Washington for a "meeting," the subject undisclosed. He was ushered into the chief of staff's office, and there, surprise, was my mother, along with two of the generals he had known overseas and his old friend Robert Sherwood. The "meeting," Marshall explained, was to present Irving Berlin, creator and driving force of *This Is the Army*, on behalf of President Truman, with the Medal for Merit "for the performance of extraordinary service to the United States Army."

"General Marshall really took a personal interest in giving this award, which touched me deeply," my father would write a friend afterward. But in the family I remember him being careful, as always, not to make too much of it. "Daddy's medal" was put away somewhere for safekeeping, not to be forgotten but not to be dwelt on, either. It wasn't an offhand thing on his part, like the couplet he had once written, and was fond of quoting, concerning awards in general, including the Academy Award he won for "White Christmas": "There goes Time with your last year's prize, / Whittling it down to its proper size." This prize and subsequent national honors were beyond time, beyond ordinary expressions of pride—the Congressional Gold Medal he received from Eisenhower in 1954 for "God Bless America," the one that perhaps meant the most, and the Presidential Medal of Freedom, the highest civilian award, which he received in January 1977 at the age of 88. But still he put them aside. That was the way he was: not necessarily the best way to be, as you got older, to wish you were still *doing* instead of being honored for past doings, long ago finished.

But in 1945, in his fifty-eighth year, already "no chicken," as he liked to put it, he was not so enamored of endless "doing," as was later implied or as I took for granted at the time. Earlier, from the Pacific, he had written my mother of an idea he had (soon abandoned) to write a book about his experience with the two army shows. And then: "Of course I will probably do nothing of the sort," he continued, "but crawl back into my shell and take up where I left off before T.I.T.A. came into my life. I seem to have lost a great deal of my self-consciousness. . . . Wouldn't it be awful if at my time of life I suddenly stepped out of character and shook off the inhibitions that shut out everything but songwriting. God forbid. It's too late I'm afraid. Besides I know too well what's best for me." Or, less ambiguously: "I am looking forward to the end of my end of *This Is the Army* and the beginning of a peaceful older age—after *Blue Skies* and the *Music Box Revue*."

The peaceful older age, as it turned out, would have to be postponed a while in favor of an irresistible offer.

30

IN THE FAMILY the saga of *Annie Get Your Gun* begins always with the sounds of "I'm an Indian Too" from behind my father's closed door at 1 Gracie Square. Then the door is flung open and nine-year-old Elizabeth, Indian names fresh in her mind from school, invited in to help with the lyric. What resulted was one of the musical's comic high spots and, as it turned out, one of the most perishable. But the author of "Cohen Owes Me Ninety-seven Dollars," "Abie Sings an Irish Song," "Yiddisha Nightingale," "Oh, How That German Could Love," "Colored Romeo," "When You Kiss an Italian Girl," "Latins Know How," etc., had always used ethnic material in his songs, and "I'm an Indian Too" seemed innocent enough in 1946. (After all, wasn't Chief Sitting Bull, Annie's adopted father, the show's real hero and the smartest of the lot?)

In reality, as anyone knows who has ever read anything about *Annie*, my father's part of the story began with yet another melancholy milestone, the death of Jerome Kern, his friend since 1912. Just arrived in New York to do the music for the new show Herbert and Dorothy Fields were writing for Ethel Merman, Kern suffered a cerebral hemorrhage on November 4, 1945, and died a week later. A day or so after the funeral, the musical's producers, Richard Rodgers and Oscar Hammerstein called on Irving Berlin, their first choice to replace Kern. Dorothy Fields had agreed, not too unhappily, to give up writing the lyrics. My father hesitated at first, not sure he should try to replace Jerome Kern, the man he honored most among the great American songwriters; not sure he wanted to give up his long-planned revue, known territory, for the kind of folkloric book musical he'd never tried before or return to Broadway with something that didn't have "Irving Berlin's whatever" at the top of the credits. He read the script, liked it, still wasn't sure he could write "hillbilly music" or music that developed a character, and over a weekend in Atlantic City tried some songs "on spec," so to speak. But he did *not* come back with the entire sixteen-song score or even most of it (a favorite myth); he came back with no less than three, maybe five, songs (the number varies according to the teller), the first always "Doin' What Comes Natur'lly" (so much for "hillbilly music"), then in no particular order "They Say It's Wonderful," "The Girl That I Marry," "You Can't Get a Man With a Gun" (so much for "character"), and "There's No Business Like Show Business" (so much for known territory, a song to rise above the immediate proceedings and become a species of anthem). Feat enough. Or as he might say, a good weekend's work.

The deal was signed. Along with waiving any special billing, my father insisted on splitting the author-songwriter royalties fifty-fifty with the Fieldses. (Normally, the split is a third each for book, music, and lyrics.) Things proceeded with remarkable speed and harmony. With the exception of two numbers, the score was finished two months later. The show went into rehearsal in March with baritone Ray Middleton, big, good-looking, the perfect Frank Butler for Merman's Annie and with a pair of lungs to match. The director was Josh Logan (who had staged *I Married an Angel* and

By Jupiter and done some last-minute work on *This Is the Army* before entering the army himself). The conductor was Jay Blackton, fresh from *Oklahoma!* and *Carousel,* who had no difficulty calling in at the last possible moment the genius arranger Robert Russell Bennett to redo all the orchestrations.

The easiest show he ever worked on, my father would say later, the happiest, most pleasant job he ever had—forgetting, perhaps, and letting all of us forget, that three days before the show was scheduled to open in New York, a wall of scenery fell at the Imperial Theatre (fortunately, no one was hurt) and while the structure was being repaired, the show, having already played New Haven and Boston, went to Philadelphia. "To look at him you wouldn't think it was fun but it was," he wired Dick and Oscar for the rescheduled New York opening. "So thanks for asking me."

Whatever my own excitement at coming into Philadelphia from Bryn Mawr, not on the usual movie binge but to see my father's new show, any first impressions are blurred in the cumulative memory of seeing *Annie* so many times I lost count. (One undimmed memory of Philadelphia was talking to Dick Rodgers at dinner, not about the show but of my own future, my plan, encouraged by my father, to dump cloistered, superintellectual Bryn Mawr, which had no music major, and transfer to Barnard, which did. There were plenty of reasons for the savvy Mr. Rodgers to warn me against such a path, not the least whose daughter I was— even if I was only testing the waters in an academic situation. I was always grateful to this man whose music I admired and loved for not being the predictable wet blanket but enthusiastically saying in so many words, "Do it. You'll never regret it.")

If I'd been asked later, I would have said that *Annie Get Your Gun,* like *As Thousands Cheer* or *Top Hat* or *This Is the Army,* was an instant, enormous hit, with its star, its surefire story, above all its trajectory of brightly hued songs, one after the other, shooting into the air like Annie Oakley's rifle pop, pop, pop, pop, never a miss. No matter how many times I went, I never tired of watching Merman play the part—the facial expressions, the gestures, the timing, the diction—hearing her get that laugh when she sang "A man may be *hot,* / But he's *not,* / When he's *shot,*" hearing her add

that pang to the "wonderful" in "They Say It's Wonderful"; hearing
Ray Middleton hold that note in "My Defenses Are Down"; never
tired of his and her punch lines. Later, my sister Elizabeth would
say, even as a child, though she loved the show, she disapproved of
the ending, Annie faking it to save Frank's pride. I cannot claim
the same feminist prescience. I took it as it came: a lover's trick.
Didn't people in love of either sex play such tricks? I even de-
fended "The Girl That I Marry"; it was meant *ironically*, a song to
define Frank's character (though I'm not sure it didn't define my
father's own male feelings more accurately than I, who was not
pink and white and did not purr, liked to think).

And all around me, month after month, year upon year, audiences shared my delight.

So it was a surprise after all this time to find that the reviews,
with the exception of Barnes in the *Tribune*, were not at all the equivalent of those for *As Thousands Cheer* or *Top Hat* or *This Is the Army*.
Lewis Nichols in the *Times*, for instance: "A good professional
Broadway musical . . . a pleasant score by Irving Berlin . . . there is
nothing like "White Christmas" or "Easter Parade" but several
which have a place a bracket or so below." Or Kronenberger in *PM:*
"*Annie* is mainly Miss Merman's show though the rest of it is competent enough of its kind. . . . Irving Berlin's score is not musically exciting." Or Morehouse in the *Sun:* "Merman often comes stridently
to the aid of a sagging book. . . . Irving Berlin's score is not a notable
one." Or Chapman in the *News:* "*Annie* is a good standard lavish big
musical . . . but it isn't the greatest show in the world. . . . Mr.
Berlin's music is okay. His lyrics are delightfully agile."

And I remember my father, the gleam in his eye, the edge in
his voice, as one after the other of those "okay" songs with "agile"
lyrics came onto "Your Hit Parade," and I wonder if that wasn't
when I first heard him say, "Critics, what do the critics know," and,
"Critics, it's a good thing they only write *about* songs and don't actually write them"—though on paper I see he was quite philosoph-
ical, writing Moss Hart, for instance, his partner in former glory,
"In spite of a few bad notices, I think all in all we got off pretty
good. In any event, I am very happy about the result."

Annie Get Your Gun, of course, would be a far greater hit than
the fabled *As Thousands Cheer*. It would run three years on Broadway

with Merman, tour the United States with Mary Martin, and play four years in London with Dolores Gray. In the postwar lineup of musicals it would take its place with the great ones—*South Pacific, Brigadoon, Kiss Me, Kate, Guys and Dolls, The King and I,* and *Lost in the Stars.* Twenty years later, in 1966, when *Annie Get Your Gun* was revived at the New York State Theater, the New York press would unanimously cheer, in the words of the earlier, unimpressed Ward Morehouse, "the greatness" of the score. And in the family it was as if we all knew, from the start, that this was the way it would be. I could have been seven or eight years old still, with my image of the golden touch, or fifteen at the opening of *This Is the Army.* With *Annie* I remember something breaking open in me, abandoning all reticence, as if saying to hell with it, I might as well go with the flow of who I am, who my father is. All of a sudden I felt so free to talk about it, asking friend after friend to join me in the family house seats, that finally one of those friends advised me to stop talking so much, I was getting to be a show-off and a bore.

But what about that score that Alec Wilder in *American Popular Song* called "probably his greatest . . . a fantastic piece of work," that was not just a crowd pleaser but admired by fellow songwriters, beginning with Dick Rodgers and Oscar Hammerstein, the feeling caught in a note from the ever eupeptic Harry Ruby: "The songs are swell, so fresh, so different from anything you have done in the last many years. In fact everyone says it's a new Berlin." Where had the energy come from, the variety, the musical invention, the grit, the grace, the sheer number? Eight certified standards ("Wonderful," "Show Business," "Naturally," "Man with a Gun," "Girl That I Marry," "Sun in the Morning," "Lost in his Arms," "Anything You Can Do"), and two more connoisseur's favorites, "Moonshine Lullaby" and "My Defenses Are Down." There was flair even in the throwaways.

Looking for an explanation all these years later, I called on Jay Blackton, conductor of all four postwar Berlin shows and my father's friend from the day he threw out those first ruinous *Annie Get Your Gun* orchestrations. "When Irving wrote a song and dictated it to Helmy Kresa, that piano part was sacred, that was the way Irving wanted the orchestra to play it, with his little answers between phrases and nothing else," said Blackton, frail and gray and so vivid in his memories it was as if that 1946 Irving were right there with us in a San Fernando Valley parlor, singing into Blackton's ear, "literally covering me with his melody as he demonstrated a song, constantly looking at me as if to share the delight of what he'd just written, always questioning, do you like it, do you *really* like it?"

And so, casting himself back to that long-ago time, smiling rather mischievously, Jay Blackton tried to explain about that score. "Leaving God out of it, the God who made him a musician in the first place, here is the picture," he said, gesturing and placing the phantoms in a room. "On one side, Irving Berlin, coming out of retirement, well, not retirement, out of the war, but still he'd been away for a while. On the other, Rodgers and Hammerstein, the new kings of Broadway, with *Oklahoma!* and *Carousel,* both huge hits, setting a new style. Now you know Dick and Irving had the greatest mutual respect. Irving called Dick a musical genius, and I remember Dick one day onstage during a rehearsal, looking at Irving pacing below, saying, 'There is America's folk song writer.' But they were not soul mates. I could feel this tug. There were those so well behaved, respectable other two and this street fighter, taking the place of Jerome Kern. Irving was a fighter you know, still the young fellow from the streets. And I would say Irving Berlin wrote this tremendous score not just for himself but for Richard Rodgers. The extra reach, again and again and *again,* to show he still had it in him."

It made sense. He was a fighter. Not noisy and brawling but quiet, dogged, and coming around from another direction is the way I thought of him when I was growing up. I see it even more clearly now. In the family one would have said that my mother, the princess, was the street fighter, my father the voice of reason. Maybe in the outside world it was the other way around. In any case, the image rang true. Something apparent even on the home front of a man always, just a bit, with his back against the wall, writing, composing, negotiating his way out of a corner.

As for Ethel Merman, the woman who launched most of those songs, who wired my father on the night *Annie Get Your Gun* opened just one word—THANKS—who would also star in his second postwar hit, *Call Me Madam*, there was never a question of how he felt about her or, to my knowledge, she about him. It was silly, he said, to talk about writing a "Merman song" when so obviously she could sing any kind of song—funny, sad, hot, sweet— and make it "hers." You'd just better write her a good lyric, that was all, because they'd hear every word in the last row of the balcony, and you'd better not write her a lousy tune, because they'd hear that tune exactly the way you wrote it.

You could hear the affection in his voice when he repeated her comebacks, her reply when asked on an opening night if she was nervous ("Why should I be nervous, I know my lines"). Or her answer to Mainbocher, the great couturier who designed her dresses for *Call Me Madam*, and asked, "What will you do about your *hair*, Miss Merman?" "Wash it," she said. You could see it on both their faces backstage, at an opening-night party, in a casual, unexpected encounter in a nightspot: something genuine, ungushy, equal. You could hear his impatience, brushing off a question about what was quite a commotion at the time, the *Call Me Madam* cast album. RCA was backing the show, and Merman had a contract with Decca; nobody budged, so there were two competing albums: Merman's with another cast; the cast's with Dinah Shore as Merman. "It didn't make a bit of difference," my father said. "They both sold."

But the moment I would remember best came many years later. It was the opening of the 1966 revival of *Annie Get Your Gun*, for which, for the fifty-eight-year-old Merman, my seventy-eight-year-old father had written a smashing new double number, "An Old Fashioned Wedding," which stopped the show in a manner, wrote one critic, "I haven't seen since the 'Rain in Spain' in *My Fair Lady*." The whole evening was electric, after twenty years *Annie* confirmed, Berlin confirmed, Merman confirmed, at nearly sixty playing a twenty-year-old and after the first shock making you believe it. At the end, there were many curtain calls, a standing ovation for Merman, an audience gone wild, and finally calls, from the stage, from out front, "Composer . . . Irving . . . where's Irving Berlin." I poked my father and whispered, "Go on, go on up there, can't you hear them calling for you?" He shook his head. "This is her night," he said, and stayed where he was.

31

WE SPENT THE SUMMER of 1946 in Bermuda, in a bright white modern house that belonged to the producer Dwight Deere Wiman. Rounded and prowed like a stage-set ship, "Landmark" stood atop the highest hill in Somerset township; from the second-floor living room, sitting on one of the outsized sofas, you could see only sky and turquoise water; wooden steps led down to a small crescent beach. "It's beautiful here," my mother wrote Mynna in the office. "Wonderful sun and swimming & cooler than in California. Think it will be good for Mr. B. so ask Mr. Dreyer not to urge him to NY but don't say I said so." It was a wonderful summer, give or take a few squalls, for all of us, the tone set in the opening weeks by the Bermuda Races, the first Newport-Hamilton race since 1938: the boats coming in, the lawn parties, the sunburned sailors, high on rum and champagne, telling of bold maneuvers, storms and near capsizings.

There were friends for Linda and Elizabeth and a gang of young people for me to run with, high-spirited, unbitchy girls setting the summer styles with tennis whites and splashy calypso prints. There were also worldly-wise boys, back from the war, taking the summer off before returning to Harvard or Columbia on the GI Bill. They were all members of a group back in New York that would become my group, the "bright young things" of this new would-be Jazz Age who'd end up on magazines, in publishing, or being published themselves. One of the boys, the brightest of the lot, yellow-haired, beak-nosed John Appleton, who could outmatch my mother in a duel of wits, would become my lifelong friend; another, a Tyrone Power look-alike, was this summer's romance, over long before the summer's end.

The sun shone, the water splashed, the calypso music blared, the bicycles spun along the twisting roads (though the Berlins also had an Austin, Jack MacKenzie at the wheel, one of the few island cars not belonging to a doctor or official); everyone argued, teased, and felt themselves brilliant. And at the center of the comings and goings were my parents, twenty years married, celebrating the success of *Annie Get Your Gun*, celebrating peacetime, having their first real summer holiday since before the war.

In the evening, in the rose-colored reflection of the Bermuda sunset, a nightly show, there were terrace barbecues, my father shaking daiquiris, suspending in his high spirits my "no hard liquor till twenty-one" promise (not acknowledging how quickly one daiquiri can lead to another), grilling the Dinty Moore's steaks, brought on the plane by one of our guests. Every Saturday we listened on the wireless to "Your Hit Parade" and learned how the *Annie* songs were doing: "Girl That I Marry" just on, "Doin' What Comes Natur'lly" still number one.

To Landmark came a typical mixture: Rhoda Clark, my mother's friend from girlhood, a soft, refined beauty with intellect and 1920s marcelled hair, many years divorced, whose composure belied the adventurousness of her life (she had spent the war in London and was still unmistakably, in pursuit of love); Peggy Pulitzer, a more down-to-earth sort, author (as Margaret Leech) of the prize-winning Civil War history *Reveille in Washington*, mother of Linda's friend Susan, a peppery lady (with coloring to match) who had a habit, not always pleasing to her pal Ellin, of taking the children's side in arguments; my father's friend, more and more his *best* friend, Irving Hoffman, the columnist, cartoonist, and leg man for Walter Winchell (Hollywood studios paid him a fortune to get an "orchid" from Walter), bringing New York gossip along with the steaks, peering at you through thick glasses as he delivered opinions on the latest book, the art of Picasso, the fate of Lucky Luciano; my aunt Joan Blake Harjes, married at eighteen to a Morgan partner, soon-to-be divorced, blond and pliant, similar to my mother in looks. "If anything happened to me, dear," my mother would begin to joke to my father, "I'd like you to marry Joan." "Maybe I'd have other ideas," said my father. "Like *who?*" said my mother, so sure of herself, so quick to bridle.

And let me not forget Tommy Murray of the Southampton clan, one of last summer's boys in uniform, with his beaming face and bumptious charm, who had become a Berlin captive, of whom my mother said, "I don't care which of my daughters you marry if you'll just marry one." (Even when he didn't, married instead his longtime sweetheart Janice Kilvert, he remained a favorite with the next generation as well, my children's buddy, the outrageous "Mr. Murray.") Marriage was a pet subject in my father's all-female

Bermuda household, and Tommy would remember Linda telling him her requirements for a husband: good looks, personality, and money. Tommy passed along a bit of advice from his own father: "Anyone who marries for money will end up earning it." My father, who'd been concentrating on his cooking, turned around and said, "He was absolutely right." My mother, taking this all in, exclaimed in a voice filled with exasperation, "*Irving!*"

Money—the forbidden subject, the one "nice people" didn't talk about—was of course being made that summer in large amounts, by my father personally and by the firm. In a depressed music business, the new, smaller Irving Berlin Music Company, thanks to the *Annie Get Your Gun* songs, was having a fine year. Money was what was paying for our Bermuda summer, for the house on Beekman Place my parents had admired since before the war and bought at last; for our whole way of life. Luckily, jokes aside, my mother's husband liked making money. He took pleasure in his deals, his reputation as a tough trader, whether for himself and his family or a cause he believed in. From a man who had given away millions during the war, there would be no apologies over getting (for himself and the Fieldses) $650,000 from M-G-M for the movie rights to *Annie*—the highest price ever for a musical, higher even than for *Oklahoma!* And if ever anyone in the family questioned the need for some whopping payment, especially for a man already in the 90 percent bracket, my mother would offer a typical bit of wisdom: "Money in the modern age is the trophy, the laurel wreath."

My father also, when not in an economizing mood, liked spending money; he didn't seem to care that much about accumulating it, though he did that in spite of himself. My mother was much the same; her expenditures and her gifts were lavish, which kept her bank account slim. Coming from opposite directions, extreme wealth and poverty, my parents met in this indifference to accumulation. Though they did not live beyond their means, they lived to the edge of those means and would say, without dishonesty, that people took them always to be richer than they were (which was rich enough).

So money mattered, whether we talked about it or not—

244 IRVING BERLIN: A Daughter's Memoir

indeed, a little more talk, in the growing-up years, might have saved me some trouble later, out there in the real world, raising a family of my own.

But hitting the songwriter's jackpot wasn't all my father was celebrating in the pink Bermuda light. As he would put in a letter to Harry Ruby (and as anyone around that summer could have sensed), "Naturally I am delighted with *Annie Get Your Gun*. I might add I am also very grateful. At my age, 'over twenty one,' this seems like a second helping. Everytime I start with a show I wonder if this is the time I'll reach for it and find it isn't there."

There is a picture taken at the Stork Club the previous fall, on my nineteenth birthday, that always brings this period back to me with a jolt: myself in a low-necked, black chiffon dress with an orchid corsage; my father in a well-cut dinner jacket, the nightclub ashtray strategically placed between us by the photographer. It is the very beginning of the *Annie* sequence. Cigarette in hand, he looks tired behind the smile but keyed up; a man with a trick or two still up his sleeve. I look pretty, in a thin phase, with my bangs grown out at last, and eager, a little too eager.

He *is* tired but about to come up with the biggest cluster of hits in his life. I *am* too eager, to begin my own life, to do my own thing, to find some boy to love—a girl, as Moss Hart liked to put it, just waiting for Mr. Wrong.

The camera does not lie.

32

MR. WRONG APPEARED one afternoon in the fall of 1946, walked in with another Mr. Wrong on a Park Avenue hen party, a Saturday bridge game, caught my eye, and came to stand behind me. Looking at my hand, and incidentally down my front, he said, "I wouldn't play that card if I were you," which caused the other girls to laugh and warn me that this tall grizzled stranger of indeterminate age didn't know how to play bridge or how to converse or how to dance, had been at war so long he had no social graces whatsoever, and watch out. A few nights later he was on the phone, asking if I'd like to take in a movie and afterward head down to the Village, to a place he knew where they played good Cuban music. I said, Why not?

At first Mr. Wrong was just another one of my "friends," the most offbeat, seven years older than me, an ex-navy flyer going to Columbia University School of General Studies on the GI Bill with a reformed black-sheep history I found alluring, and shared only sparingly with my family. His name gave off an aura of money and high society; and his crowd was fast, a bunch of Mr. Wrongs, and Mrs. Wrongs as well, with a few friendly exceptions: older, richer, wilder than the Bermuda crowd I traveled with; people I knew were bad news from the number of times I read about them in the gossip columns but still found intriguing. My Mr. Wrong was the most un-conventional member of the group, the one who ran away from home at seventeen to join the peacetime navy, who'd been at Pearl Harbor when the Japanese attacked. Now the former school dropout was pulling down As and Bs, and resuming his place in not-so-polite society, the jester who made the others laugh.

"Flashy," my mother commented the first time she met him. "That ring, that suit. So odd given the family. But not flashy in per-sonality, I agree." (He had been on his best behavior.) "Rather shy. With a bit of humor, I suspect." So my mother smiled for a season upon Mr. Wrong because, like her, he was part old New York, part Irish (his immigrant grandfather had made a small fortune, dwin-dling fast, in the Colorado copper mines); because he was a Catholic; because his aunt had been a bridesmaid in her own par-ents' wedding.

And my father: He was in Hollywood much of the winter and spring of 1947, working on the movie *Easter Parade*, and writing songs, for the first time, for Judy Garland. On a week home he would not even have registered this new fellow picking me up for a date, said by my mother to be "nice," with a good war record—there were so many fellows around.

So winter turned to spring, and Mr. Wrong was still around, speaking for half my dates instead of one in four, become a neces-sity instead of a choice.

Then it was another California summer, another Santa Monica

beach house, everything as always, it seemed, except for a sad absence: Jack MacKenzie had died of a stroke in the spring of that year. There was a visiting O'Brien, my cousin Morgan this time. There were friends, parties, the mixing of the generations; a dance at the Goldwyns' in honor of Sammy's coming of age; a gala at the Zanucks' in honor of Gen. Mark Clark; "the game" in evening clothes with Danny Kaye and Gene Kelly (when he broke his ankle Kelly would be replaced in *Easter Parade* by Fred Astaire); Harold Arlen playing his low-down piano, taking requests for "Blues in the Night" and "One for My Baby"; my father playing some of his songs for the movie: "It Only Happens When I Dance with You," "Better Luck Next Time," and the one inexplicably his favorite, "Fella with an Umbrella"; my playing the Gershwin preludes for Oscar Levant, who said, "Not bad," a high compliment from Oscar; my father and Fred Astaire loose in the fun house in Venice with Elizabeth, Fred, Jr., and a pack of eleven-year-olds who were worn out long before the two of them.

But I was out of sorts not only because my favorite date was a continent away but because Linda, at fifteen, was suddenly a dark-haired beauty with many admirers among Hollywood's teenage set and maybe I was a bit jealous. (Though the admirers were mostly kept at bay by my ever-vigilant mother).

In the family the categories had now been made. I was "the smart one," Linda was indeed "the pretty one," also "the funny one," and Elizabeth was "the one with a heart like a pat of butter." In fact, when not overweight, I had my own brand of good looks, though I needed to work on my sense of humor. Pretty Linda, who didn't like school, was plenty smart, as was Elizabeth; who, though kind to animals and children no one else liked, an unusually good-hearted little person, had an edge to her; a hint of the presence, along with the quick tongue, that would serve her well in the years to come.

So there were the two younger sisters coming up fast behind me, and ahead was my scintillating mother, finishing up her second novel, *Lace Curtain,* a saga of a Catholic family that looked already to be a possible best-seller. She seemed to me the cleverest woman alive, a self-educated marvel who not only charmed but also outargued anyone she felt worth the effort, on subjects of which she knew nothing. Maybe I was a bit jealous of her too.

My father, sensing my mood, and maybe not sorry for an excuse to be on the move himself, suggested a few weeks for the family in Honolulu, a vacation away from my vacation. It seemed to work. "Feeling better?" he asked me on the ocean voyage home after witnessing me at the piano entertaining a large group in the ship's salon. "Definitely," I said, tanned, thinner, a spoiled darling once again—with barely a season to go.

Four months later, my mother tells my father she thinks it would be a good idea if they took me, just me, to Mexico for the Christmas holidays. "She is talking marriage," says my mother, her smile quite faded, "and I am not sure this is marriage material." "*What?*" says my father, who only a fortnight earlier, at my twenty-first birthday party, talked to Mr. Wrong about the navy, thought him a nice enough guy, understood he was my new beau, nothing too serious. Hadn't we just been in Hawaii? There is a look, and my father does as he's told, makes the arrangements in Mexico and further agrees for me to take a leave from Barnard and spend the winter with them in California "thinking things over." The year 1925 all over again? Not exactly.

What had cinched matters, where I was concerned, was the discovery that Mr. Wrong had a talent, the Holy Grail in our family, a gift for portraiture. This word of praise came from no less an expert than a trustee of the Museum of Modern Art, an old friend of my mother's who disclosed that before he ran away to sea, Mr. Wrong, one of her favorites, had done wonderful drawings of all his summer friends. Confirmation of this was in the lady's own living room, striking charcoal portraits of her sons. "You should get him back to it," she told me. I planned to, I said, though the artist himself said what he needed was to finish college and get into a business, preferably far from New York, south of the border if possible; marriage might have to wait.

Mexico City was my first whiff of foreign travel. Mexico City was Art: what a good place for me and Mr. Wrong! Though my parents had been there before and knew all about Aztec and Mayan ruins, they did not know about what was going on today. It was my pleasure to enlighten them about Rivera, Orozco, and Siqueiros. With their friend Pauline Poniatowski, who owned a gallery, we went one afternoon to Orozco's studio and left with two purchases, a gouache of Aztec Indians for me and for my parents a bright and hectic fiesta scene (which turned out to be *The Day of the Dead*). Another acquaintance, A. C. Blumenthal, developer of Acapulco, brought Diego Rivera to our suite at the Reforma. Huge and genial, the ex-revolutionary asked to paint Mr. Berlin's portrait. The last artist my father had actually sat still for was a nameless Russian in Palm Beach, before he married my mother. He turned Rivera down but later commissioned him to do the cover for the sheet music of "In Acapulco." (The painting, a beach scene, called "too cartoonish," was never used; it was also, with its mixed couples, considered too advanced for the American South, where sheet music still sold in quantities.)

"She's having such a good time, seeing there's more to the world than New York City, Mr. You-know-who" said my mother. "You should take her to London. Don't you have some business there?" "*What?*" said my father, still not through with *Easter Parade* and eager to get started on *Stars on My Shoulders*, his new Broadway musical with the timely theme of a retired general who becomes a political candidate. Heading for his sixtieth birthday, he had no plans, clearly, for slowing down. We settled into yet another cottage on the grounds of the Beverly Hills Hotel, where I practiced the piano, read the galleys of *Lace Curtain*, getting so swept up in the story of a mixed (Catholic-Protestant) marriage that I forgot my own mother had written it. I also wrote Mr. Wrong, who was now sending me furious letters because my parents had had the audacity to remove me from his grasp. The letters were supplemented by hour-long telephone calls on my father's bill.

In late February we returned to our elegant five-story Georgian brick house on Beekman Place, in whose golden and nut-brown paneled library Mr. Wrong and I were reunited.

Nobody but me wanted us to be engaged, though Mr. Wrong was now prepared to pay that price for hanging on to me. There were notable impediments. On the groom's side, anti-Semitism lying not too far beneath the surface, vehemently denied but still there, the inheritance of prejudice he shared with most of his upper-class friends. On my side, it wasn't just being married by a priest, agreeing to raise my children as Catholics. (There were real questions about that from my father and from me as well.) It was the grave suspicion that this charming wild man was held together with toothpicks, as my girlfriends had warned, a concern shared by his own family.

One man-to-man conversation was enough for my father to determine that he indeed was Mr. Wrong. My father asked what kind of a job he was planning to get, an ordinary enough question to ask of a prospective son-in-law, but his answer was vague. Maybe advertising, maybe import-export, or maybe something in South America. Why advertising? asked my father. Because his family had connections. Why South America? Because he had friends down there. Why not build on his drawing ability? Because that was ancient history. Or his experience as a pilot? Because he never wanted to see a plane again; he had been in one crash, which cured him (not downed by the enemy but, this being Mr. Wrong, joyriding).

My father didn't understand my interest in him, at least not till he caught the two of us one night standing in a doorway at Beekman Place, not saying anything, just looking at each other. Then he understood all too well and suggested I take another summer away. He was now saying things like "You have nothing in common with that fellow" or "Okay, so you have a language, but believe me, that gets very old very fast if you haven't anything else" or "You think it's romantic, me and your mother in reverse, it has nothing to do with me and your mother."

And I said, "You'll see, once we're married everything will be fine," a thought not uncommon in those days among girls in love with boys back from the war, who were having a hard time readjusting.

Wearily, a few weeks after his sixtieth birthday, in a letter to Uncle Joe enclosing clippings of my engagement announcement, my father summed up: "We of course just gave out the simple statement but the *Times* and *Herald Tribune* gave it the usual society works. There is some humor in it to find my father and mother in the society column. . . . The excitement has died down and things are pretty normal. None of it seems to faze Mary Ellin, who takes everything in stride. She is, as you know, terribly in love. As Ellin puts it, 'If anything happened to the electricity in our house we wouldn't have to worry because Mary Ellin could light up the whole house by herself.'" By now, for me, the lights were flickering. And my father was not being entirely candid, even with his best and oldest friend.

Now I see the two of us on my wedding morning, July 3, 1948. I am at the piano, where I have been sitting, letting off steam since a little after six A.M. People have begun coming into the living room, the maid with the vacuum, the caterer bringing flowers, Elizabeth and Tenny. Everyone is surprised to see the bride calmly sitting there playing when a few hours hence some sixty people are due to arrive for a noon ceremony and lunch. "Given the friends and relatives on both sides, it's sixty here or six hundred at the Waldorf," my mother has said, "and frankly my girl"—she didn't have to finish the sentence—"you're lucky, given how we feel, to be getting a wedding at all."

Not till my father, in a bathrobe, unshaven, uncombed, comes in to see what is going on do I finally stop and stand up to say good morning. "You are something on your wedding day," he says, giving me a rueful look. "A very cool cookie."

For an instant we look at each other, hazel eyes staring into brown. "It's not too late," he says in his raspy morning voice, so softly I wondered if I had heard correctly. "We can still call it off."

He departs, only to be replaced by my mother. "Everyone has enjoyed your concert," she says briskly, "but there's a wedding taking place this morning. You need to eat something." The night before, she had been in tears. Now she is dry-eyed and smiling, giving me a clear blue gaze, resigned to the knowledge that only by marrying the man will I get over him.

A year later, almost to the day, I was back with the family, mother, sisters, Tenny, on my way to Reno to get a divorce.

33

NO DUDE RANCH, no ogling cowboys for this particular unhappy bride, but a cottage (one of several needed to accommodate the family group) at the Cal Neva Lodge on the shores of Lake

Tahoe, just a few houses away from Aunt K, Uncle Bob, and little Bobby Hawkins. My father joined us for weekends as work permitted, just as if it were another interesting family summer in a pleasant new place.

My mother, now working on a biography of her grandmother Marie Louise Mackay, used the time for research in the University of Nevada library, in Virginia City, where the Mackay home was a museum, in the ghost mining town of Downieville, California, where Marie Louise's first marriage to the handsome, alcoholic Dr. Bryant ended in young widowhood. For my sisters it was an active lakeside summer, with jolly Aunt K to organize, ten-year-old Bobby to be nice to, and Uncle Bob to grill the steaks as the sun set behind the towering ponderosa pines.

But my father, I could tell, was angry. He had been an angel all year; my mother, too. Never a word of reproach, never a single "I told you so," only support and understanding. They let me come to a decision without heckling. They took pride in the way I managed, during the year of my marriage, to graduate from Barnard with honors; to land a job (forget that M.A., forget vague dreams of a career in music) at Time Inc. But now that I was safely back in the fold, my father let himself go a bit. He took abrupt leave of conversations that he had sprinkled with my least favorite phrases, *"not a bit of it"* (meaning you don't know what you're talking about) and *"wait a minute"* (preceding "are you telling me," the opening of a diatribe); chewing me out for speedboating around the lake with some young local, shouting that I wasn't even divorced yet and what did I think I was doing. No, I couldn't go on a double date with my just-married cousin Katherine, he said, and no, I couldn't spend a few days at a dude ranch on Pyramid Lake with Shana Ager, the future Shana Alexander, daughter of his colleague Milton ("Happy Days Are Here Again") Ager, also getting a divorce. I could go for the day, period. Only the weekend the Goldwyns came was I released to accompany young Sam on an evening of gambling at Cal Neva Lodge. But my resentment was mostly show. My interest in the opposite sex, in the pursuit of pleasure, had come to a dead halt. I preferred to be by myself, to read and worry that Time Inc. might think better of employing me as an editorial trainee, married one year, divorced the next, and off on a leave of absence even before I'd begun my job.

When the divorce came, it was shockingly quick. Uncle Bob presented me to the judge. I answered a few questions, petitioned to take back my maiden name, signed the paper the bailiff pushed toward me, and it was over, a half hour at the most. Afterward I threw my wedding ring, according to tradition, into the Truckee River and went with my mother into a café, where, at ten-thirty in the morning, we each had a Bloody Mary.

But here is what, in my memory of the year 1949, I had completely forgotten: another reason for my father's abrupt temper and haggard look. The very week the rest of us headed West on the train for Nevada was the week *Miss Liberty*, score by Irving Berlin, book by Robert Sherwood, directed by Moss Hart, opened in New York and was almost unanimously panned, the first full-fledged flop in four decades of Berlin Broadway hits.

Miss Liberty had drifted always unanchored in my mind somewhere between *Annie Get Your Gun* and *Call Me Madam*, a poor lost show about the French girl who did or did not pose for the Statue of Liberty, with its capable but nonstellar leads, Eddie Albert, Allyn McLerie, Mary McCarty. There were stories afterward of high hopes and terrible second-act problems, of Robert Sherwood getting drunk to relieve the pain of a tic douloureux and unable to do the necessary rewrites. There was Moss Hart, observing his falling-down state one night in Philadelphia, saying, "There goes the ball game"; and the sad truth that it wasn't the best work of anyone except Jerome Robbins, who stopped the show with his choreography for "The Policeman's Ball."

Years afterward, my father would still talk of how they could "fix" *Miss Liberty*, especially when walking about Paris with his half-French son-in-law, Edouard Emmet, Linda's husband, recalling how the Paris parts of the show had worked, with the wonderful Motley costumes, straight out of Toulouse-Lautrec, the Robbins cancan, the pretty waltz "Paris Wakes Up and Smiles," and the rowdy, cynical "Only For Americans." And Kitty Hart would remember the excitement in the early, hopeful weeks, Irving calling Moss three or four times a day. "Doesn't it *bother* you, all these telephone calls?" Kitty would ask her husband. And Moss would say, "Oh, no, he always has something so interesting, so funny, so helpful to say."

As for the score that the critics called "competent," "professional," but "reminiscent," my father predictably took pride in the setting he gave to Emma Lazarus's "Give Me Your Tired, Your Poor" and was pleased as he should have been, with "Let's Take an Old-Fashioned Walk" and "You Can Have Him." Later, in an album of 192 handpicked songs from over 800 published possibilities put together for family and friends, he included nine from *Miss Liberty*.

But his special favorite, and what in the end I remember best about *Miss Liberty*, was the song that stopped the show in Philadelphia and was knocked out because it was too modern, too idiosyncratic, didn't belong. Sassy, low-down, funny "Mr. Monotony," a holdover from *Easter Parade*, another period piece where it hadn't belonged. (There exists a classic outtake of Judy Garland singing it.) I can see my father still, at one of the Beekman Place pianos, the Steinway upright in the paneled library, the grand piano in the pale blue living room, the funny piano in his top-floor workroom, a wicked gleam in his eye singing "Monotony," a play on words, a play on melody, a built-in joke in the way the clever words fit the one-note beat, the first minimalist song. "Mr. Monotony": a thumbing of his nose at the year's two failures, his and mine.

PART EIGHT

REPRISE

Celebrating *Call Me Madam* with *(l. to r.)* Howard Lindsay, Russel Crouse, and Ethel Merman.

34

THE WEEK I WENT to work for Time Inc. as a lowly editorial trainee was the same September week a brief, bleak notice, blowing any cover I might have assumed mine, appeared as a milestone in *Time*, the weekly newsmagazine:

> Divorced: by Mary Ellin Berlin Burden, 22, brunette daughter of songwriter Irving Berlin and Postal Telegraph heiress-novelist Ellin Mackay (*Lace Curtain*) Berlin, socialite Dennis Sheedy Burden, 29, after 14 months of marriage, no children; in Reno.

Walking down the corridors of my new place of work, I felt like a big red *D* had been embroidered on my new gray flannel dress and a tag hung around my neck: *Irving Berlin's Divorced Daughter*. With that introduction (no one in *Time*'s history had made her way into the milestone column and into the halls as a try-out researcher in the same week), who would ever take me seriously? Who would understand that I wasn't some spoiled, feather-brained brat, but the really quite bright victim of a momentary derangement? Well, wasn't I? But it didn't take me long to understand that at *Time* or *Life* or *Fortune* nobody cared, nobody really read the magazines that carefully except for their own sections, and if they did? In this glamorous place, everyone, all of those knowledgeable, with-it people, had stories, secrets, pasts, most of them a lot more interesting than mine. What better place to start afresh, prove to the world and the family I was back on track, than this, where I soon found everyone agreed with my romantic assessment. And so I affected an air of irony, the office pose of choice, and assumed it made me just like everyone else.

That illusion lasted till day's end, when instead of returning to a fourth-floor walk-up shared with two other working girls I 257 returned to the best address on sought-after Beekman Place, with a butler, chef, and several maids in attendance, an uninterrupted view of the East River, and my parents, waiting to greet me.

But behind that elegant Georgian facade, things were not so easy. True, there were a couple of friends also waiting at home: Linda, in her senior year at Chapin, all of a sudden my contemporary and confidante; Elizabeth, turned thirteen, all of a sudden real company and more acute than was suitable in any thirteen-year-old. This rapprochement between me and my younger sisters pleased my parents, though they were not so easily pleased these days. Having suffered gamely through the years of my courtship and marriage, they were having, and who could blame them, a delayed reaction. They gave me full credit for the honors degree and the job, but as far as they were concerned, having made one disastrous mistake, I could be expected to make another. They were watching me, as my mother put it, "like hawks."

With a divorced daughter back home and a sixty-one-year-old husband, my mother was making a big thing now of being middle-aged. She had put her pretty hair up in a dowdy style that her daughters deplored, that she called "appropriate" to an older face, though, in fact, hers was still remarkably youthful. She played the distinguished no-nonsense matron to the hilt, caring for her daughters still in school, writing her book about her forebears, working for the Girl Scouts as vice president in charge of public relations, inviting the cream of the older scouts, in their green uniforms, to Beekman Place for tea, keeping all the while that beady eye on her own eldest child. Above all, she fussed about the well-being of her husband, who did not see her as a matron but as his own darling Ellie, the bright spirit of his life, who "breaks her neck," as he put it, for everyone, especially him, having, as the 1940s ended, a clearly difficult time.

There were other setbacks for my father that flanked *Miss Liberty*. *Stars on My Shoulders* indefinitely postponed, eight good songs into the files. Judy Garland, who was to be the great movie Annie, sick on pills and booze, a dazed wraith fired by M-G-M and replaced by Betty Hutton (hardworking but no Garland). True, he was "all hot about" the idea Howard Lindsay and Russel Crouse had brought him: Ethel Merman playing Perle Mesta, Harry Truman's madam ambassadress to Luxembourg and Washington's reigning hostess. He seemed to enjoy the running of his publishing house (now exclusively Berlin songs); he took an interest in the Music Box Theatre, the God Bless America Fund, the newly established Irving Berlin Charitable Fund. Still my mother watched him, not like a hawk, like a woman increasingly concerned for the man she loved. And it pleased her to see him enjoy the Beekman Place house, especially his new toy, the projection room, commonplace in Hollywood, rare in New York. After dinner when friends came, a few at a time—the Harts, the Crouses, the Sherwoods, Leland and Slim Hayward, Irving Hoffman, Anita Loos—a movie was shown in the library.

So they were occupied, my parents, but not nearly busy enough. They still had time to worry about me. They hovered. They were nice. They were too nice. They were impossible. They threw a terrific party in my honor, "Happy Birthday and Welcome Home, Mary Ellin," to which I made the mistake of inviting an interesting new male friend, the artist Alajalov, a friend I was proud of—sophisticated, talented, and one (foolishly) I thought would impress and reassure my parents. Not exactly.

The day after the party I was summoned to my mother's bedroom, my father not in view, my mother talking for both of them. It began to spill out. Had I not given my poor tired father enough grief for one year? This was no boyfriend for me, fifty at least (in fact, he was only forty-seven), and dangerous, she continued, though I might not realize it, my father's White Russian look-alike, short, wiry, black-haired, high-cheekboned. He wasn't *my* type, I said, not exactly tactful, he was the best kind of pal, that was all, smart, amusing, too old to be a threat—to no avail. I had done enough damage. The orders were issued, the limits defined. I was on probation, and there was nothing for the moment I could do about it. They wanted me home; and whether I thought so or not, I needed home. So my talented, continental buddy was dropped.

But there was more to it than that. Under the surface, not very far, was the inescapable linkage; my mother's allusions to my father being "down"; really *very down* since his sixtieth birthday. And I didn't have to be told what else had hit him hard, on top of turning sixty, a lot harder than *Miss Liberty,* which he had brushed off like the professional he was. Later, doctors would tell her what should have been obvious to all of us, that my father's depression came from pushing himself without let up during the war and never taking that six months, or even six weeks, off. But at the time, we genuinely believed that the cause, coupled with "sixty," was me—my terrible in-and-out marriage and all it implied; someone thought to be very bright proved to be very stupid, someone thought to be Miss Capable, severely fallible; and beyond, the reflection of a divorce on the good name of a family that till that moment had seemed to contradict the world's assumptions that the children of the famous were destined to lead disorderly lives. A pall had descended on a happy household, and my mother and I willfully, willingly, collaborated on the grandiose fantasy that I, the oldest child, was its cause. There was nothing for me to do but figure out what my father wanted and do it.

If my father was depressed, my own melancholy some days was profound.

The office was my escape and, as it turned out, after considerable maneuvering, the solution.

It was deadline night in the back-of-the-book section of *Time:* only an ex–Time employee from the company's mid-century prime could know what that meant—hurdles and tension to match Beekman Place. All around me, in a vast, windowless region known as the bullpen, were sounds of furious activity: clacking typewriters, voices on the telephone, copyboys hurrying by, occasional too-hearty laughter.

I was not laughing, though, or typing or talking to anyone on the phone. Sitting there in my eight-by-ten cubicle, I could only think of the origin of the term bullpen, told to me jokingly by an old-hand researcher: that this was the place in the stockyards of Omaha or Chicago where cattle waited for transportation to their slaughter.

A researcher-at-large, otherwise known as a "floater," I was filling in for the regular music researcher who was on a week off; trying to write up a luncheon interview with the Weavers, the popular folksingers who happened to have the week's number-one record, "Goodnight, Irene." Hardly a major item, but it might have been a cover story on the great Toscanini himself and I the writer instead of his humble assistant, for all the balls of paper on the floor. My first job and I was flubbing it.

Now my writer—tall, blond, and frowning—emerged from one of the offices that ringed the bullpen and stood over me. "When will you be done?" he asked impatiently.

"Soon, soon," I answered, turning to look at him, close to tears. With his blue button-down shirt, slightly loosened tie, and green-blue eyes, he was the kind of good-looking, not-too-smooth boy who was, God forbid, my type. Except his voice was not the prep-school voice—sharp, nasal, slightly snotty, that had usually issued from the mouths of my type. It had a midwestern twang to it.

Uninvited, he read what was in the typewriter, glanced at the finished page on the desk. "But that's fine, I'll take that," he said, giving me a smile that was more friendly, less sure of itself than your usual blond-boy grin. He was nervous, too, I thought, not that long on the job himself. "Finish it up. You have a good eye, Miss Berlin. A good ear."

Something lifted in me. I started to type again, hard, with a beat, like the woman in the next cubicle, the one I'd been hating for her efficient clatter.

So I remember my first encounter, in the spring of 1950, with Marvin Barrett, back-of-the-book floater like myself, transplant from Des Moines, Iowa, by way of Harvard, the U.S. Navy, and a year on a ranch in Southern California, and my husband-to-be. (Our marriage is now in its forty-third year.) Marvin's memory, which he would later share with our children when they asked how we met, was a quicker take. "I was sitting in my office, minding my own business, when this brunette in a green plaid dress came in with a pad and pencil to discuss the week's stories. 'Who is that good-looking girl with the loud voice?' I asked my office mate when she had departed. 'That is Irving Berlin's daughter,' he replied. 'It is my observation that the children of the famous often have loud voices. They probably have a hard time making themselves heard.' 'Well, she seems like a nice enough kid,' I said, or something like that. These historic meetings are hard to recollect."

Over the next six months my future husband met his future mother-in-law (who approved even if she couldn't remember where it was he had come from) and future sisters-in-law (who said he'd do) and other members of his future extended family (A fine lad with a head on his shoulders, said Tenny), but not my father. Depressed or not, feeling his age or not, my father was very busy, busy the way he liked best, working on a show. Rescue of another sort.

Call Me Madam, produced by Leland Hayward, directed by George Abbott, did not happen with the same ease, the same creative burst, as *Annie Get Your Gun*. It was a show, my father would say later, he worked harder on than any other. Everyone concerned worked harder than they had expected, given the foolproof idea, the adventures of a U.S. ambassadress to the mythical duchy of Lichtenberg—so recalls Anna Crouse, Russel Crouse's theaterwise widow who shared with me Russel's diary jottings of the day. The script written by Lindsay and Crouse with painful slowness, and sent off scene by scene to the composer, now in Nassau, who writes the first of the songs slowly, slowly, though the songs themselves are not slow, have a wake-up sound to them . . . "The Hostess with the Mostes' on the Ball," "The Best Thing for You," "Marrying for Love," "Can You Use Any Money Today?" "Very good," Russel writes, in his diary, of song after song, "a show stopper . . . a sure hit." And, more important, "Irving calls to say that Ethel loves the songs and she gets on to confirm this in true Merman fashion." Irving responds in kind about the script and writes the rhythmical, flag-waving "Free" to underscore the comedy's serious side. As the play gets finished, the score signs off, or seems to, with "It's a Lovely Day Today," to be sung by the new boy in the show, Russell Nype, such a whimsical, romantic young man's song—how could someone sixty-two remember? By August, when the show begins its out-of-town tryouts, the score already delivers a message: *I'm back in top form.*

And then the story my father liked to tell, that everyone liked to tell. How they had a very bad second act, "especially in my department," he would write his favorite sounding board, Harry Ruby, afterward. "The best song in the score I wrote in New Haven after we opened. It's nice after all these years to know that you can still reach up there and find it when you're in trouble."

"All afternoon working on our new second-act stuff," Russel Crouse noted, "and below us Irving Berlin toils over new tunes. We hear his notes as they are put together tortuously . . . a late night." And then, the next afternoon, "great elation" when they hear Russell Nype and Ethel Merman sing "You're Just in Love," that "best song" written overnight, the finest double number Irving Berlin has written since "Play a Simple Melody" for *Watch Your Step,* his first show in 1914. (By now, recalled Anna Crouse, Leland Hayward had taken his stroll around Yale, observed the current campus look, and told Nype to get himself a crew cut and a pair of horn-rimmed glasses, the right look and the right song—the character's making.)

The work went on in Boston: another number, written in an afternoon, "Something to Dance About"; other songs dropped ("Mr. Monotony" for the third time). Rumblings of postponements, advice (not taken) to replace Paul Lukas, the male lead, a fine actor with no voice; the ending, called overly preachy about moneybags America treading on little countries' feelings, finally lightened. (" 'Free' out and all our comment and it plays well," noted Russel. "All happy but Lindsay and me. We have lost something.") Changes welcome and hurtful that helped turn a half-good show into a smash hit.

I saw *Call Me Madam* first in Boston, the invitation an old time gesture, though I liked to give it a newer interpretation: that my job had made me all of a sudden someone whose opinion counted. Before the show my father and I had dinner in the Ritz dining room, where a tall, reddish-haired, drop-dead-handsome man stopped by our table. He and my father exchanged pleasantries—how's your mother, how's your father, give them my best. Though introduced, I didn't catch the name, distracted by the young man's brilliant white smile. "Who was *that?*" I asked. "Jack Kennedy. Joe's boy," my father answered. "He's in politics. Good-looking, isn't he?" A brush with future history, remembered because in my paranoia I heard an unspoken implication: Now there's a young man a father could be proud to call his son-in-law.

As for the show, I knew they were still working on it. After I went to bed there would be a late conference in someone's suite.

But it seemed to me finished, altogether terrific—Merman, the songs, the situation, and a show stopping such as I hadn't witnessed since *This Is the Army* when the star and the sweet-voiced boy in horn-rims sang the new—just put into the second act—double number: the roar that greeted "You're Just in Love," the first time around, the second, the third, and then I lost count.

My father was fine! He wasn't down anymore! He *couldn't* be down anymore! And so when after the New York opening I heard him talking of taking a cruise somewhere to "get some rest and a little sun," I hinted that instead he might take me to Europe, where I'd never been. I had some time off saved up. My mother proposed a boat trip to Italy. When the sailing was canceled, my father, clearly exhausted, just wanting to flop, agreed, with his typical generosity, to take me, anyhow.

35 _____

IT WOULDN'T SEEM the best present a twenty-three-year-old divorcée might ask for, the best way to spend her saved-up time off. But there it was, as I wrote my parents afterward in a long thank-you letter, "the most wonderful three weeks of my life." For more than one reason.

The gift, first, was simply being there, in Europe at last, waking up in the Crillon Hotel, throwing back the curtains and beyond, blue gray in a faint drizzle, was Paris—*Paris*—lodestone of all my readings and dreams, city of St. Louis and Richelieu, Marie Antoinette and Napoleon, of the Hunchback and D'Artagnan and Chauvelin and Jean Valjean, of Toulouse-Lautrec and Daumier, of Hemingway and Gertrude Stein. I had never been so excited, and made no secret of it then or later, for I was hopelessly uncool and got that uncoolness straight from my father, whose own capacity for enthusiasm was as boundless as his capacity for melancholy. He understood exactly about waking up in Paris, and later in Rome and still later in London; he remembered exactly how he had felt on his own first trip to Europe in 1911, at just my age, telling me wonderful stories about how it was to be young and on top of it, in London and Paris before World War I.

It was also exciting being there with my particular father, with his insider's knowledge of Europe's great capitals and his magical, ever replenished gold money clip filled with francs, liras, and pounds to pay for the best hotels and those lunches and dinners in the finest restaurants that were the real focus of every day. "What do you think was the best meal we had?" he'd ask on the plane home, as eager as if he had cooked each one himself. It sometimes seemed that he had, given all the instructions to headwaiters, the barging into chefs' kitchens. I thought of the fish soufflé at the Tour D'Argent, the fettuccine, sticky with cheese and cream, at Alfredo's, the Irish stew at George's, the entire *menu* at a tiny bistro outside of Paris where we went with Alexander Korda, where, in honor of American guests, the enormously fat proprietor-chef ended his feast with baked Alaska. Maybe the best dinner of all, I said, was at Korda's own London flat—tiny sweet oysters, chicken in casserole, a Grand Marnier soufflé as tall as a top hat, accompanied by a greenish Alsatian wine. Even if it wasn't the best, the surroundings made it seem so—the paintings glowing on the walls, a Renoir child, a de Hooch interior, the silver, the polished wood, the host's impish face, his accent, as he told stories in the candlelight. ("A charming charlatan," my father said of his dear friend Korda, the genius moviemaker, as if it were a compliment.)

So that kind of lively company was certainly part of my grand tour, as it had always been part of being Irving Berlin's daughter— as much a delight as the hours I spent, gloriously, freely, sightseeing by myself, shaking off the experts, the friends my father pressed upon me when he wasn't up to taking me himself, saying I liked to go off with my guidebooks and my own thoughts for company. And though he said, "Well you're a funny kid," I knew he was secretly pleased that I was on my own.

But just as interesting, though less easily articulated, was the gift of my father himself, undiluted, without my mother, without my sisters, the longest he and I had ever been in each other's company unmediated except, I should note, for Bill Curto, my father's barber, invited to come along to see his native Italy, keep my father shaved and slapped to life each morning with hot towels, and perform, after a fashion, the traditional services of a gentleman's gentleman.

And what was that self in the fall of 1950? A sixty-two-year-old man, forty years famous, freshly in the news because of *Call Me Madam,* "glad to be back in town with a hit," as he told a London reporter, but plainly exhausted, in Europe for a bit of business and to show his daughter a good time, restless, uncertain about what next, up one minute, down the next.

For the first time, head on, I experienced my father's sleeping habits, which were everything I'd ever been told. The verdict each morning in a hoarse, mournful voice: "I haven't slept at all." Or, "God, I have such a hangover," and I learned this didn't mean my sober father, a moderate drinker always, had drunk too much, just that he had taken two sleeping pills and hadn't slept them off. Sometimes he would say, "I haven't slept a wink, but I feel fine." One night he actually got two good hours, then misery when the trick (one pill, reading till he got sleepy) didn't work again. "Of course it's tragic not to sleep," I wrote in that letter to my parents, with the blitheness of youth and one who generally got eight hours a night. "But it was hard to restrain a giggle when I saw that Chaplinesque figure come into my room with the disorderly curly hair sticking up and the small brown feet sticking out of rumpled yellow pyjamas."

I was not amused, however, if my father appeared too early, wanting to share with me some passage from the third volume of Churchill's memoirs, his current reading (my father did not devour books like my mother, but when he read, he *read*), and especially not when he placed an ancient hot plate on my crowded bedside table, plugged in the frayed cord, which gave off ominous blue sparks, and announced he was making me a "real cup of coffee." Though he didn't blow us up, I was less than appreciative, calling the hotel coffee just fine. The truth dawned on him (he, too, was having a learning experience): "You certainly aren't very pleasant in the morning," he muttered in disgust one day, turning on his heels.

Making coffee reminded my father, as did most things sooner or later, of my mother. "Your mother is really wonderful," he said, half-laughing, half-admiring. "She's the most uncomplaining woman I've ever known. She's almost as bad a sleeper as I am, but she's so unselfish, you never hear about it—she'd bawl the hell out of me if she knew how much I talk about not sleeping—anyhow, she's never learned to make coffee. I've tried to show her how, but she says it's too late. She'll wake up at five and suffer for three hours till she can get someone to make her breakfast."

Rarely a day went by when my father didn't find some way to bring my mother into the conversation. In and out of shops he went, on the Rue St. Honoré, on Bond Street, looking for the right present, anxiously asking, Would she like this? For years I had been listening to her miss him. Now I was listening to him miss her: a confirmation of something that was the rock base of my growing up, my parents' relationship, something I valued as deeply as I sometimes resented it. Now, in my travel euphoria, I found it touching. Besides, "your mother" was only one of many topics. Afterward I had the sense we had covered vast territory, past and present, that Europe with me, through my eyes, brought back to my father his own young self, bursting with tunes and rhymes and ideas, eager to learn and better himself. He hadn't lost that eagerness yet, peppering me with questions, not all of which I could answer, about what I was seeing. I talked a lot about my job, I remember, which I took extremely seriously, not sure exactly where it was leading, only that I liked reporting, interviewing people like Mitch Miller, the Columbia Records A & R man, and Bob Merrill, the new young songwriter who'd written the year's silliest hit, "If I Knew You Were Comin' I'd've Baked a Cake," and most interesting in future terms, the new boy with a voice, Eddie Fisher, who earlier that year had made a striking nightclub debut at Bill Miller's Riviera. A sweet, shy, handsome kid, I said of twenty-one-year-old Eddie, who didn't croon but "sang out," as he put it, like his idol Al Jolson, and like Jolson had started singing in a synagogue. (My next encounter with Eddie, four years later, would be at the Hollywood Bowl, where he had sung, among other selections, his, and my father's, latest hit, "Count Your Blessings." Later, fans mobbed the limousine in which we rode off, my father, my husband and I, Eddie, and his bride, Debbie Reynolds. Still later, at Mocambo's, Eddie had given another concert from our table, his arm around Debbie, no longer shy, though still quite sweet).

There was something else, too, I told my father during one of these heart-to-hearts: that people said I wrote well, even if it was only research for someone else's polishing. And my father nodded, gave me a look, as if he, too, remembered my moment of truth. How finally after years of school plays, in male and villainous roles, I finally had my chance at Barnard as Kate in *The Taming of the Shrew* and made a mess of my big speech. Afterward, when I begged for reassurance, my father (who had always encouraged me) said, and I accepted it, "Darling, you're brilliant and pretty, but let's face it, you are not an actress. Maybe you should write, like your mother."

It was a summing up, that trip, of all the years of him and me as good companions, give or take a few moments. There was however a missing element, let us be frank, in the most wonderful three weeks of my life so far. However good a companion a father may be, he is, after all, only a father. Paris after dark was a disappointment, especially the night Leland and Slim Hayward, also at the Crillon resting up from *Call Me Madam*, brought to dinner Montgomery Clift. We had little to say to each other, Monty, the dashing ne'er-do-well of *The Heiress*, and I, the *Time* researcher; and he had even less to look at. (Fresh from sightseeing I was wearing that same green dress I wore in the office.) Slim's hope we'd go out dancing came to naught. The only young man to invite me out in Paris was the pale, mannerly son of Albert Willemetz, president of SACEM (the French ASCAP), translator of my father's lyrics for thirty years, most recently of *Annie du Far-West*. In restaurants, in the entr'acte of *Annie*, in the Montmarte boîte where Patachou sang, in the office of Patachou's boyfriend Maurice Chevalier, it was "cher Albert" and "dear Earving," talk, talk, talk, with me translating Albert's jokes into English, the plot of *Call Me Madam* into French, cozy as could be, two old friends who doted on each other. And I couldn't believe it when dear Earving said he wasn't letting me out alone with any young Frenchman, never mind whose son he was, how meek and mild he appeared.

But in Rome, ah, that was different. My memories are almost all of a young man, though the first few evenings were my father's, the night we arrived curiously charged as he showed me around the city, its monuments lit up for the half century. He had already been back to Rome once since the war, with my mother and sisters. But I remember a tone of voice, a look on his face, as he pointed out the sights, something beyond excitement at my excitement, something that prompted me to recall a photograph of him, one of my favorites from the *This Is the Army* years, tanned, uniformed, the Colosseum behind him. "A long time ago, Mary Ellin," he said.

Then, one morning, Marvin Barrett appeared in the lobby of the Excelsior Hotel to take me sightseeing, a tall, young American with a camera around his neck, my sometime partner on a story, like me, on his first trip to Europe. My father, out of his yellow pajamas, dressed at an unusually early hour, was in the lobby, too, wanting to check out this "office friend" who had made a good impression on the rest of the family. They shook hands and exchanged a few words; my father said there was a car at our disposal and to enjoy ourselves, deciding on the instant, rightly or wrongly, that here was someone to be trusted.

The young man with the camera was not quite as simple and straightforward as he appeared. He was complex, quirky, and soul-searching, a poet posing as a writer for *Time*, a real handful, I would discover, the subject for a whole other book. But he could indeed be trusted. Of that there has never been a question.

So my future husband and I saw Rome together and, like so many Americans before and after us, fell in love with a city, though not yet with each other, but let the relationship expand as we snapped each other in archways and squares, read to each other from guidebooks, and at lunch in a sunny trattoria window, over a bottle of Soave Bolla, talked of art and history and ourselves; and at a certain point I said to this friend who could be trusted what I couldn't say to my father no matter how close we got, "I'm well. I never thought I'd be really well again," having never admitted to anyone that I hadn't been well, hadn't for a minute taken the events of the past few years "in stride," as I wanted my family to think.

One night the three of us had dinner at Alfredo's. "Curiosity and kindness, those were the two things I noticed first about your father," Marvin says of that long-ago occasion. "Both surprised me, that a man so talented and celebrated should be so interested in what others thought and did and so considerate of their feelings. I remember him asking me questions that did not embarrass or trick me, that I could answer. I also remember, as the evening began, this gray-haired man coming up to the table, a onetime matinee idol named Tullio Carminati, Grace Moore's costar, I believe, in *One Night of Love*, now on his uppers with a none-too-clear political past. Your father's steady friendliness never wavered. Then, after Tullio left, your father excused himself and went into the kitchen to consult with Alfredo about our dinner."

Then it was *arrivederci Roma* and on to London for a final smashing week, at the end of which my father found at last a present worthy of my mother, the famous Staffordshire cows, three rows of them, twenty-seven in all, spotted in an antique shop window. "Just the thing your mother would love for the Welsh dresser in the dining room," my father said, and asked "How much?" When the dealer told him, he said that was pretty reasonable. "Really? Most people think that's pretty dear," said the man. The price it turned out was for one pair. My father bought all twenty-seven.

On the plane home, trying awkwardly to express my thanks, I reported a conversation I'd had with friends, met for a drink at Claridge's. "How do you happen to be in Europe?" one of them asked. "Does your father have business?" "Well, yes," I said. "He's interested in organizing a London company of *Call Me Madam*, and in Paris he talked to Willemetz," and then I broke off, saying sheepishly, "Really he took the trip for me. To be nice."

At first my father brushed this off with a smile. "I think you've got a pretty nice old man, too." Then he added, more seriously, "I'll tell you exactly how much was me being unselfish. I didn't want to fly to Paris, I didn't feel like seeing a lot of people, I just wanted some sun. It was a letdown to get on that plane. That part was unselfish. But once we got there I got a big kick out of watching you see Europe for the first time. I liked to see the way you handled yourself, the way you were with my friends, the way you could take care of yourself. And I think we got on pretty well, too, which pleases me."

It would be the story of his life, more and more, avoiding people, places, events, dreading them, but when cornered, by a sense of duty, concern for someone else, business, he rose to the occasion and, though later might deny it, managed to have a grand time himself.

And I cannot take it as insignificant that in the middle of my grand tour, because it was time, whether he realized it or not, whether he knew what he was doing, my father gave me his blessing and, as much as I was able to accept it, my freedom.

_____ 36

SHORTLY AFTER being done, for the moment, with me, my father took my mother to Hawaii, to celebrate their silver wedding anniversary. Along for part of the time was Linda, on holiday from the American Academy of Dramatic Arts, now the designated actress of the family. She remembers a beautiful house, parties, our parents having a good time with each other and with friends—Uncle Joe, Eddie Mannix, maybe the Goetzes. In a photograph, sitting under a palm tree, they look relaxed, amused at life and themselves, nothing fancy: a good-looking black-haired man in shorts, a pretty lady with a topknot in printed beach pajamas and a shell necklace. A 1951 picture to add to the twenty-four others my mother had given my father in a foldout silver picture frame, twenty-five units, each one engraved with a bar of a song, holding a photograph of that year, of them, of us children as we came along: 1926 ("Always"), 1927 ("Blue Skies"), 1928 ("The Song Is Ended"), and so on. No one remembers my father's twenty-fifth anniversary present to my mother (what could you give the granddaughter of the Comstock Lode on her silver anniversary?), though we all remember the thirtieth, a double pearl ring; the fortieth, a ruby; the fiftieth, a plain wide Cartier gold band.

"We had a lovely time, yes," my mother would say later of that anniversary trip, then hesitate. "But." A gesture: a little up and down . . . you know.

Twenty-five years for my parents was a confirmation, as if any were needed, of the impregnability of their marriage. It was also the winding down of an incredible spree—a spree not without its hard times, and one very dark stretch near the beginning, but seen in hindsight as unbroken. And for my father, 1951 marked the end of a run of forty years. How much more did any man have in him? A lot more, my father would have said, if he could just get feeling better, just get some sleep; that "peaceful older age" always receding, a point receding to infinity.

"I'm really getting steamed up again," he had said during one of those evenings in Paris with the Haywards, outlining an idea for a revue designed to play equally well in New York, London, and Paris, set in the present, future, and past, with the past including old songs of the First World War, and before and after, which had been hits in Europe.

But in my memory, after our return, my father the songwriter goes underground. He is audible, of course, on the stage of the Imperial Theatre, where *Call Me Madam* will run till June 1952; in nightclubs, where orchestras play "It's a Lovely Day Today" and "You're Just in Love" ad nauseam. He is there at the Tony Awards, winner for *Call Me Madam* for best musical score. (*Guys and Dolls* won best musical.) There is an Irving Berlin television special in September 1951, with Margaret Truman closing the show singing "God Bless America." (In the Cub Room of the Stork Club, where we gathered afterward, my father was called to the telephone. On the other end, just like the running gag in *Call Me Madam*, the president of the United States, saying how much he liked the show and thanking Irving Berlin for being so nice to his little girl.) There is Irving Berlin, the Eisenhower supporter, introducing at a Madison Square Garden rally "They Like Ike," a new version of "I Like Ike," with its new last line: "Even Harry Truman says that he likes Ike." There are, always, "White Christmas" and "Easter Parade' and new records of old songs—"Maybe It's Because I Love You Too Much," "I'm Playing with Fire," "How About Me?"—songs that appeal to the smoky-voiced cabaret singers of the early fifties. There's talk of movie deals, the *Call Me Madam* movie, a movie to be called *White Christmas*, a movie about show business, deals on, then off, then on again. Of course, he must be writing *something*, you think, and it seems merely very sweet when he summons you up to his top-floor study not to hear some just finished song but to see what he has on his easel, his latest oil of riotously colored flowers in a bowl, what he really seems steamed up about these days. ("I agree with you that I shouldn't keep painting the same picture," he wrote Irving Hoffman, who had started him painting shortly after his sixtieth birthday as a kind of therapy. "But as I look back on my early songs, I realize I kept writing the same tune.")

In reality, 1951 is a lost year for songs, and most of 1952 as well. In reality, I'm paying scant attention to my father's struggles, being almost entirely involved in my own affairs—my job, my love life (which does not always run smooth), my battle to move into my own apartment.

My most vivid memory in this period is of the visit we paid Pablo Picasso, in his Vallauris studio, in June 1951—a revealing glimpse at mid-century of two singular men, the presiding artistic genius of the twentieth century and the world's most famous writer of popular songs. I had spent my life observing my father in the company of celebrated people—songwriters, Broadway and Hollywood stars, playwrights, authors, directors: his peers. I had seen him at ease with Somerset Maugham and Charlie Chaplin. But I had not seen him in the company of one of those larger-than-life figures, with President Roosevelt, say, or General Eisenhower, the king and queen of England, or the pope. I was not around the famous night at Russel and Anna Crouse's when he and Eugene O'Neill met and sat at the piano till three in the morning. I had never observed him with someone he not only admired but might be in awe of. This was a first.

How I got to meet Picasso, and Chagall as well, how my father happened to take me to Europe for the second time in six months, was a typical Beekman Place comedy. A trip to Paris I'd planned with a friend, a recent divorcée like myself, scuttled by parental arm twisting; my father looking cross and avoiding my eye; my mother, a dragon in a pink-satin bed jacket, puffing smoke and breathing fire, relaying my "poor" father's apprehensions and commands; my inability to tell them to go jump in the lake (that what I needed at this moment was to put an ocean between me and Marvin Barrett); my further inability, shortly thereafter, to turn down an invitation from my father, feeling guilty because he had gotten his way, to accompany him to Paris for the wedding of "cher Albert's" son (that same young Willemetz he'd forbidden me to go out with) and then on to the Côte D'Azur, to the Hôtel du Cap for a week of sun. I went, I enjoyed, I returned to New York with my trophies, from lunch with Chagall an autographed silkscreen, a pair of lovers, in violets and greens, floating above a town; from that visit to Picasso ten pages of notes; from all those two- and three-star restaurants, ten extra pounds, a real *tanta*, though not a word from my father.

Lunch with Chagall and assorted members of his family in Vence was easy, familiar territory. There was talk of art, music, and Russia, two famous Russian Jews, whose families hailed from the same part of the old country, a year apart in age, enjoying each other's company. But Picasso's hillside studio was a rocky Parnassus.

Seventy years old, surrounded by his beautiful young family—twenty-eight-year-old Françoise Gilot in ponytail and black sweater, laughing, keeping things genial; four-year-old Claude, a rumpled urchin; Paloma, two, plump and solemn—Picasso was Gjon Mili's genie sprung to life: the swarthy skin like thin creased leather, the bald dome fringed with dirty white hair, the dark eyes, alert, observant, cautious. He greeted us warmly (he and my father had met briefly in Cannes the previous summer with Irving Hoffman), demanding on the instant that we admire a line of blue-and-white vases on the terrace wall, notice the contrast between the pottery and the view of blackened tile roofs, distant green hills. But those eyes, so full of knowledge, had little warmth.

The tour began, room after room of works soon to be famous: the plaster goat with a red-clay vase for an udder, the pregnant woman with pottery breasts and stomach, not yet cast in bronze, the family portraits, the Vallauris landscapes, some in earth colors, some bright and clashing, the plates and vases, the outpourings of a man in the "older years" on a new creative splurge, the artist explaining, demonstrating, answering questions. (René Batigne, director of the Picasso Museum, interpreted, but gestures said as much as words.) Busy taking mental notes, I left the talking to my father, who, as quick as he was, had met a master of quickness. When he admired a group of small clay figures, the artist put them on a turntable, one by one. "There, that is how you should see them, turning"; when he admired a shelf of pottery, like ancient Greek vases, Picasso picked up his favorite, a bull on one side, nude women on the other, turning it gleefully. "See the bull, then quick, the women, good, isn't it?" Then plunging the vase into a bucket of water, holding it in the sunlight: "See it glisten, see how the red looks better!" When, looking at the family portraits, my father asked how long the children kept still in a pose, Picasso answered, "They never pose; it's all memory." Some of the painted children were quite unpleasant, with green faces and swollen heads like a fun-house reflection; others more realistic. But this was Picasso; ordinary reactions were suspended.

Almost everything we saw had been done in the last year, a lot of work. What was his working day, my father asked, one professional to another, all of a sudden. From lunch till nine or ten at night, the artist answered. Most mornings he went down to Golfe Juan to swim. Otherwise, he rarely left Vallauris except to go to Paris on business, visit Matisse in Nice, or attend bullfights in Nimes. ("The way some people go to the movies. I don't care if it's good or bad as long as it's a bullfight.") Mostly he worked. "Creation, that is my fun," he said.

The great artist, I was making a mental note, was a charming host, but his gaiety was too deliberate, artificial, like a man performing for small children, and he never asked a question, only answered them. But then my father was giving his own company performance now, not artificial, just typical: spinning a fantasy, as the tour finished, of a musical comedy set in Vallauris, with its famous pottery kilns, its presiding artist, its recent flash of notoriety, as the place where Rita Hayworth and Aly Khan were married; a musical for which Picasso would design the sets. Briefly Picasso joined in the fantasy, recalling the days when he had designed sets for Diaghilev ballets, asking fondly after his old friend Stravinsky, who lived in Hollywood—a question finally—though my father could only answer that he didn't know Stravinsky, that was not his world. And then reality. "You go away tomorrow," said

Pablo Picasso to Irving Berlin. "I stay here. We make an operetta together? *C'est drôle, ça.*" And a grumpy mention of having been refused a U.S. visa.

Then Françoise came to the rescue with an anecdote, apocryphal, perhaps, but it restored the artist's good humor. How a visiting American millionaire was shown a Picasso canvas by Ramié the potter (executor of Picasso designs) and asked, "How much?" Picasso's agent in Paris took care of all transactions, said Ramié, but he did not believe this picture was for sale. "Forget the agent," the man responded, "I'll give you any price you ask." When he reached $100,000 (a substantial amount in those days) and Ramié still shook his head, the visitor asked in honest bewilderment, "But then why does he do it?"

Everyone beamed as Batigne began taking pictures against the view of tile-roofed houses and hills in the noontime sun. But hanging in the air as the two famous men embraced twice, French fashion, was the question that would never be satisfactorily answered, for either the artist or the songwriter, however much money their work commanded—not why but what. What made him do it in the first place? And most mysterious of all, where? Where did the talent come from?

If he had felt ruffled by Picasso's prickliness, my father gave no sign. He appeared at ease, as he always had to me, whatever the encounter. My sister Linda, describing a similar perception, would use the French expression "*Il est bien dans sa peau*"; literally, he is comfortable in his skin; more broadly, he is comfortable with who he is. Which did not mean, in my father's case, he might not inwardly, physically, be ready to jump right out of that skin. A lifelong interest, at any rate, began that day in Vallauris. And if, in later years, you wanted to give my father a present he would truly appreciate, you would give him the latest Picasso book, hot off the Paris or New York presses.

My days as Miss Berlin are coming to an end. Two final scenes.

The first a night at Beekman Place, in the late winter of 1952. My parents are about to set out for California, where my father is to begin work on two movies, *There's No Business Like Show Business*

and *White Christmas.* I am home for a farewell dinner. Things seem
to be looking up for me. I have my own apartment. At work, I've
landed a permanent and delightful post as books researcher, out of
the bullpen, into my own office with all those books; my boss is
Max Gissen, one of *Time*'s major characters, a jazz buff who in his
spare moments is writing a book about Louis Armstrong. Weekly, a
notable quartet of reviewers arrive to drop their copy, argue over
fact and opinion: Irving Howe, Nigel Dennis, Anthony West, and
Brad Darrach. Nonetheless, my own spring plans include, yet
again a trip to Europe with a friend. Finally, at twenty-five, living
on my own, I cannot be told no, but things are scratchy. "Come and
see me upstairs," my father says, leaving the table before dessert.
In bed, surrounded by books, magazines, pills, and Kleenex, he
looks small and sorry for himself.

"What's the matter?" I ask.

"I have a cold, that's all," he answers. "But you. What gives
with you? What good is running away going to do? Why don't you
and that young man make up your minds, yes or no, and be done
with it?"

I have no answer, or no answer I care to give. How to explain,
even if I dared, or wanted to, to a man of my father's age and generation the complications of romance in the early 1950s?

"If it's not right, it's not right," he presses. "If it is—you need
someone to take care of you. With someone to take care of you, you
could accomplish a lot. Have a family. Write, Write for publication, not just research for someone else to use. Make something of
yourself."

But the exact words are not what I remember as much as the
frustration and helplessness because he can't make it well or force
me to make it well. He can't be in control.

"Everything's going to be fine," I said finally (words he has
unfortunately heard before).

"If I didn't believe that . . ." What a ham he is. Are those tears
I see in those dark eyes or merely the cold?

The second scene, with my mother, comes in late summer, in
Lew Beach. Things on the home front seem brighter than they did
in the winter. Returned from California, where work has been on
scripts rather than songs and the atmosphere (so my sisters would

report) gloomy, my father is back where he belongs, at the piano. Two letters recall the changed air. A note, brief, perky, dated August 27, 1952, to Irving Hoffman: "I just wrote my first song for the movie *White Christmas*. This will be sung by Bing Crosby and the title is 'Sittin' in the Sun Counting My Money.' See you later." (Twenty years later, Alec Wilder would single out this neglected song, dropped from the movie and released as a single, as one of his favorites: "It's as if Berlin had just finished writing the end of a release when a great jazz improvisation drifted in through the open window . . . and so affected him that he said in effect, 'Oh, the hell with conventional forms . . . I'll just wail!' ")

A few days later my father wrote Joe Schenck: "First let me tell you I feel just great. I've had several nights of good sleep without too much help. Also for the first time in a long time the work is coming faster and better. I'm enclosing a lyric of a song I finished here which I am going to publish immediately. . . . You have always said that I commercialized my emotions and many times you were wrong but this particular song is based on what really happened . . . some time ago, after the worst kind of a sleepless night, my doctor came to see me, and after a lot of self-pity . . . he looked at me and said, 'speaking of doing something about insomnia, did you ever try counting your blessings?' "

My mother, whose moods swing with my father's, who is pleased about "Count Your Blessings," is reaching out, would like to be friends, in a way that isn't so easy with a touchy, grown-up daughter. She and I have gone on one of those cross-country walks I found excruciating as a teenager but now enjoyed. She is asking about Marvin. I tell her he has left the magazine and is in San Diego with his parents, free-lancing and starting a novel. I do not tell her the exact circumstances of Marvin's leaving, that meeting one deadline too many, he has had a major fit, not unknown in the offices of *Time;* though he has not thrown his typewriter and a ream of copy out the window or turned himself in at Payne Whitney (the psychiatric branch of New York Hospital, where rumor had it there was a reserved Time Inc. suite), he has in his own way made quite a splash. But my mother is not a fool. "That magazine may not have been the right place for him," she says. "So much pressure. Will he come back to New York and look for another job?" "That depends."

And after a bit, unaccountably, for I didn't discuss my private life with my mother these days, "He and I have to decide, I guess."

"Well, yes, that would be good," my mother says mildly. "Not decided, you don't seem terribly happy. I suspect you love him, and why not, he's very lovable, he shares your interests, he's everything Mr. Unmentionable was not, and handsome to boot. You'd have beautiful children."

"He also has problems." I hesitate. "He gets depressed. He has very bad nerves."

"Your father gets depressed and has very bad nerves," my mother says a few paces later. "They often go with talent." Neither of us is being entirely candid, but candid enough. I felt I had been given a form of permission, and though I never would have admitted I wanted or needed it, in fact, I did.

As for my father, who'd made his points earlier, the thing I remember him saying, steadily, ever since my first debacle, was that he hoped when I remarried, I'd just go off and do it, as he and my mother had.

And so we did it. One evening in Ensenada, Mexico, after a day of sightseeing and dithering, with a thick fog rolling in from the Pacific, we knocked on the mayor's door. His witnesses were out seeing a Rita Hayworth movie, he said, but they could sign the license later; and that was that.

The next morning, October 15, 1952, at lunchtime in New York, I telephoned home. Linda answered and passed me on to my father. "That's wonderful," he said. He would reach my mother at the Colony restaurant; she would be very happy, too. Later, my mother would tell me what my father told her that day, something that seemed to me silly but sweet. "I was so afraid," he said, "that Mary Ellin would waste her whole youth."

37 _____

A P O S T S C R I P T :

In the late fall of 1952, stopping off in New York long enough for me to quit my job, and for both of us to receive everyone's congratulations and a large wedding check, Marvin and I took off for Italy to start our new life together. We settled into a small pink casa on a hillside just beyond the main thoroughfare of Taormina, Sicily. Four tiny rooms and a view. We established our rent, fifty dollars a month, and what we paid our maid, somewhat less, and our image. To the merchants, the café owners, the nice expatriate Californian at the other end of town, we were the new, young Americans, not the first struggling writers to land in this town on a shelf between mountains and sea, with a Greek theater and a backdrop of Mt. Etna. (D. H. Lawrence and Frieda had lived there, exchanging frying pans and rolling pins in a villa visible from our front door; Truman Capote had passed our gate on his way to market with his Pekingese in his shopping basket). We settled in for a busy winter and spring.

And then the telegram arrived from New York: My parents, Linda, and Finny (my mother's dearest holdover from her youth) would like to join us for Christmas.

We joked, there went our cover, we squirmed, we were flattered by their attention, we were appalled. Underneath we understood what was up. They wanted to make sure that everything was all right. Postcards and letters were not enough. They had to see with their own eyes and unfortunately at the same time be seen.

So they arrived and settled into the largest suite in Taormina's largest and grandest hotel, the San Domenico, where the staff, however used to illustrious visitors, snapped to attention. Our California friend, briefly cross ("Why didn't you *tell* me?"), had the family to dinner and exchanged stories with my father about their mutual friend Mary Martin, with my mother about the very rich of Santa Barbara. Whatever was going on with my father back home (nothing too good in terms of those very ragged nerves and the grim knowledge that Uncle Ben was dying of cancer), he was his enthusiastic-on-the-road self. On Christmas Eve he went out onto the

Corso Victor Umberto and bought for my mother at Panarello's antique shop the single most expensive item available in town, a
necklace of rough-cut emeralds and brilliants with a carved emerald pendant. For himself, from Taormina's famed cobbler, he ordered a half-dozen pairs of hand-sewn shoes. Word traveled up and
down the Corso and along the little side streets: Extraordinary
Americans have arrived; expensive objects are being bought. My
mother alternately charmed and terrorized the hotel manager, himself one of Taormina's holy terrors. Linda drew stares, whistles, and
unsuitable invitations from liquid-eyed Sicilians wherever she
went. Finny beamed upon us, the newlyweds, exclaimed at Mt.
Etna but was scandalized at the pagan flavor of Sicilian Catholi-
cism. In my father's honor, at the town hall, a mandolin concert was
given—massed mandolins, every mandolin in Taormina, playing a
jangling medley of Sicilian and Irving Berlin tunes. The auditorium
was packed with our new fellow townspeople.

A few evenings later we were joined at the local nightclub by
Ruth and Mark Schorer, old friends of Marvin's from Harvard,
down from Florence (where Mark was researching his biography of
Sinclair Lewis). We danced to "Luna Rossa," "Les Feuilles
Mortes," and "What'll I Do?" And though nothing really personal
was said that night or any other, my father made it clear that whatever it was he'd come to check out, he was satisfied. "So did I do
all right?" I said to him, oh so lightly, at a moment when it was just
the two of us, walking ahead of the others arm in arm; not quite
sure what I meant by that, only that I wanted some concrete token
of approval, some final expression of forgiveness for whatever it
was I had put him through. "You've done fine," he said.

Nine months later, we returned to New York, I seven months
pregnant, Marvin with a completed novel (yet to see print, though
subsequent Marvin Barrett publications are many). In November
our daughter Elizabeth, first of our four children, first of my parents' nine grandchildren, was born. For my mother's birthday the
following March, her fifty-first, my father was photographed in our
apartment with the baby. Engraved, in his handwriting, on the picture's gold frame, was the announcement of a new era: "For
Granny, from Grandpa and Elizabeth Esther."

A few years later he wrote his first grandfather's song, a pretty, lilting tune, a perfectly turned lyric:

> *I can hear a parrot*
> *Singing in a garret*
> *I can hear it sing*
> *Who's the sweetest thing?*
> *Elizabeth Esther Barrett.*

Some spoilsport pointed out that parrots don't sing. My father said he didn't care; for his oldest grandchild a parrot would sing.

GRANNY
AND GRANDPA

MY FATHER LEFT an amazing legacy of songs that he hoped would survive, like those of Stephen Foster, into another century. With my mother he also created a family, one that would give birth to new families, stretching into time, widening, no end in sight. Already to the nine grandchildren have been added, by way of my three daughters, five great-grandchildren. "Your father cares about three things," my mother liked to say when we were growing up, "his work, his wife, and his children, not necessarily in that order." ("His country," I suppose, went without saying.) My father only commented from time to time, "We are a funny family," saying it with wryness and affection both.

But a family we were, no question, in a long-ago time that seemed less long ago when I first tried to summon it up in the form of a thirty-page letter to my father on his seventieth birthday.

It was not a birthday to celebrate. In the mid-1950s, his ragged nerves, lack of sleep, and general dilapidation—all those problems triggered or aggravated by his wartime exertions—had culminated in a severe depression, far graver than the walking depression of the "dry spell"; a nervous breakdown that would last several years, involve periods of hospitalization (at New York Hospital, at Silver Hill in Connecticut), and cause him to say he was retired.

What bright moments there were in these years concerned others. My mother's long-awaited book about her grandmother, *Silver Platter*, out at last, well reviewed, on the best-seller list. My sister Elizabeth's graduation from Vassar. Linda's marriage to Edouard Emmet, a boy she had known for years, a family favorite, whose dark looks and quizzical manner had something of my young father about them; who had taken a Wall Street job to earn money, though what he wanted to do was paint (and today does just 285 that). The birth of more Barrett babies—Irving, Mary Ellin, and Katherine Leah following Elizabeth Esther—beautiful children all, just like my mother said we'd have; four of them, the magic number in my generation.

It was in Lew Beach that my small children began to know their grandparents—my indefatigable mother, who knocked herself out giving them a good time, my casual country father, who, even in the worst of his depression, could come to life for the children, a nice old grandpa who retreated for part of each day to the tea house, now a studio, to paint; not a clue, my daughter Elizabeth would say, not till she was eight or nine, that he was a world-famous man. "If the children didn't come, I knew it would be the end," my mother said later.

My father would pull himself out of that black depression, emerge from "retirement" in 1962, to do, heaven help him, *Mr. President*. But in the late 1950s, things seemed very bleak.

Hoping to cheer him up, I sat at my desk in the tree-shaded old house in Wilton, Connecticut, where Marvin, now a *Newsweek* editor, and I were raising our young family. And I tried to answer some questions. They were the ones that had been put to me by various reporters, writing their own pieces in honor of that milestone, Irving Berlin Turns Seventy. Always the same. "Did you see a lot of your father as a child? Did you do things together? Was he interested in your day-to-day activities? Can you *have* a normal family life with a great man?" The answer was yes, emphatically, demonstrably yes. In the course of my reminiscing, I tried to sum up what I felt my parents had stood for and what they meant to me and my sisters.

"In your own partly old fashioned, partly liberal way," I wrote, "you raised us to think for ourselves, to be industrious and kind, to be realistic about our advantages but not to feel superior, to respect authority but to recognize and beware of bigotry. You gave us the best of two worlds and made it impossible to be really snobbish about anything. Or at least, if we were, to know it was wrong. . . .

"Above all, I suppose the best thing you did for us was to be happily married, not just married for better or worse as so many parents are. Whatever your differences may have been you presented a united front. You had a good time together and you somehow drew us into that good time. You never complained about each other or tried to get us to take sides. Occasionally you spoke sharply to each other . . . but should we children chime in, watch out.

"In an age and in a world where broken families were the rule, you gave us a sense of the family unit and the continuity of family life. Of course there were between us the usual battles of the generations. . . . But there was always, even in the worst fights, a basic feeling of support. In the last analysis, Mamma and Daddy would come through."

That seventieth birthday letter, my father said, pleased him more than anything that had ever been written about him. It was, in a sense, the genesis of this memoir, and portrait of the parents of my youth, in the great years of their life together. A time, perhaps, to write "the end."

Except there are thirty-one years to go—more than a generation of years before I would find myself in that haunted attic on Forty-sixth Street, where this story began. The entire second half of my parents' marriage.

Those speeded-up years were difficult ones. They are not easy for me to talk about, especially from the mid-1970s on. And yet having come this far, I cannot quite walk away. The Irving Berlin I knew when I was growing up didn't suddenly disappear, to be replaced by some sort of reclusive misanthrope. It wasn't like that. As always, the view from outside in is different from the view inside out.

Within my parents' less than peaceful older age were splendid moments, touching moments, or simply loving, funny ones, many of them connected with that new generation of little people filling up the house in Lew Beach. There is pleasure in being reminded by my daughter Katherine of the way my mother entertained her grandchildren, in town or in the country, as she had once entertained her children, organizing games and expeditions, taking them to museums and the theater, instilling in them the family love of books, reading to them, making up stories (it seems no coincidence that all three of our daughters are writers); the way she looked after them when Marvin and I went to Europe or California, on assignment or holiday. There is pleasure in remembering my father as Elizabeth, that oldest grandchild, remembers him. "I know that the adjective currently applied to Irving Berlin's later life is, at best, 'reclusive,' " she wrote me recently from Los Angeles (where she lives with her husband, the composer Sasha Matson, and our two Matson grandsons). "I can only say that as a child and teenager, I had no problems with his need for privacy. It made sense to me. He seemed shy and sometimes left a room abruptly but he was never harsh or angry, never told us to keep it down or behave. He allowed us to tease and question him. There was black in his hair, he had a quick wit and energy, and seemed younger than some of the other grandparents I knew. He cooked steak on the outdoor grill. He shared a bowl of ice cream at midnight in the kitchen. He watched TV. He fished and painted. He pinched cheeks, literally, and told us girls we were smart and pretty. When surrounded by us, he seemed to enjoy our vagaries with affection and a wise objectivity."

From the hard times that began for my father in the 1950s there would be no brilliant emerging or triumph of an obvious sort, as there had been thirty years earlier, after the "dry spell." But there was, for a while, anyhow, a triumph of the spirit, in private, in public.

I was away in 1961, the year the depression lifted. Marvin's magazine life had taken us to Chicago for a venture few will remember, Hugh Hefner's *Show Business Illustrated*. By the time we returned to New York (Mr. Barrett now in a new, high-risk job as managing editor of Huntington Hartford's *Show*), the miracle had happened.

At seventy-three my father appeared to be his "old self," feisty, full of pep, looking as always younger than his age. He had a little more weight around the middle, and his later look was in place: face squarish rather than sharp and bony, thick, dark-rimmed glasses, hair and brows black indeed. (The gray in his hair wouldn't be apparent until his late seventies.) He was every inch the songwriter, working on a new show with Lindsay and Crouse—*Mr. President*. The subject seemed just right for the older Irving Berlin, a U.S. president in his last month of office, facing retirement. There were echoes of that shelved musical *Stars on My*

Shoulders (and one of its songs, "It Gets Lonely in the White House"); echoes of the movie *White Christmas,* with its retired general. But this was to reflect glamorous new times, the high-style White House of JFK (for whom I.B., reverting to his Democrat origins, voted). It is painful, given the outcome, to remember that spring and summer of 1962, the old-time mixture of nerves and excitement; excitement notwithstanding rumblings from Boston that the reviews were bad, that much work needed to be done. But with Leland Hayward producing, Josh Logan directing, how could they *not* get it fixed? There was worry, yes, as the show headed for Washington, caution in my father's voice, but hope, too, though maybe that was for my benefit.

"The success or failure of a show," Howard Lindsay would say later, "is settled when somebody says, 'Wouldn't it be a great idea. . . .' Perle Mesta was. This wasn't."

And then a memory of my father at that ghastly opening night in Washington, a Kennedy affair benefiting their favorite charity, and at the party afterward at the British embassy, so quiet, so gracious, sitting beside my mother, chatting with the vice president, the Crouses, asking fourteen-year-old Lindsay Ann Crouse for a dance. ("Do you do the twist?" she asked when the beat changed. "No, dear," he said, returning her to the table.) Next day, in a hotel suite, surrounded by newspapers, he was even quieter, trying to put a brave face on it, brushing off Russel Crouse's remark "Well, Irving, *you* can't complain." (The Washington press had a few kind words for the score.)

As for myself: I remember all around me, as we left the theater, the forced smiles of Washington friends and acquaintances, the embarrassed murmurs of "lovely songs." I had a cold feeling at the pit of my stomach because I knew the worst, Marvin taking my hand very hard because he suspected the worst, though, loyally, saying, "I *like* it." And then, on the grand embassy staircase, I was introduced to Ethel Kennedy, who gave the biggest unforced smile and said, "It was great, just great, how proud you must be of your father." If she was only being polite, I didn't care; she had enabled me to walk into that ballroom with my head high.

A half-dozen years later, some months after the tragic 1968

campaign, when I worked for Robert Kennedy, I had reason to write Ethel, and I reminded her of this encounter. "I meant every word," she wrote back—or so I recollect. "We played and played the record and to this day 'The Secret Service Makes Me Nervous' is our family theme song."

Listening to that record with my children, in the living room of our garden duplex on West Eleventh Street, was one of my own memories; not letting on what the world thought because the kids thought *Mr. President* was great, their first experience of "grandpa's show"; and after a number of hearings I could almost think it was great, too; Nanette Fabray singing "They Love Me," Jack Haskell and Anita Gillette singing "Empty Pockets Filled with Love," the next to last of my father's double numbers, and an item called "Song for Belly Dancer." (The children knew that one by heart: "In ancient Si-am, / Women like I-am . . . indoors or on the street, / No woman dances with her feet.")

What can you say when an old showman's last musical, instead of being, at the least, a good, strong farewell, like Cole Porter's *Silk Stockings* or Kurt Weill's *Lost in the Stars*, is an unprecedented dud? You can say that the old showman took the humiliation with dignity, he shrugged it off, and he didn't sink back into depression, though he would never again be the real "old self" I'd once known. Instead, he wrote a batch of new songs, a score he said was one of his best, for *Say It with Music*, the movie in the works throughout the sixties, and finally called off, victim of a changing management at M-G-M, a perception in Hollywood that musicals were finished and that Irving Berlin, in his sixth decade of songwriting, was old hat. (Not so, concerning at least four of those fresh-sounding *Say It with Music* songs, which may find their way yet into some cabaret singer's repertory.)

For my parents the 1960s were hard but not frozen. They still traveled. They spent time in California. They went south in the winter. They visited the Emmets, who had moved to Paris, Edouard's boyhood home. In London, in September 1963, they checked into Claridge's and gave a wedding for Elizabeth Irving, their youngest, to the English book editor Edmund Fisher. (The marriage would end in 1969.) More babies arrived, Caroline, Ellin and Edward Emmet, and Emily Fisher.

Summers in Lew Beach continued and would continue throughout the seventies. "What I remember was this welcoming, man-of-the-earth grandfather who made me feel my ethnic origins, Jewish from the bottom up," my daughter Mary Ellin said recently on the phone from Washington, D.C. (where she lives with her writer-husband Steve Lerner, pursues her own free-lance magazine career, and takes care of two-year-old Benjamin). "This guy with thick glasses, talking two inches from your face—'how are you? What are you reading?'—and as we got older, 'What boys are you seeing?' Very basic, a real straight shooter who made you feel special. Sure he could be in a bad mood sometimes, but he was always glad to see us, a warm, crusty man who played cards, taught us to fish, and occasionally made fun of Granny's manners lessons. 'On the Lower East Side we called it the boardinghouse reach,' he'd say, demonstrating." My son Irving remembers the time he told Grandpa he needn't worry about his fame; he was even bigger than the Beatles. Grandpa, who admitted "Yesterday" was a first-rate song, was so amused he gave him a hundred-dollar bill. He also told Irving that his long hair reminded him of some Chinese fellow at Mike Salter's café and reassured my mother: "Don't worry about it, Ellin, in ten years his hair will be as short as mine."

Throughout the sixties my mother worked on a new novel, *The Best of Families*, a nostalgic tale of old New York, and read it, chapter by chapter, to my father, who said, "Wonderful," or, "You don't need all that." But she continued to call her writing a sideline (not entirely truthfully concerning *Silver Platter*, which she had taken seriously and talked about a lot). Her real life, she'd say, was as a wife, a mother, and a grandmother—and, since the mid-fifties (she didn't have to say), a Catholic, a very ardent Catholic returned to the fold.

In 1966, when I presented my parents with the manuscript of my first novel, *Castle Ugly* (a scarier brand of nostalgia, love and murder in the 1930s, on the Long Island dunes), my mother wrote me a beautiful letter. My father invited me up to his top-floor digs at Beekman Place and said it was "wonderful" but I didn't "need all that" at the end; there were two twists too many. (I didn't take all his advice, but I made some changes.) "I'm proud of you," he said. What else could he have said? But I would have known (and did with a later book he liked less well).

The year 1966, when Elizabeth, our oldest, became a teenager and Katherine, our youngest, entered first grade, marked my parents' fortieth wedding anniversary and the twentieth anniversary of *Annie Get Your Gun,* with its Lincoln Center revival and its showstopping new song, "An Old Fashioned Wedding," my father's last hit. Two years later, there was the *Ed Sullivan Show* celebrating his eightieth birthday.

Then, in 1969, *Say It with Music* fell through, and he really did retire, though he continued to write songs, which (once he stopped going to the office) he dictated to Helmy Kresa over the phone till Helmy lost his hearing; and lyrics, which he dictated to Hilda Schneider, the last of these only two years before he died.

Little by little, as the world knows, my father became a recluse, seeing only his immediate family (and not all that often), though nothing happens overnight. In the first part of the seventies there were events that brought him out still. The remarriage, in 1970, of my sister Elizabeth to the New York lawyer Alton Peters, who was, and is, a guiding light of the Metropolitan Opera. The birth of the last Berlin grandchild, Rachel Peters, the following year. The prisoner of war dinner at the White House in the spring of 1973, his final public appearance, singing "God Bless America" for the country's latest set of veterans (for a night Watergate headlines put on hold). His last photo session, in September of 1974, with Jill Krementz for *Life.*

In the early seventies he still had a few New York pals to go to dinner and a movie with. (My mother no longer went to the movies, saying they neither amused nor pleased her, though she still read widely, at the age of seventy James Joyce's *Ulysses,* saying to really appreciate it you not only had to know Homer and Shakespeare; you had to be a Catholic). I remember thinking it sporty that my father, in his mid-eighties, went with Abe Berman, his theatrical lawyer, and Harold Arlen to see *Last Tango in Paris.* "Very long, very dirty, Brando brilliant," he said when I asked for his critique.

We talked a lot about criticism in that period because I was the book reviewer for *Cosmopolitan.* He read my column every month and made comments, generally favorable. And I would not forget the evening he took me upstairs after dinner to see his latest painting, he said, but in fact to talk about *The Best of Families*, coming out in the spring of 1970. "You like your mother's book," he challenged. "Yes. I've told you so ten times." "Are you going to review it?" "Yes," I answered, "I loved it . . . thank God." "Say that," he said. "Say just that." Which I did. In a diary I kept at the time, I made a note of the whole conversation, how he talked that night more personally than was his habit. About an idea he had for a show, except he hadn't the energy to mount a whole show. "I'm tired, Mary Ellin," he said. "Damn it, your old man has about had it." I put my arms around him a little awkwardly; we had a hard time as a family being demonstrative. "You know I love you," he said. "I know. I love you." And then, "Well, darling, I think I'll lie down for a while. You go downstairs to Marvin and your mother. Try to cheer her up. It's not so cheerful always these days being married to your old man."

It was also around this time that my father said, "Remember how upset I was, what a fuss I made, when your mother went back into the church? I'm glad now she has that."

The next year, Irving Hoffman, the friend my father depended on most, died. A grim gathering in a West Side funeral parlor, Irving's longtime lady friend Gertrude Bayne weeping, my mother trying to steady her with small talk, my father ashen as we sat through eulogies of dreadful, forced jollity. A few years later, Abe Berman died. The last pals who got him out of the house going, one by one. Then Harold Arlen became ill with Parkinson's disease. For the final six years of his life, he and my father talked almost daily on the telephone, conversations recalled to me by Ed Jablonski, Arlen's biographer and latter-day caretaker: how when Harold was having a bad day, Irving could make him laugh; how Irving would call up and say, "Turn on CBS"—or NBC, or whatever— "hurry, they're playing one of your songs."

Grandchildren, young people growing up fast, continued to catch glimpses of the old time charmer and enthusiast. There was Elizabeth Barrett, in transition from Sarah Lawrence to Santa Cruz, bringing to lunch at Beekman Place a friend, named Priscilla, who confessed to feeling blue; Grandpa wrote her a poem about love around the corner (which later was read at her wedding). Or Emily Fisher, fourteen, spending relaxed weekends with her grandparents while rehearsing the Spence School production of *Guys and Dolls* (she played Sky Masterson); listening to Grandpa, now ninety-three, talk about the original *Guys and Dolls,* about the stars and the great Frank Loesser score. "He was genuinely excited I was doing that show," she'd recall. (He was excited when Katherine got into Harvard, when Mary Ellin entered Columbia Journalism School where Marvin for many years had been director of the Du Pont program; excited by something Elizabeth had written, by a painting Irving, now in art school, had sent. He was that enthusiastic Jewish grandpa. He was also, of course, Irving Berlin, an American icon, an object of perpetual curiosity. But that's another story: the problems, two generations removed, of having not a famous father now but a famous grandfather.)

With the rest of the world, my hidden-away father kept in touch by phone. Along with what old friends or relatives remained, there were younger "telephone friends" like Ed Jablonski and Leonard Gershe, the screenwriter, and the musical-theater historians Stanley Green, Miles Kreuger, and Robert Kimball (who was helping organize the Berlin musical archives). But friends were only a part of a vast network of callers, for my father continued to run his business from home.

The character he presented in his eighties and nineties depended to some extent on who was at the other end of the phone. To strangers, or acquaintances who wanted something he didn't want to give, he was a disagreeable, out-of-touch old man who said no and guarded the use of his songs, of everything to do with him, beyond reason. And though some reports of this character are exaggerated, I cannot claim all were (or that I did not have my own experiences, over the phone, of that cranky, difficult old man). I can only say that whether it was unreasonable—or indeed mistaken —or not, it was his artist's prerogative to do with his songs what he wanted and his loss, as well as the public's, if he was wrong—and to note that for some callers he continued to be a thoughtful professional and a realist who had a keen awareness of what had happened in the musical world. "It was as if I owned a store and people no longer wanted to buy what I had to sell," he told Robert Kimball in the late 1970s. "Everything changed. The world was a different place. The death of President Kennedy, the Vietnam War, the social protest. Music changed, too. The Beatles and other groups reached audiences I couldn't. It was time for me to close up shop." He said no to himself first, recalls Kimball. When he said no to others, "it was not so much hostility as frustration and anger at himself, because he couldn't be there to make sure every part of a project was right." Or, as the ever-loyal and protective Hilda Schneider would say, "Mary Ellin, when you get old, it's easier and safer to say no."

Though my father never returned to the blackness of the 1950s, he was gloomy a lot of the time, which, though not inevitable in old age, is hardly unusual. "Wait till *you* get old and see how *you* like it," he and my mother would say. There were periods when my father was convinced he would be forgotten, that it was a laugh to think people would sing his songs in the next century. There were also times when his spirits would rise, when he'd write a lyric he liked, go to the piano, talk about a show even—one more show at the Music Box—only at his age how could he do a show, his way. "Oh, he still can *write songs*," my mother would say, "but he was never one to drop a score on a producer's desk and run." Unwilling to admit what she probably understood better than anyone: that by the time he reached eighty, after sixty years of songwriting, and why not, he was flickering out. And living with himself, flickering out, was a form of hell—for both of them.

But I prefer to think of something Helen Hayes told me about those last years when I visited her two springs before she died. How once she had telephoned my mother, who was in Lew Beach, and asked, "What do you do up there?" My mother replied, "Irving likes to fish. He paints. We walk. We read in the evenings, occasionally watch television. [Their favorite program was *All in the Family;* they saw themselves as Archie and Edith and me and Marvin, God help us, as Gloria and Meathead.] Sometimes the grandchildren come and it's lovely having them and we miss them when they leave but it's nice to be alone." It seemed peaceful, Miss Hayes said. "I felt the program Ellin outlined for him was enough."

In 1983 my parents left the Catskills for the last time and withdrew completely into Beekman Place, closing the door behind them. Even family visits were discouraged and eventually stopped entirely. My aged father took care of my mother, whose health had failed. Little things at first, a bad leg, a broken knee, then more serious symptoms, osteosclerosis, hardening of the arteries. Both had nurses. A doctor came every few days. His own health was terrible from the neck down, my father said, though his head was as clear as a bell. Linda, in New York in the winter of 1987, settling her daughter Ellin at NYU, remembers him erect and in charge as he answered the door, complaining about all the problems he was having getting proper household help. (What he didn't want, he made it plain, was help, hovering help, from his children.) They also talked about China, where she and Edouard had recently been. What was it like? Did they enjoy it? Questions, always questions, about the world out there, about the family.

On the day I turned sixty, I had a question for my father: "Do you realize how old I am? What do you think of that?" I asked when I called to thank him for my birthday check. There was a pause, a beat. Then, "Well, a year and a half from now," he said, "if I make it, I'll be a hundred." So. "Take it in stride, kid." He also said, "I wish I'd known at your age I was going to live so long, I'd have taken better care of myself."

Six weeks later, on their sixty-first anniversary, he sent my mother flowers with this card:

HAPPY ANNIVERSARY
61—We've just begun
62—There's me and you
63—There's you and me
64—And there is more
65—We're still alive
looking forward to 66,
love, Irving

A few days after my father's ninety-ninth birthday there was a milestone of another sort: Our daughter Elizabeth presented me and Marvin with our first grandchild, and my parents with their first great-grandchild, Peter Barrett Matson.

And then, the winter before the spring of my father's 100th

birthday, my mother had a stroke. The door to 17 Beekman Place was opened wide, and my sister and I found ourselves at last caring for our ailing, aged parents, as we had wanted to and which they had resisted till the last possible moment. Under painful circumstances, things were normal. We came and went freely, brought things as needed. Linda arrived from Paris and stayed for a while. My mother began seeing her grandchildren. Aunt Gwen came and her old friend Consuelo Vanderbilt, Mrs. Clarkson Earl. (Neither could remember how long it was since they'd been to the house.) "I'm so glad to see you, I've missed you *terribly*," said Mrs. Earl. "I've missed you," said my mother.

"You look pretty, Mamma," I said on the afternoon of my father's 100th birthday. And she did, in white pajamas piped in pink, a ribbon holding back her still-plentiful gray hair. "Thank you, dear," she said. "I'm so happy to see you," I said, holding her hand. "I'm happy to see you," she said in the halting voice of someone who is learning to speak again after a stroke. "Though . . . sorry . . . for . . . the reason." She also had not lost her edge. When I asked one day if something was bothering her, for she seemed in pain, she said, "Yes, the . . . *New* . . . *York* . . . *Times.*"

And so, on May 11, 1988, the two of them had dinner on trays in the library, and I believe cake and a sip of champagne, surrounded by flowers from relatives and other well-wishers like Kitty Hart, Rosemary Clooney, Frank Sinatra, Bob and Dolores Hope, Helen and David Brown (and no jokes about the room resembling a funeral parlor). Meanwhile the rest of the family was lined up fourth-row center for the big 100th birthday concert at Carnegie Hall.

Then, maybe a week later, came the scene that has haunted me ever since. With an infection and a fever, on top of a bad reaction to his birthday, my father had had what his nurse called "an episode." He wanted to see me, to tell me something, she said, but must warn me that he was confused as to where he was. "He thinks he is in a hotel somewhere," she whispered.

In actuality, he was sitting in his red-leather bedroom chair, in a pair of blue pajamas, wrapped in a cashmere blanket. A small, very small, man whose narrow face, pale olive, curiously smooth, nose pared to the bone, had the look of a carving, except for the live steel-gray hair and defiantly dark brows. In his liquid-eyed youth he looked Italian; now he was a very Jewish looking, very old man, reunited with his forebears.

He was barely able to see. Some months earlier he had agreed to have a cataract operation; then at the last minute, dressed, ready to go, he panicked. Nonetheless, he seemed to be looking straight at me, seeing me with sunken but still intense eyes. And though confused, he was, within his confusion, firm-voiced and precise. "I want you to tell your mother everything is fine," he said. "I'm still out of town on this business matter. Explain to her. It's nothing for her to worry about, just a business thing. I'll be home in a few days." "Of course," I said. "And give her my love," he added, "Be sure to give her my love." "Oh, I will." And again to the nurse, "Be sure to give Mrs. Berlin my love."

We went downstairs to my mother. "I just saw Daddy," I said. "How is he?" she asked; she had been told he had a slight bug. "He's fine," I said. And before I could get the message out myself, "He wanted me to be sure to give you his love," said the nurse.

At that my mother got that look, a raised-eyebrow look, you might say, a "really?" look. The look with which she had silenced three living generations.

"I *know* I have that," she said slowly and firmly.

They were not the last, but they were the most heartfelt words I heard her say.

Two months later, I stood by my 100-year-old father's bedside with my sister Elizabeth. And we told him—Elizabeth, with extra-ordinary grace, doing most of the talking—that our mother—his Ellin—had died during the night.

It was the hardest thing I have had to do in my life.

The following December, the day after Christmas, my father had a stroke. He was in a coma, the doctor told us, and would not wake up. There was no need to move him to the hospital. Every-thing could be done at home, which was where he had said he wanted to die. But he surprised everyone in a week by opening his eyes and saying he felt cold. It was like that eight-year-old news-boy, Linda said, who should have drowned but didn't and was recovered from the East River, still clutching the pennies he had earned that day.

He lived for another nine months, and I had the pleasure of telling him that "Mr. Monotony" had made it onto the stage at last, most successfully, by way of *Jerome Robbins' Broadway* and that he had a second great-grandchild by way of Katherine and her writer husband, Benjy Swett, a baby girl named Rachel. "Good," he said to both pieces of news. He didn't have a lot of words since his stroke, but "good" was one of them. (It is a pity he didn't live long enough to say "good" to the arrival of Benjamin Wesley Lerner, James Irving Matson, and Nicholas Berlin Swett.) Another word was "okay," said after I'd been there for a while. The way he said it made me laugh. "You mean I've talked enough for one day," I'd say. "Yeah," he'd say. But he looked forward to his daughters' visits, said his chief nurse, and final friend in a lifetime of friendships, the wonderful Ellen Duncan, who had been with him for five years; he asked for us when we weren't there, and when we said we loved him, he got the words out in return.

On my last visit, the day before he died, September 22, 1989, I had two items for him: that his two-year-old great-grandson Peter liked to dance to "Alexander's Ragtime Band" (I'd just returned from visiting the Matsons in Los Angeles) and that the play going into the Music Box, *A Few Good Men,* was being coproduced by his old friend David Brown, who thought he might have a hit. "Good," said my father to both pieces of news, the voice faint now, barely audible. "Good."

But enough now, as he would say with a ghost of a ghost of a Yiddish inflection.

It is two years later. I am back where my journey into the past began, at 29 West Forty-sixth Street.

The building has been sold. The top floor is empty and swept clean. It is hard to remember the way it was—the boxes, the trunks, the debris, the gloom. The sun is shining through the front windows and skylights and to the side. The front room is bright in the afternoon, in September. The corridor is bright. Only the back room is muted and shadowy. Facing north, it must always have been muted, a good bedroom for someone who slept late. The top floor does not lose its potency, its spectral air, even in bright light. But it is no longer sad, or is sad in a different way. The new owners will no doubt gut the space. And that will be that. Finished. Leaving, I'm leaving an empty stage, a set ready to be struck.

But for a moment, no more than a few seconds, but those seconds fill my whole mind's eye and ear, I imagine not the end but the beginning. The stage fills up with furniture, there the refectory table, there the Persian rug, there the little Georgian desk with the cubbyholes, there the armchairs, the long sofa, the piano, the lamps with ivory figurines, all those objects my sisters and I grew up with, which are now ours. Books fill the shelves, the gold of the leather bindings catching the light; the dark floors gleam.

It is the spring of 1924. About to celebrate his thirty-sixth birthday, my father is the most famous songwriter in the world, He has lived such a life already that Alexander Woollcott is writing a book about him. Everything he does, it seems, succeeds (but causes him constant worry; for a man on top of the world, he is singularly modest). The third of his *Music Box Revue*s has just closed after a successful eight-month run, though it wasn't quite so dazzling as the first and second; the next one has to be better. He has a new hit song, "What'll I Do," a sweet, sad Jazz Age waltz that is different from waltzes before the war, different from other waltzes he himself has written, a waltz not for wheeling, even a slow, stately wheel, but for dancing close. Another new song, "Lazy," is also different from anything he has written before, a meandering, lackadaisical song that never repeats itself in melody or lyric. When he isn't working, he has a dandy social life, the sort that suits him, casual, last-minute; he has old friends he can count on; he is finally recovering from his mother's death, summer before last. Life is busy, exhausting, perpetually interesting, a challenge (if you are at the top, where else is there to go but . . .). Life suits him just fine. Only he has been a bachelor a long time.

The story is about to begin.

Acknowledgments

MY FIRST THANKS go to my husband, Marvin Barrett. Without his loving support, his editorial advice and on many occasions real hands-on editing of the manuscript in progress, his willingness, time and again, to put his own work aside to help me with mine, I would not have been able to do this book. Nor could I have written it without the support and encouragement of my wonderful Simon & Schuster editor, Alice Mayhew. Her enthusiasm matched my own; she got me started, helped me lay out a plan, cautioned when cautioning was appropriate, made suggestions when I needed them, stood back when I didn't, and at the end gave me a crucial piece of advice that I had the good sense to follow.

Next I want to thank my sisters, Linda Emmet and Elizabeth Peters, for their generous approval of my project and for agreeing that I should have free access to the Irving Berlin papers we jointly own, in particular to the correspondence between our parents. I'm further indebted to Linda for the many times she jogged, amplified (and periodically corrected) my memory of the childhood experiences we shared. I want to thank my brother-in-law Edouard Emmet for putting down on paper his vivid recollections of my father and for his thoughtful comments on the manuscript. Thanks also to my brother-in-law Alton Peters for invaluable background on the Mackay art collection and my grandfather's last years, on the legal intricacies of this complicated family history, and for straightening me out on some major facts.

I thank my children Elizabeth Matson, Irving Barrett, Mary Ellin Barrett Lerner (who said "let us help"), and Katherine Swett, for their contributions to the final section of the book. I'm grateful to Elizabeth, too, for her long and evocative letter about her grandfather and for her astute queries on the manuscript.

Though this book in essence is a memoir, I knew from the

start I would supplement my own recollections with those of others. Many family members contributed background. From my father's side, I thank my cousin Russell Baline and his wife, Edythe, not only for hours of reminiscences but for historical material on the Balines, and for the sharing of valuable early letters from my father to his sister Gussie (which Russell has given to the Library of Congress). I am also grateful to my cousins Lilyan and Sophie Robinson, to the late Irving Kahn, and his sister Mildred Kahn Breitbart (who not only told me fascinating, sometimes painful, stories but sent me many family pictures).

On my mother's side, first thanks to Mrs. John W. Mackay— "Aunt Gwen"—who filled in my knowledge of the years before I began to remember with her lively reminiscences, and with rare pictures and letters. My thanks also to my cousin Morgan O'Brien for his thoughts and quips, and my cousin Katherine O'Brien Grau for her wonderfully written account of the summer of 1945.

In the course of writing this book I talked to many family friends and business associates of my father's. I am deeply indepted to the late Hilda Schneider, my father's devoted secretary for the last forty-three years of his life, keeper of the lore and the files, who until her final illness and death last year was always there to offer assistance and advice.

Next, I'd like to thank Robert Kimball, the musical-theater historian, for sharing recollections of his telephone conversations with my father in the 1970s and 1980s; for augmenting my knowledge of songwriters and shows in general; and for being around with the answers to any questions I might pose. I could not have done without his professional reading of my manuscript. I'd also like to thank two other musical experts and latter-day "telephone friends" of my father's: Edward Jablonski, biographer of Harold Arlen and the Gershwins, and Miles Kreuger, president of the Institute of the American Musical (who shed light on the always shadowy early Berlin years in Hollywood).

My special thanks, as well, to my old friend Samuel Goldwyn, for the help he gave me with the California sections of the book, the hours of conversation, the insights into my parents' natures, the revisiting of old Hollywood haunts . . . and for the loan of his assistant, Sandra Thomas, who arranged for me to see everyone in Los Angeles I wanted to see and go everywhere I wanted to go.

I'm indebted to Anna Crouse and Kitty Carlisle Hart for their recollections of my parents in the postwar years, and to Anna for putting on tape the *Call Me Madam* portions of Russel Crouse's diary.

Many others contributed to this project, in the form of interviews, shared letters, diaries, news clips and photographs, tours of houses where I once lived—so many I can only list them and thank them all for their time and interest (though some of them, most sadly, like Hilda Schneider and Irving Kahn, are no longer alive to thank). My list includes Shana Alexander, Don Ameche, Alan Anderson, John Appleton, Scott Berg, Pandro Berman, Jay Blackton, Seymour Bricker, John Campbell, Joan Caulfield, Elizabeth Rappleye Cooke, Mr. and Mrs. Royce Diener, Helen Devine, Leonard Gershe, Mynna Granat, Charles Hamm, Helen Hayes, Robert Hector, John B. Johnson, Jill Krementz, Maurice Kussell, June Levant, Carlene Lawrence, Katherine Cromwell Moore, Hugh Morton, Esther Rydell, Timothy Seldes, Walter Scharf, Karen Sherry, Max Wilk, Fay Wray.

Among a group of wonderfully supportive friends, I'd like to give special mention to Edna Lerner and the late Max Lerner. Max began encouraging my writing nearly thirty years ago; how I wish he were around to enjoy the completion of this book. Thanks also to Shirley Hazzard and Francis Steegmuller for helping me retrace *This Is the Army*'s Italian tour (and introducing me to off-season Capri as a great place to work).

For help with research I'm indebted to the Library of Congress (in particular to Raymond White, one of the custodians of the Irving Berlin archive), the Performing Arts Library at Lincoln Center; the New York Society Library; the Rogers Memorial Library in Southampton and the Easthampton Free Library; the Houghton Library at Harvard University, repository of the Alexander Woollcott papers (and archivist Melanie Wisher); and the State Historical Society of Wisconsin, location of the Moss Hart papers (and archivist Harold L. Miller). My thanks also to Gabriel Morgan, Kurt Reighley, and Jim Furgele, to Janet Reitman for her stalwart checking of the manuscript, and to Natalie Goldstein, my picture researcher.

Official acknowledgments to the estate of Irving Berlin appear on the permissions page. But I would also like to give personal thanks, for their support, to Frederic B. Ingraham, the Morgan Bank officer in charge of our estate, and to Theodore S. Chapin, executive director of the Rodgers and Hammerstein Organization, who manages my father's catalog. Thanks also, for many services rendered, to the R & H staff, in particular Lisa Alter, Cindy Boyle, Bert Fink, Nicole Gillette, Maxyne Lang, Montsy Martynek, Kurt Reighley (again), and Vince Scuderi.

At Simon & Schuster, I'd like to thank Sarah Baker, Alice Mayhew's assistant, for her sensitive line editing of my manuscript, for seeing me into print with intelligence, good humor, and a minimum amount of fuss, for being generally splendid. Thanks also to my copy editors, Lydia Buechler and Frank Lavena, for a complex job well done, and to Eve Metz and Edith Fowler for putting together so elegantly the photographs that illustrate the story.

Finally I want to thank my friend and agent Lois Wallace, who liked the idea of this book, conveyed her positive feelings to others, read the manuscript section by section, and never failed to make me feel, with her eloquent enthusiasm, that what I was doing was eminently worthwhile.

Permissions

Index